Bullying in Different Contexts

Bullying has a tendency to be associated with aggression between children in the playground, but bullying and abuse can also be observed in other social settings. *Bullying in Different Contexts* brings together, for the first time, leading international researchers to discuss these behaviours in a wide range of settings, including preschool, school, the home, residential care, prisons, the workplace and cyberspace. The authors provide background to the different contexts and discuss the impact and types of interpersonal aggression and the characteristics of those involved. A final chapter collates the findings from each context to draw conclusions on the similarities and differences between the behaviours, risk factors for involvement and theoretical approaches to explain bullying. This original volume will further our understanding of bullying and inform preventative and intervention work. The authors seek to show how research from diverse settings may inform our understanding of the bullying phenomenon as a whole.

CLAIRE P. MONKS is a Senior Lecturer in Developmental Psychology and a member of the Research Centre for Children, Schools and Families at the University of Greenwich.

IAIN COYNE is an Associate Professor in Occupational Psychology in the Institute of Work, Health and Organisations at the University of Nottingham.

Bullying in Different Contexts

Edited by

Claire P. Monks

Iain Coyne

CAMBRIDGE
UNIVERSITY PRESS

CAMBRIDGE UNIVERSITY PRESS
Cambridge, New York, Melbourne, Madrid, Cape Town, Singapore,
São Paulo, Delhi, Dubai, Tokyo, Mexico City

Cambridge University Press
The Edinburgh Building, Cambridge CB2 8RU, UK

Published in the United States of America by Cambridge University Press,
New York

www.cambridge.org
Information on this title: www.cambridge.org/9780521132596

© Cambridge University Press 2011

First published 2011

Printed in the United Kingdom at the University Press, Cambridge

A catalogue record for this publication is available from the British Library

Library of Congress Cataloguing in Publication data
  Bullying in different contexts / [edited by] Claire P. Monks, Iain Coyne.
    p.   cm.
  Includes bibliographical references and index.
  ISBN 978-0-521-13259-6 (pbk.) – ISBN 978-0-521-11481-3 (hardback)
  1. Bullying. I. Monks, Claire P. II. Coyne, Iain.
  BF637.B85B8572 2011
  302.3–dc22
  2010040407

ISBN 978-0-521-11481-3 Hardback
ISBN 978-0-521-13259-6 Paperback

To Graham and Alexander for all of your love and
support (CPM)

To Emma, Amy and Joshua for their love, intelligence, humour and patience (IC)

Courage is fire, and bullying is smoke.

Benjamin Disraeli

No one can make you feel inferior without your consent.

Eleanor Roosevelt

Contents

Figures

Tables

Contributors

PARVEEN AZAM ALI is a PhD student and was awarded a coveted University of Sheffield studentship to research gender relations in the Pakistani household. Her work is being is co-supervised by Paul Naylor.

CHRISTINE BARTER is an NSPCC senior research fellow at the School for Policy Studies, University of Bristol. She has published widely on a range of children's welfare issues and has also authored a number of methodological papers on including young people within social research. Christine undertook the first study on peer violence in residential children's homes. Her most recent research, the first in the UK, explored young people's experiences of partner exploitation and violence in their intimate relationships.

KATE BEAMER is a graduate student in the Department of Education at the University of Calgary, Canada. Her research interests centre on the education of undisclosed adolescent female child sexual abuse survivors using a hermeneutic model of narrative inquiry. She also works with Christine A. Walsh analysing research data on issues relating to women's poverty, homelessness and elder abuse.

THOMAS CHESNEY is a lecturer in Information Systems at Nottingham University Business School. He has a PhD in information systems from Brunel University, an MSc in informatics from Edinburgh University and a BSc in information management from the Queen's University of Belfast. He is a fellow of the Higher Education Academy. His research interests centre on technology adoption in the home, particularly socialising in virtual worlds.

GABRIELLE D'AOUST is completing a master's degree in social work at the University of Calgary, Canada. She has assisted with community-based research projects exploring issues affecting youth and older adults in Ontario and Alberta. Her current research interests include processes of forgiveness and reconciliation in post-conflict communities.

JANE L. IRELAND is a professor in forensic aggression research, chartered psychologist, forensic psychologist and chartered scientist and fellow of the International Society for Research on Aggression. She published the first book on prison bullying in 2002, followed by the first edited book on this topic in 2005 and is responsible for over 60 publications, the majority of which are on bullying- or aggression-related topics.

PAUL B. NAYLOR is a senior research fellow in the Institute for Health Services Effectiveness, Aston Business School, Aston University. Since taking up a research career 12 years ago he has published more than 20 book chapters, web articles and peer-reviewed journal articles. Most of this work has been on bullying amongst children and anti-bullying peer-support systems in school, but also addresses workplace bullying and interpersonal racism.

ROSARIO ORTEGA is a professor of psychology at the University of Cordoba, Spain. She has researched extensively into the causes and nature of interpersonal violence. She was director of two national projects (SAVE and ANDAVE) that created new models to prevent school bullying. She designed and co-ordinated the Educational Program for the Prevention of Bullying in Schools with the Andalucian government and is currently directing a project examining various forms of aggression and violence in Andalucian schools (VEA). She is a founding member of the European Observatory on Violence, the International Observatory, as well as the Observatory of Brazil and the Observatory of School Convivencia, recently created by the Spanish government. She has published numerous books and peer-reviewed journal articles in this area and has been an invited speaker at conferences as well as to government officials.

LAURIE PETCH is a chartered educational psychologist, lecturer and co-course director for the doctoral course in educational and child psychology at the University of Sheffield. He currently practises as an educational psychologist with a local authority in the north of England. Laurie's research interests centre on existential perspectives in applied educational psychology. His PhD examines school-based interventions for children with high anxiety.

IAN RIVERS is Professor of Human Development at Brunel University. He is the author of over 80 articles and book chapters dealing with various aspects of bullying behaviour, and particularly homophobic bullying in schools. He is the 2001 recipient of The British Psychological Society's Award for Promoting Equality of Opportunity in the UK, for his work on bullying behaviour and its long-term effects. Ian was previously Professor of Applied Psychology at York St John University, and visiting fellow at the Centers for Disease Control and Prevention, in Atlanta.

VIRGINIA SÁNCHEZ is a lecturer in developmental psychology at the University of Seville, Spain. She has been involved in european research programmes on school violence and has published scientific articles relating moral emotions to involvement in bullying behaviour.

PETER K. SMITH is Professor of Psychology and Head of the Unit for School and Family Studies at Goldsmiths, University of London. He is co-editor of *Bullying in Schools: How Successful Can Interventions Be?* (Cambridge University Press, 2004). He currently chairs COST Action IS0801 on cyberbullying.

CHRISTINE A. WALSH is an associate professor of social work at the University of Calgary, Canada. Her research interests include the examination of interpersonal violence across the lifespan, including the victimisation of older adults and ethno-cultural issues related to interpersonal violence. She conducts participatory action research and community-based research with populations affected by issues of poverty or violence, and has authored more than 50 journal articles and book chapters.

1   A history of research into bullying

Claire P. Monks and Iain Coyne

General overview of and rationale for the book

Bullying is widely recognised as being a problem, not only for those individuals involved, but also for the organisation within which it occurs and the wider community. Few people can be unaware of bullying, either having been involved in it (as a perpetrator or target), having witnessed it occurring or seen it reported within the local or national media. Although bullying has long been recognised as an issue that warrants concern and action, empirical research on the topic only really began in the late 1970s. Since this time, there have been many books and journal articles published on this important topic. Work on dealing with and preventing bullying has come from many different quarters, from governments creating laws for dealing with and punishing bullying, and drawing up legal guidelines for institutions to follow with the aim of preventing bullying, to practitioners developing models of intervention and prevention work with those suffering or at risk of being involved in bullying.

We currently have an established body of research focusing on the nature and extent of bullying, as well as highlighting some of the risk factors for involvement in bullying (both individual and situational) across a number of different contexts. Much of this research could be criticised as being somewhat atheoretical and descriptive. However, the authors within this volume have drawn on theory in an attempt to develop models to further our understanding of the phenomenon. The merits of this approach are that not only does it assist in our conceptualisation of these behaviours, but it also enables us to develop more focussed and perhaps more appropriate and effective intervention and prevention programmes.

We suggest that 'bullying' does not only occur within peer-relationships in schools, but can also occur within many different social contexts and in a variety of relationships. This book brings together, for the first time, leading international researchers to address the concept

1

of bullying during childhood, adolescence and adulthood. We examine bullying in preschools (Monks, Chapter 2), schools (Smith, Chapter 3), residential care (Barter, Chapter 4), families (Naylor, Petch and Azam Ali, Chapter 5), dating relationships (Ortega and Sánchez, Chapter 6), prisons (Ireland, Chapter 7), the workplace (Coyne, Chapter 8), among older people (Walsh, D'Aoust and Beamer, Chapter 9) and in cyberspace (Rivers, Chesney and Coyne, Chapter 10).

The rationale for this book is that, although most published work on bullying has focused on what occurs between children in schools, there is now a growing body of research which has highlighted the fact that behaviours which could be described as bullying occur in a number of other settings and relationships (e.g. Monks *et al.*, 2009). However, little research has focused on similarities and differences between the different contexts, and researchers have tended to operate within their own domain. This book begins to draw this, often disparate, research together and consider how the commonalities and differences may help advance the general research area of bullying. Second, there is currently a move towards applying theoretical frameworks to bullying, although this is still in its infancy and has, in the main, focused on school bullying. This book attempts to add to the debate by considering theoretical approaches which may make useful contributions to our understanding of bullying in all contexts. We try to draw together this research and theory from the different chapters in Chapter 11 (Coyne and Monks).

What is bullying?

Research into bullying has its origins in work with peer-to-peer bullying among schoolchildren. Research in this field began in Scandinavian countries and the original term used in the literature to describe this behaviour was 'mobbing' (Olweus, 1993). This term originally came from ethology and was used to describe a group of birds attacking an individual bird. It was adopted to describe aggression among schoolchildren, as early research focused on groups of children attacking individuals. However, later, Olweus acknowledged that one-on-one bullying was actually more common than the group versus the individual, and the English term 'bullying' became more prevalent in English-language publications.

Work on school bullying has defined bullying as 'a systematic abuse of power' (Smith and Sharp, 1994, p. 2). Farrington (1993) notes that bullying can be physical or psychological and that it is an act which is intended to hurt or harm another person. The defining features of bullying which distinguish it from general aggression are that it is repeated and that there is an imbalance of power, with the victim in the weaker or more vulnerable position. This definition is generally agreed upon by researchers into school bullying, but there are some who argue that behaviour does not necessarily have to be repeated to be bullying, as a one-off incident may be so upsetting and damaging to the target that they then live in fear of it being repeated (e.g. Besag, 1989). When young people, teachers and parents are asked their views, they do not always share this definition of bullying held by researchers. Monks and Smith (2006) found that young children tend to have an over-inclusive definition of bullying compared with adolescents and adults. They were more likely than older participants to conflate aggression and bullying, focusing less on the need for repetition or an imbalance of power (see Smith, Chapter 3).

Research examining this phenomenon in different countries has had to take into account the different terms used in different languages and different cultures. There are even differences between countries with a shared language. For example, in English-speaking countries, the term 'bullying' is more commonly used in the United Kingdom than in the United States, where 'victimisation' is more frequently used. Smith et al. (2002) examined the terms used to describe behaviours similar to bullying in 13 different languages. They found that some languages did not possess a word with an identical meaning to 'bullying'; for example, the closest word in Italian is 'prepotenza', which also covers behaviours such as fighting (where there is not necessarily an imbalance of power or repetition). Smith et al. noted that this disparity in terminology, which may also be used in questionnaires to ask about the prevalence of these behaviours, may affect cross-national comparisons of reported levels of 'bullying'. This may reflect differences in behaviours, but may also simply reflect linguistic differences in some cases (Smith and Monks, 2008). For example, in Italy, behaviours which meet the definition of 'bullying' are observable, although there was no single term to describe bullying in Italian. In the case of Italy, the term 'il bulismo' has now been adopted to describe bullying behaviours. In terms of the impact this has on research, researchers tend to either provide a definition of the phenomenon for participants to refer to, or they ask about experiences by providing examples of specific behaviours, rather than using a term such as 'bullying'.

Types of bullying

Historically, when looking at school bullying, research initially focused on physical attacks and tended to view bullying as a behaviour which occurred between boys. However, this has expanded to include verbal bullying (including threats, name-calling and taunting) and damage to property. More recent research in the 1990s highlighted the related concepts of social, relational and indirect bullying. Social and relational bullying refers to behaviours which are aimed specifically at attacking or causing damage to the target's relationships with their peers. Indirect bullying is used to describe bullying which occurs behind the recipient's back (and includes behaviours such as rumour-spreading). The overlap can be seen here, with rumour-spreading being indirect, but also social and relational in nature. Social/relational bullying can also be direct in nature, referring to direct social exclusion where an individual is told face-to-face that they cannot join in.

This illustrates that the term 'bullying' encompasses a wide variety of negative and potentially harmful behaviours in the context of young people's relationships with peers. However, we argue in this book that 'bullying' can be used to describe behaviours which are exhibited in a wide variety of relationships and social contexts. This 'systematic abuse of power' described by Smith and Sharp (1994, p. 2) can be seen throughout the lifespan from preschool to older age, and across different relationships – peers, family, partners, colleagues, employers/employees – and in a variety of contexts – preschools, schools, families, residential care, dating relationships, prisons and the workplace. Some of the behaviours exhibited are similar to those reported among schoolchildren. However, others are more sinister, such as sexual abuse/harassment.

'Bullying' is not a term that is widely used in all of these contexts to describe these behaviours; in some, the term 'abuse' or 'harassment' is more commonly used. However, it is argued in this book that, although historically work in these areas has come from different research traditions and backgrounds and has used different terminologies, essentially we are talking about behaviours which involve similar features, antecedents and outcomes. We do not argue that a traditional school-based definition of the term 'bullying' should necessarily be used to label all of these behaviours in these different contexts, but we do argue that by considering them as having commonalities we can then draw together findings from often very separate research traditions, looking at theory and practice which may better inform our understanding of these behaviours. Our final chapter poses the question of whether current definitions of bullying restrict our ability to look at these other areas in order to consider common features and discusses whether we need to reconsider our conceptualisation of bullying.

Current state of research

From an early focus on peer-to-peer bullying in schools, research has broadened its approach to explore other examples of bullying behaviour. Research has also begun to examine bullying-type behaviours across a broader age range. Much of the school bullying literature has focused on children aged eight years and over. However, more recently, researchers have started to look at younger age groups, including pre-schoolers, in an attempt to identify the origins of these types of behaviour. Peer-directed aggression does occur among these very young peer-groups, but it does not meet the definition of bullying used in the school bullying literature and outlined above. The research reviewed by Monks in Chapter 2 indicates that this aggression does not appear to be repeated over time, with one-off incidents fairly common, and little research has focused on a power differential between victim and aggressor. As a result, the term 'bullying' does not tend to be used to describe these behaviours, but rather terms such as 'peer-victimisation' or 'unjustified aggression' are employed instead to mark the difference in definition. However, as Monks argues, these behaviours may in some cases mark the early beginnings of bullying as it is known in school.

When examining bullying among children, but within a context away from school, the residential home, Barter (Chapter 4) notes that research does not tend to use the term 'bullying' to describe aggressive and violent behaviours. Instead, the term most commonly used is 'peer violence', which is broader than bullying and describes the four main types of violence identified within this context. These are: direct physical violence (which includes hitting, slapping, etc.), physical non-contact (invasion of privacy, dirty looks, etc.), verbal abuse (name-calling) and unwanted sexual behaviours (such as inappropriate touching and rape). Although there has long been concern regarding children's experiences within care, this is only a relatively recently studied area.

Other research examined within this book has come from well-established and distinct research traditions. In particular, this is the case when looking at investigations focused on aggression and violence within family contexts and within the context of couples. Aggression and violent behaviour within these contexts has long been the focus of concern and research. This research has often been carried out completely separately from and in parallel with research on bullying and has rarely used the term 'bullying' to describe aggressive/violent behaviours within these relationships or contexts. Most commonly, the terms 'abuse' or 'domestic violence' have been used. However, although Naylor and colleagues (Chapter 5) and Ortega and Sánchez (Chapter 6) note that the behaviours exhibited in these contexts are somewhat broader than the traditional definition of bullying, they argue that many have strong similarities to 'bullying'. The key similarities are in the imbalance of power which exists between the aggressor and target, with the recipient of the aggression often being in a more vulnerable position and less able to extricate themselves from the situation for a variety of reasons. Furthermore these behaviours are rarely one-offs and are often repeated. Naylor and colleagues examine abuse within various relationships in the family context: intimate partner violence, child exposure to domestic violence, abuse of children by adults and sibling abuse. These forms of abuse and violence can take a variety of different forms, depending on the type of domestic violence. Naylor and colleagues note that child abuse by an adult can be conceptualised as neglect, emotional abuse, physical, mixed and sexual. Sibling abuse can take emotional, physical or sexual forms. Ortega and Sánchez (Chapter 6) note that dating violence shows some similarities to domestic violence (and much of the literature in this area is influenced by the literature on domestic violence), including behaviours such as verbal aggression, psychological aggression, physical and sexual violence. Ortega and Sánchez go further and draw direct links between involvement in bullying of peers and bullying of girlfriends/boyfriends.

Fairly recently, researchers have begun to examine bullying among adults (in the workplace and in prisons). It was only in the 1990s that organisational and forensic psychologists started to survey participants about their experiences of behaviours which could be considered to be bullying. The research coming from the workplace tradition tends to use the terminology 'bullying', 'harassment', 'victimisation' or 'mobbing' interchangeably, with each describing behaviour which fits the definition of a 'systematic abuse of power'. Behaviours described by researchers within the work environment include personal attack (physical, but more commonly verbal or psychological), work-related (providing impossible deadlines) or social exclusion (isolation). Within a prison setting, the term 'bullying' is commonly used to describe behaviours between inmates and between staff and inmates, and includes behaviours such as physical, verbal and indirect attacks. However, in Chapter 7 in this volume, Ireland argues that the definition of 'bullying' as occurring within prison is somewhat broader than the concept used in schools and can include thoughtless behaviours which may not be intended to be bullying by the perpetrator, but may be perceived as such by the recipient. She argues that the imbalance of power may not be necessary and that some individuals may voluntarily enter into relationships where this imbalance of power exists (e.g. with loan sharks).

Additionally, perhaps given the enclosed nature of the environment, the *fear* of repeated attack may be sufficient for behaviour to be considered as bullying, without actual repetition of the behaviour being necessary.

Research at the other end of the age range has looked at elder abuse (see Walsh and colleagues, Chapter 9). Despite the relatively established tradition of research over the past 30 years examining elder abuse, there has been very little looking at bullying within this age group. Again, the term 'bullying' is not often used when examining behaviours among this group, with the preferred term being 'elder abuse'. This term again reflects the somewhat broader types of behaviours described, although most of these behaviours may display the characteristics of bullying – repetition and the vulnerability of the recipient. Walsh refers to five main types of elder abuse. Physical abuse can take the form of hitting, force-feeding or the use of physical restraints. Sexual abuse includes any sexual contact without the full knowledge or consent of the older person. Emotional or psychological abuse includes behaviours such as harassment, threats and insults, as well as behaviours such as ignoring and isolation. Financial or material abuse refers to the improper or illegal use of the older person's resources and includes theft and the forging of financial or legal documents. Neglect describes behaviours such as failure to provide adequate care for the older person, such as food and drink, clothing, hygiene, etc. She also notes that there are some types of abuse which are now becoming more recognised, such as medical abuse (the overmedication of older adults) and systemic institutional abuse (the provision of inadequate care by governments, such as pensions).

A very new and growing area of research is focusing on bullying behaviours carried out via new technologies – cyberbullying (see Rivers *et al.*, Chapter 10). Studies of cyberbullying have focused on the use of technology as a medium to bully, predominately via mobile phones and the internet. Via mobile phone, this behaviour includes intimidating or silent calls, as well as harassment via SMS or MMS. Additionally, via the internet bullying behaviours have been described including the creation of slam-books (nasty websites about someone), posting unpleasant pictures/videos of individuals online, harassment via social networking sites, email or instant messenger, and griefing (cyberbullying) in online virtual environments (ibid.). Although this type of bullying is often less physical than those experienced in the other contexts described, it can also contain a physical element, such as 'happy-slapping'. Studies of cyberbullying have included participants ranging in age from primary school pupils to adults, although most research has focused on secondary school students' experiences. Currently, there appear to be a number of slightly different conceptualisations of cyberbullying in the literature. However, most of these focus on there being some intent to harm, with some definitions being adapted almost directly from definitions of traditional bullying (with the sole addition that the behaviour is conducted via electronic media) and including repetition and the power imbalance identified as key features of bullying.

The developmental process of research into bullying

Early research in each of the contexts initially focused on providing a description of the phenomenon: the types of behaviour reported, the prevalence and incidence rates. This is important in order to obtain information about what is happening (if anything) within particular social contexts and relationships and to provide an insight into the types of behaviour individuals may be exhibiting and experiencing. Once the 'problem' has been highlighted, research then tends to move on to examining the risk factors for involvement in these types of behaviour in an attempt to understand why some people may be at heightened risk for involvement in these relationships and which types of context may promote the occurrence of these behaviours or support their continuation. The next step is to examine, preferably longitudinally, the precursors and outcomes of these behaviours, in order to better understand the nature of the phenomenon. This then leads on to the development of theories. The development of models and theories regarding bullying is important, not only in furthering our understanding of the phenomenon, but also in informing the design of prevention and intervention programmes. The final phase of research culminates with controlled evaluations of these prevention and intervention programmes. The literature reviewed by the authors within this volume indicates that research is clearly at different stages of development within each of the contexts and relationships addressed, with the most obviously developed research body in the context of school bullying.

What is also important, and highlighted in this book, is the use of a multidisciplinary approach to examining bullying in these different contexts. Research reviewed by the authors in this volume comes from a wide variety of research traditions and backgrounds. These include psychology, education, sociology, feminism and social work. In general, researchers within these areas have been working independently of each other, with little communication across the different fields of research. As a consequence, one of the main aims of this book is to draw together what is known about bullying in these disparate contexts and from these different research cultures to enrich our understanding of this issue. The hope is that, by furthering our understanding of bullying and by drawing out any commonalities (and differences) found in this behaviour, as well as potential risk factors for these problems, we may be better placed to develop overarching theories related to this issue. The clear aim of all research in this area is to move towards the development of appropriate intervention and prevention programmes, and the more information available about the problem itself, how it manifests and what may trigger it, the more it will be possible to be able to do so.

The current book

Within this book, the authors review literature on behaviours which are either termed bullying or meet the definition of being a 'systematic abuse of power' within a variety of social contexts and relationships. These are organised somewhat chronologically, beginning with Chapter 2 on preschoolers, Chapter 3 on school bullying, Chapter 4 on bullying in children's residential homes, Chapter 5 within families, Chapter 6 within dating relationships, Chapter 7 in prisons, Chapter 8 in the workplace. Chapter 9 focuses on elder abuse. Chapter 10 looks at an emerging and relatively new phenomenon related to bullying – 'cyberbullying'. The research covered in this volume covers the lifespan, from preschool to older age, across a variety of social relationships: with peers (during childhood, adolescence and adulthood), family members, boyfriends/girlfriends, co-workers and employers/employees.

There are some areas of research into bullying-type behaviours which have not been addressed in this book, but may also shed light on our understanding of bullying across a variety of contexts. Research exists which has looked at bullying within organisations such as the National Health Service (NHS) in the UK (e.g. Quine, 2001, 2003; Steadman *et al.*, 2009) and the Church (Lee, 2007), examining the experiences of nursing staff, junior doctors, hospital dentists and the clergy. Research has also examined the nature and extent of bullying within other organisations such as the army (Ostvik and Rudmin, 2001). Other work has examined harassment and abuse experienced by individuals within contexts such as sport. Although the term 'bullying' again seems to be reserved for those experiences of children (see Bullying UK), there is a body of research on harassment, abuse and maltreatment experienced by individuals involved in sporting activities: coaches, athletes, officials and parents (e.g. Stirling, 2009). The inclusion of these (and other) developing areas of research was not possible within the current volume, although it is likely that they could contribute to the shared knowledge of bullying and its prevention.

Bullying is a term that describes behaviours which can vary quite markedly in type (from physical to verbal or psychological), but what they have in common is that they are aggressive behaviours which are intended to cause harm or distress to the recipient. They are also characterised to some extent by an imbalance of power between aggressor and recipient, which means that it is difficult for the victim to defend themselves or escape further victimisation. Within this book we propose that bullying is not simply a behaviour which can be seen within our schools. We suggest that unpleasant and aggressive behaviours can be reported across the lifespan, from preschool to older age, and that they can take place within a variety of social contexts and relationships. These behaviours may be conceptualised as bullying and abuse, but current rigid school-based definitions of bullying do not allow us to capture fully behaviour in these other settings. In Chapter 11 we discuss three possible ways forward, ranging from a stance promoting disparity across contexts, through one arguing for commonalities, to one suggesting unification. Although research has come a long way, as we see in the chapters there is more to do. This book provides an account of the state of play for bullying and abuse and, although the coverage of this book is not exhaustive (as noted above), it does address the most developed fields of research on this topic.

REFERENCES

Besag, V.E. (1989). *Bullies and Victims in Schools*. Buckingham: Open University Press.

Bullying UK. www.bullying.co.uk/index.php/young-people/advice/bullying-in-sport.html (accessed 20 January 2010).

Farrington, D.P. (1993). 'Understanding and preventing bullying'. In M. Tonry and N. Morris (eds.), *Crime and Justice: An Annual Review of Research*. Chicago: University of Chicago Press.

Lee, A. (2007). 'Why the church must confront the bullies'. *Church Times*, 7528, www.churchtimes.co.uk/content.asp?id=40909 (accessed 20 January 2010).

Monks, C.P. and Smith, P.K. (2006). 'Definitions of "bullying": age differences in understanding of the term, and the role of experience'. *British Journal of Developmental Psychology*, 24: 801–21.

Monks, C.P., Smith, P.K., Coyne, I., Barter, C., Ireland, J. and Naylor, P. (2009). 'Bullying in different contexts: commonalities and differences'. *Aggression and Violent Behavior: A Review Journal*, 14: 146–56.

Olweus, D. (1993). *Bullying at School: What We Know and What We Can Do*. Oxford: Blackwell.

Ostvik, K. and Rudmin, F. (2001). 'Bullying and hazing among Norwegian army soldiers: two studies of prevalence, context, and cognition'. *Military Psychology*, 13: 17–39.

Quine, L. (2001). 'Workplace bullying in nurses'. *Journal of Health Psychology*, 6: 73–84.

    (2003). 'Workplace bullying, psychological distress, and job satisfaction in junior doctors'. *Cambridge Quarterly of Healthcare Ethics*, 12: 91–101.

Smith, P.K. and Monks, C.P. (2008). 'Concepts of bullying: developmental and cultural aspects'. *International Journal of Adolescent Medicine and Health*, 20: 101–12.

Smith, P.K. and Sharp, S. (eds.) (1994). *School Bullying: Insights and Perspectives*. London: Routledge.

Smith, P.K., Cowie, H., Olafsson, R., Liefooghe, A.P.D. *et al.* (2002). 'Definitions of bullying: a comparison of terms used, and age and sex differences, in a 14-country international comparison'. *Child Development*, 73: 1119–33.

Steadman, L., Quine, L., Jack, K., Felix, D.H. and Waumsley, J. (2009). 'Experience of workplace bullying behaviours in postgraduate hospital dentists: questionnaire survey'. *British Dental Journal*, 207: 379–80.

Stirling, A.E. (2009). 'Definition and constituents of maltreatment in sport: establishing a conceptual framework for research practitioners'. *British Journal of Sports Medicine*, 43: 1091–99.

2 Peer-victimisation in preschool

Claire P. Monks

There is an extensive body of research which has examined the bullying behaviours of schoolchildren during middle childhood and adolescence (see Smith, Chapter 3). Fewer studies have focused on children during preschool/kindergarten (between the ages of three and six years in most Western countries). Preschool settings may vary considerably within and between countries and attendance at preschool is not compulsory in most countries. However, according to UNICEF (2008), in developed countries, approximately 80 per cent of children in this age range spend some time in out-of-home child-care settings. Therefore, it is clearly important to explore the development of children's relationships with peers (including peer-victimisation) at this point.

The comparative lack of research with preschoolers is probably a reflection of the methods used to ask about bullying, which, in the main, have employed anonymous self-report questionnaires (e.g. the Olweus Bullying Questionnaire), and which are inappropriate for use with young children because of their more limited reading and writing skills. During the last decade, researchers have developed new methods of finding out about bullying and have begun to investigate these behaviours among younger children. Researching these behaviours among children during preschool/kindergarten (when their first peer-relations may develop) may provide insights into the ways in which peer-victimisation develops and provide us with methods of dealing with it early on, before it becomes an established part of a child's social repertoire.

This chapter will describe the nature and extent of peer-victimisation in preschool. In particular, it will focus on the differences and similarities between behaviours exhibited during the preschool years and behaviours reported later on in childhood. It will then go on to examine some of the correlates of aggressive and victimised status, including peer-relations, family factors and individual differences. Implications and suggestions for interventions and future research directions will be proposed.

Nature and extent

Researchers in different continents, including Europe (e.g. Monks *et al.*, 2005; Ortega and Monks, 2005; Perren and Alsaker, 2006; Smith and Levan, 1995), North America (e.g. Ladd and Burgess, 1999; Ostrov, 2008; Snyder *et al.*, 2003), South America, Australasia (e.g. Russell *et al.*, 2003) and Asia (e.g. Nelson *et al.*, 2006; Shahim, 2008; Shin and Kim, 2008), have found that some young children behave aggressively towards their peers.

This research has shown that the aggressive behaviour exhibited by young children differs in a number of ways from that shown by children during middle childhood and adolescence. During early childhood, children are most likely to use direct forms of aggression, which occur in a face-to-face encounter and can include physically aggressive behaviours, such as hitting, kicking and pushing, and verbally aggressive behaviours, such as name-calling or threats (Monks *et al.*, 2003). Young children may also employ relationally aggressive tactics to damage peer-relationships (e.g. Crick and Grotpeter, 1995), with the majority using direct forms of relational aggression (such as socially excluding someone by saying 'You can't play with us!') as compared to indirect forms of aggression (e.g. rumour-spreading), which characteristically go on behind the victim's back or are via a third party (Monks *et al.*, 2003). Research in Finland has indicated that there is a developmental change in the types of aggression used by children and adolescents, with older pupils using more indirect forms of aggression (e.g. Björkqvist *et al.*, 1992). It is thought that these are more sophisticated forms of aggression (as they may require more honed social skills on the part of the aggressor), which make it much more difficult for the aggressor to be identified (in some cases, even by the victim).

As is found among older groups, there are gender differences in the roles taken by boys and girls and the aggressive behaviours they use and experience. Boys are more likely than girls to be bully-victims (Perren and Alsaker, 2006) or aggressors (Monks *et al.*, 2003). Crick *et al.* (1999) and Ostrov and Keating (2004) found that, among preschoolers, physical aggression was more commonly experienced (either as an aggressor or target) by boys and that girls were more likely to use and experience relational aggression. Perren and Alsaker (2006) used a combination of peer-and teacher-reports with a sample of Swiss five- to seven-year-olds, and noted that 8 per cent were victims, 14 per cent bully-victims and 15 per cent bullies. Using peer-reports within a UK sample of four- to six-year-olds, Monks *et al.* (2003) found that between 13 and 22 per cent were victims and between 22 and 25 per cent were aggressors.

These findings, although providing different absolute values, suggest that more children are implicated, both as the perpetrators and targets of these behaviours, within younger groups than compared to school-aged groups (see Smith, Chapter 3). However, as a result of the differing methodologies employed, the extent of peer-aggression among preschoolers has not been directly compared with older, school-aged groups.

Smith *et al.* (1999) note several reasons why younger children may be more likely to be the targets of peer-aggression. First, there are more children who are older than them who could victimise them. Second, young children may not have adequate coping skills to avoid victimisation. Third, young children may 'over-report' bullying. Indeed, research has shown that young children have a more over-inclusive definition of bullying than older children and adults (Monks and Smith, 2006; Smith and Monks, 2008), and are more likely to consider behaviours such as fighting or where there is no intention to harm (but with a negative outcome) as bullying. This may lead to teachers/parents perceiving them as 'over-reporting' bullying.

There is general consensus regarding the stability of aggressive behaviour over time, with stability reported over a period of four months and one year for peer- and self-reports (Ladd and Burgess, 1999; Monks *et al.*, 2003) and over a period of four to five months for teacher-reports and observations (Ostrov, 2008). Ladd and Burgess (1999) also report some stability of aggression over two years based on teacher-reports (from kindergarten to Grade 2; five to seven years old). In contrast, the stability of being a target of peer-victimisation is less agreed upon. Monks *et al.* (2003) and Kochenderfer and Ladd (1996), based on peer- and self-reports, suggest that many children are targeted briefly, but that few are repeatedly targeted over time. Further, longitudinal self-report data (Kochenderfer-Ladd and Wardrop, 2001) and observational research (Persson, 2005; Snyder *et al.*, 2003) have found that few young children are consistently victimised by their peers. However, teacher-reports indicate some stability of the victim role over one to four or five months (Crick *et al.*, 1997; Ostrov, 2008).

It is likely that differences in the reported stability of victimisation may be related to the different methodologies employed by researchers, with different methods contributing unique variance (Pellegrini and Bartini, 2000). Monks *et al.* (2003) found that four- to six-year-old children's peer-nominations for the role of aggressor showed some agreement with teacher-reports of aggressive behaviour in their pupils, but that there was low agreement between peer- and teacher-reports for victim status. Ladd and Kochenderfer-Ladd (2006) found that peer- and self-reports of victimisation showed little concordance before the age of seven years.

The differences in the stability reported for victim status by children and teachers may indicate differences in awareness of behaviours and/ or differences in the ability to identify and report victimised behaviours. It is possible that teachers are less aware of who is victimised by peers, as it often occurs out of sight of members of staff, and it is also possible that children may be more aware of who is currently being targeted by aggressive peers and their reports may reflect the more fluid nature of peer-victimisation at this age (with few children consistently being victimised, but many experiencing transient victimisation). Alternatively, young children's reports of victimisation may be reflecting their more limited ability to identify behaviours in their peers, in particular behaviours which may not directly impact on them personally (Ladd, 2006). Unlike an aggressive peer, a classmate who is victimised is unlikely to impact on your own experiences within preschool.

Researchers have attempted to explain the apparently low stability of victim status, but relative stability of the aggressor role as reported by data from peers and observations. It has been suggested that initially on entering the peer-group some children may behave aggressively towards a variety of peers in an indiscriminate way. It may take some time before they identify the most 'rewarding' victims (children who may not defend themselves effectively) and limit their aggression to them (Perry et al., 1990). Additionally, Hanish and Guerra (2000) have noted that young children find it more difficult than older children to identify withdrawn behaviours in their peers, and so young aggressors may find it a challenge to identify victims who are less able to defend themselves successfully. Furthermore, Schäfer et al. (2005) noted that the dominance hierarchies within classrooms during the early years of school are less stable than those found in older groups, which could mean that younger victims may find it easier to 'escape' further victimisation and the label of 'victim'.

This raises the issue of whether we can call this behaviour 'bullying'. As mentioned in Chapter 1, 'bullying' is generally taken by researchers to mean an intentional aggressive behaviour, which involves an imbalance of power between the aggressor and victim and is *repeated over time* (e.g. Farrington, 1993). However, this repetition does not appear to be present among younger children. This has led some researchers to suggest that, although these behaviours may be indicative of behaviours which may later become 'bullying', we cannot call them such during preschool (Monks et al., 2003). Researchers have used terms such as 'unjustified aggression' (Ortega and Monks, 2005) or 'peer-victimisation' (Kochenderfer-Ladd and Wardrop, 2001) to describe peer-directed aggression in preschool.

Important research in Finland with adolescents (Salmivalli *et al.*, 1996) indicated that bullying is rarely a dyadic interaction between bully and victim, and often includes other children in roles which may support (either directly or indirectly) or counter the bullying (see Smith, Chapter 3, for more on this research with school-aged pupils). Research which has examined whether peer-victimisation during the preschool period can be described as a 'group process' has suggested that this is unlikely. Monks *et al.* (2002) found that few children were identified using peer-, teacher- or self-nominations as taking the more 'peripheral' roles in peer-aggression (such as assisting or encouraging the aggressor). This may relate to the nature of children's peer-relations during the period between three and six years. Children's friendship groups are less stable at this age than is found among older groups, which suggests that these supporting roles in aggression may become more apparent as the dynamics of children's social interactions become more established (Smith and Monks, 2005).

Risk factors

Studies with older pupils have identified some risk factors for involvement in bullying, and researchers working with preschoolers have also explored these factors in relation to involvement in peer-victimisation, either as an aggressor or victim. By examining these characteristics in early childhood, we may learn more about what might place children at risk of involvement in peer-victimisation early on. Additionally, by focusing on preschoolers we may then be able to pull apart some cause and effect variables, which will be more difficult to distinguish once these patterns of behaviour become more established. By understanding these we will be better placed to develop age-appropriate intervention and prevention programmes with young children.

The characteristics explored by researchers have included family factors, peer-relations and social-cognitive abilities. Based on the research reviewed earlier regarding the relative stability of the role of aggressor, it would be suggested that aggressive preschoolers may show some similarities to those who are aggressive at school age. However, if there is low stability of the role of victim, this implies that the majority of children who are identified as victims in preschool will experience this transiently and it would be less likely that they would exhibit similar characteristics to their older counterparts.

Family factors

The family is often the first socialisation environment a child experiences and is thought to have an influence on the ways in which children develop social skills. The research in this area has focused on the impact of attachment on involvement in peer–victimisation, parenting styles and exposure to family conflict.

Aggression and attachment

A substantial body of research has looked at the link between attachment quality and aggression with peers among older groups. Early avoidant attachment has been found to be related to later hostility and aggressive relationships (e.g. Bost *et al.*, 1998). Attachment theory would suggest that the attachment formed with the primary caregiver (usually a parent) provides the child with a template (or 'internal working model') for future relationships. A child with an insecure attachment may be more at risk of responding to others insecurely, displaying hostility and aggression or withdrawal (e.g. Bowlby, 1973).

Troy and Sroufe (1987) used contrived play settings with four-and five-year-old children and found that those who were bullies in these play settings were more likely to be insecurely attached (based on assessments using the Strange Situation at 18 months). Monks *et al.* (2005) found, in a group of four- to six-year-olds, that more aggressors than victims or defenders were identified as being insecurely attached as assessed concurrently using the Separation Anxiety Test (although this difference did not reach significance). They found that 36.8 per cent of aggressors, 60.0 per cent of defenders and 66.7 per cent of victims were securely attached. Casas *et al.* (2006) also examined attachment security of the preschoolers in relation to relational and physical aggression. They found complex relationships between attachment security and aggression dependent on the gender of child and parent. Boys who were physically aggressive were less likely to be insecurely attached, whereas girls who were physically aggressive were more likely to be insecurely attached to their mother (but not their father). With regard to relational aggression, girls who were relationally aggressive were more likely to be insecurely attached to their mother, and relationally aggressive boys were more likely to have an insecure attachment to their father. Casas *et al.* do not provide firm conclusions to account for these findings, but do note that it is clearly important to consider gender in studies of the effects of family relationships.

A longitudinal study in Switzerland examining the relationship between children's parental representations and their behaviour (Stadelmann *et al.*, 2007) found that there was a relationship between parental representations and children's conduct problems and prosocial behaviour. They found that negative representations of the parent at age five were predictive of later conduct problems (including externalising behaviour), and that positive representations of the parent were linked to later prosocial behaviour. However, they did not look directly at bully/victim status and did not examine the behaviour of the children at age five in relation to their representations of their parents.

Other researchers have looked at the relationship between disorganised (D) patterns of attachment and early aggressive behaviour. Shaw *et al.* (1996) found that disorganised attachment at 12 months and maternal perceptions of the child as 'difficult' during their second year were related to disruptive behaviour at the age of five. Children with both of these risk factors showed significantly more aggressive problems as preschoolers than those with only one risk factor. Moss *et al.* (1996) reported that children classified as D were more likely to be perceived by teachers as having behaviour problems than their secure peers, both at the time of the assessment and two years beforehand. Moss *et al.* have put forward a theoretical link between this pattern of attachment and externalising behaviour problems. This association takes the form of the child focusing on controlling non-reciprocal behaviour patterns in an attempt to bring some kind of stability to their world.

Aggression and parenting styles Parenting styles are thought to have the potential to influence children's behaviour; that is, with the child learning from their parents' behaviour how to act in social situations (e.g. Bandura, 1973). Parenting may also reinforce antisocial or aggressive behaviours, explicitly by rewarding the child for aggressive acts, or implicitly by ignoring aggressive behaviour by the child and thereby being seen by the child as condoning it (e.g. Baldry, 2003). Paterson and Sanson (1999) also note that a child on the receiving end of harsh and power-assertive parenting may react with anger and frustration, which could lead to aggressive behaviour with peers. They found that, among a group of five- to six-year-olds in Australia, externalising behaviour (including aggression) was related to an interaction between inflexibility in the child's temperament and parental punitiveness. They suggest that a child who has an inflexible temperament may be more at risk from punitive parenting and may be more inclined to 'act out' when faced with punishment from the parent.

More recent studies have made the distinction between relational and overt aggression in relation to parenting practices. Nelson and Crick (2002) have suggested that parents' use of psychological control techniques with their children, such as love withdrawal ('if you don't do what I say, I won't love you anymore') or erratic emotional behaviour, show similarities to relational aggression among children and adolescents – with both involving the manipulation of relationships.

Additionally, there may be sex differences in the parenting styles which are related to aggression in children. Using Baumrind's (1967) classification of parenting styles, Casas *et al.* (2006) found that there were complex interactions between the sex of child, sex of parent and type of parenting predictive of aggression in the child. They found that for boys, relational aggression was predicted by maternal permissiveness and paternal authoritarianism, whereas, for girls, use of authoritarian types of parenting by both parents or maternal permissiveness were predictive of relational aggression. Further, for girls, lower levels of physical aggression were related to maternal authoritative parenting (for boys, this was less clear-cut). However, for both boys and girls, psychological control was related to each type of aggression.

Within a Chinese preschool sample of five year olds, Nelson *et al.* (2006) found physically coercive parenting was related to aggressive behaviour by boys and psychologically coercive parenting was related to aggressive behaviour by girls. They note that these types of parenting are related to *both* physical and relational aggression in the children. Although a specificity hypothesis might suggest that physically coercive parenting would be linked to physical aggression and that psychologically coercive aggression might be linked to relational aggression, this was not found to be the case. Nelson *et al.* suggest that boys and girls may be more sensitive to different forms of aversive parenting and that psychologically coercive parenting is similar to relational aggression between peers. Previous studies have found that relational aggression is reported as being more upsetting to girls than to boys, and Nelson *et al.* postulate that this may also hold true for the parent–child interaction, with this type of parenting being more likely to result in aggression of any type in girls. In contrast, they note that boys are more concerned by physical dominance within the peer-group and suggest that physical aggression would be more upsetting to boys and physically coercive parenting may be more provocative to boys and have a more negative influence on their behaviour.

Russell *et al.* (2003) looked at parenting practices and preschooler aggression in Australia and the USA. They confirmed previous findings that girls were more relationally aggressive and that boys were more physically aggressive and also found differences in the types of parenting received by boys and girls; boys received more authoritarian parenting and girls more authoritative parenting. They suggest that, from this type of parenting, girls might pick up a focus on relationships. This may be a positive thing, leading girls to be more prosocial (as found by this and other studies), but this focus on relationships may also lead to relational forms of aggression. For boys, the type of aversive parenting they experienced had more of a focus on physical coercion and was more punitive, which might lead to physical aggression.

Other studies have highlighted cultural differences in parenting practices (e.g. Deater-Deckard and Dodge, 1997), leading researchers to explore the links between parenting and child aggression in different cultures. Deater-Deckard and Dodge examined the relationship between the use of physical punishment by parents and the child's level of externalising behaviours (as rated by teachers). They found that there was a consistently positive and significant correlation between the extent to which parents used physical discipline and child externalising behaviours (including aggression) within a European-American sample from kindergarten to Grade 6. However, the correlation between the two variables did not reach significance in an African-American sample. They suggest that these findings may relate to the different views of the use of physical discipline in the two cultures and propose the 'misfit' hypothesis in an attempt to account for this. They note that, in a culture where physical discipline is deemed as a 'normal' part of parenting, it is less likely to be viewed by the child as signifying hostility or rejection on the part of the parent, and, therefore, may be less likely to lead to negative child outcomes. Additionally, they suggest that, in cultures where physical discipline is an accepted form of parenting, parents within this culture who use it may be doing so in a controlled and reasoned manner. Whereas, when it is used in a culture which generally frowns upon its use, it may reflect parenting that is 'out-of-control'.

However, some authors have suggested that what is important in affecting child behaviour is the child's interpretation of the parenting and whether they perceive the parenting as a rejection by the parent, rather than the particular parenting style *per se* (Khaleque and Rohner, 2002). They argue that the association between perceived rejection and child aggression should be demonstrable across cultures. So, there may be some subtle cultural variations in parenting, but the key negative factor would be rejecting parenting. Nevertheless, Nelson *et al.* (2006) found that physical punishment by parents is related to aggression in children even in cultures where it is seen as a 'good' form of parenting (and so not rejecting). Lansford *et al.* (2005) examined the relationship between child aggression and parental use of physical discipline in a number of countries where the normativeness of the use of physical discipline varied. They found in all countries that there was a relationship between the use of physical discipline and aggression in children, but that this was weaker (yet still significant) in countries where its use was seen as more normative.

Aggression and family conflict In addition to examining attachment quality and parenting styles, researchers have also looked at the impact of exposure to conflict (either parent–parent or parent–child) within the home. In a stringently controlled study (controlling for potentially confounding variables such as socioeconomic status, violence within the community and maternal life stressors), Ybarra *et al.* (2007) reported that preschoolers who were exposed to domestic violence did not show high levels of externalising behaviours, but rather exhibited internalising behaviours. Schwartz *et al.* (1997), in a study focused on adult aggression and conflict (rather than domestic violence), found links between early exposure to these behaviours during the preschool period and later aggressive behaviour. In their longitudinal study of boys, following them from the age of five years for four to five years, they reported that aggressors at age nine to ten years were more likely to have been exposed to adult aggression and conflict, but were unlikely to have been the targets of that aggression. However, this study did not examine the links between exposure to interparental aggression and aggression displayed by the child during preschool.

Ostrov and Bishop (2008) used a combination of observations, teacher and parent reports and found that parent–child conflict was linked to relational and not physical aggression by the child. They suggested that perhaps parent–child interactions are more focused on relationships rather than on instrumental goals, and that this gives the child more insight into relational rather than physical forms of aggression. However, as with other cross-sectional studies, it is important to note that the parent–child conflict may predate the child's relational aggression but, equally, it could be that the relational aggression exhibited by the child may be a trigger for parent–child conflict.

Taken together, these findings suggest that there may be important effects of attachment, parenting and conflict within the family on children's aggressive behaviour. There may be gender-specific pathways, with girls being more affected by psychological control and boys by physical coercion. Many of the studies, particularly those examining the impact of conflict, have been cross-sectional in design, making it impossible to draw firm conclusions about the direction of the relations; does conflict cause child aggression or does child aggression precipitate conflict? Controlled, longitudinal studies are needed to explore this further.

Victims and family factors There has been less focus on the families of those children who are victimised by their peers during preschool. Schwartz *et al.* (2000) carried out two longitudinal studies into the relationship between parenting factors and victimisation by peers. They confirmed the link between early harsh environment and later victimisation but additionally found that friendship moderated the link between parenting and victimisation. Those children who had few friends and had experienced an earlier harsh environment were at risk of victimisation by peers. In contrast, those who had experienced earlier difficulties in their home, but had friends, were less likely to be victimised. Schwartz *et al.* suggested that it could be that having friends helped children to develop social competencies which they may otherwise have lacked and would have left them more vulnerable to peer-victimisation. Alternatively, it could be that having friends is a 'marker', indicating resilience in these children to experiencing a difficult background. However, this research explored the relationship between family factors prior to entering kindergarten with behaviour during Grades 2 or 3 (ages eight or nine years). The studies did not examine the relationship between family factors and victimisation in preschool.

If victim status during preschool is not a stable experience for many children, then we would expect that most children identified as 'victims' at this age would not show the same vulnerabilities as older victims. Research with older children has found that children who are victimised by their peers are more likely to be insecurely attached to their caregivers. Attachment theory would suggest that insecure attachment would mean that children may respond to their peers with hostility (aggression) or by withdrawing (perhaps leaving them open to victimisation). Monks *et al.* (2005) found that young victims, aged four to six years, did not show this pattern of insecurity, with the majority, around two-thirds, showing secure attachments with their primary caregivers. However, Troy and Sroufe (1987) found that victims in their sample of four- to six-year-olds were more likely to be insecurely attached. This difference may be related to the different methodologies used; Troy and Sroufe (1987) used contrived play settings to identify whether children were bullies or victims, whereas Monks *et al.* (2005) used nominations of their behaviour by classmates. The use of contrived play settings by

Troy and Sroufe may have identified those children who are particularly at risk of peer-victimisation in a very brief peer-interaction. In contrast, the use of peer-nominations in the research by Monks *et al.* may have identified the large and varied group of children who actually experience victimisation in the peer-group over a longer period of exposure in a more naturalistic setting.

Peer-relations

As well as examining family relationships in relation to peer-aggression, researchers have explored the role of relationships with peers. One of the most commonly used methods of assessing children's peer-relations has been the sociometric nomination procedure developed by Coie *et al.* (1982). This involves each child identifying the three classmates they 'like most' and the three classmates they 'like least'. Using this method, it is possible to assign most children to one of five sociometric status groups: popular, average, rejected, neglected (not nominated as like most or like least) and controversial (highly liked by some and highly disliked by others).

Aggression and peer-relations Wood *et al.* (2004) highlighted that at age four to five years, externalising behaviour was positively correlated with peer-rejection, indicating that those who exhibited higher levels of externalising behaviour were more rejected by their classmates. Slaughter *et al.* (2002) noted that, when age and IQ were partialled out, social preference was negatively correlated with aggression and positively correlated with prosocial behaviour among four- to six-year-olds. Ladd and Burgess (1999) found that aggressive behaviour during the first years of school (ages five to seven) was related to relationship problems, including low peer-acceptance and higher levels of teacher–child conflict. Ladd and Burgess (2001) reported significant positive correlations between aggression and peer-rejection during kindergarten (ages five to six), $rs = 0.33$ (autumn), 0.44 (spring) and Grade 1 (ages six to seven), 0.34 (spring).

Wood *et al.* (2002) found that rejection by peers was related to non-compliant behaviours, hyperactivity and withdrawal among preschoolers. They propose that children's behaviour problems may place them at risk of being rejected by classmates – as these behaviours may make them less appealing playmates. However, their study was cross-sectional in design and it is possible that rejection by peers may lead to or indeed exacerbate behaviour problems.

Monks *et al.* (2003) and Ortega and Monks (2006) showed that preschool aggressors in England and Spain were likely to be socially rejected by their classmates. It is perhaps not surprising that very young children view peer-aggressors negatively. At this age there is a general consensus among children that aggressive behaviour towards others is 'wrong' (Huesmann and Guerra, 1997). This would suggest that young aggressive children may be socially rejected by their classmates as a consequence of their behaviour or that social rejection may result in this aggressive behaviour (if no one likes me, why should I be nice to them?) or exacerbate an existing behaviour problem. However, this study was also cross-sectional and firm conclusions regarding causality could not be drawn.

In order to examine this link, Keane and Calkins (2004) obtained parental reports of children's behaviours before they started school (at ages two and four years) and looked at these in relation to their behaviour at school and peer-status with classmates (at age five years). They found that externalising behaviours prior to school entry predicted aggressive behaviours in school. They additionally found that there was a link (for boys only) between externalising behaviours before starting school and peer-rejection at school, but that this was mediated by current aggressive behaviour. These findings suggest that it is the aggressive behaviour that leads to peer-rejection, although they do not rule out a cyclical effect of peer-rejection leading to further aggression.

The existence of a cyclical relationship between peer-rejection and aggression was supported by Dodge *et al.* (2003). They examined the relationship between aggression and social rejection between the ages of five and eight years. As later confirmed by Keane and Calkins (2004), they found that aggression was related significantly to social rejection. In addition, they report that peer-rejection led to an increase in aggressive behaviour among children who were already aggressive. In contrast, it did not have that effect for children who were not initially aggressive. Taken together, these results suggest that peer-rejection is a particular risk for aggressive children, which may result in them displaying increased levels of aggressive behaviour during the early years of school.

Braza *et al.* (2007) looked at the relation between sociometric status and behaviour from the opposite direction. They made observations of preschool children who had been identified as having different sociometric statuses within the peer-group, examining their social behaviours with others, in particular, their aggression, sociability and involvement in hierarchical play. They found that popular children showed high levels of sociability with peers, but lower levels of aggression in their interactions, and spent more time engaged in hierarchical play. In contrast, rejected children were less sociable, and displayed higher levels of aggression in their interactions with peers and were less likely to be involved in hierarchical play. They suggest that this may reflect children's standing within the dominance hierarchy of the class and proposed that popular children are already at a high level within the dominance hierarchy and do not need to use aggressive strategies to promote their social standing. These popular children instead settle any dominance struggles through the use of hierarchical play. In contrast, rejected children may be trying to better their social standing within the peer-group through the use of aggressive strategies.

Research has also explored the link between relational aggression and peer-status in preschoolers (Crick *et al.*, 1997). They found that girls who were relationally aggressive were more likely to be socially rejected by peers. Ostrov *et al.* (2006) confirmed the relationship between relational aggression and peer-rejection in an observational study, but noted that relational assertion (manipulating relationships for gain, without harm, hostility or anger), e.g. 'Because I said so!', was related to later popularity. Although generally it has been found that young aggressors tend to be socially rejected, Hawley (2002, 2003) has noted that, in situations of resource competition, a strategy which involves both prosocial and coercive patterns (children Hawley calls 'bistrategic controllers') can enhance a child's social dominance within preschool groups. She found that children who used this strategy were liked by other children. However, those children who used solely coercive patterns did not show this peer-popularity.

Roseth *et al.* (2007) examined the relationships of aggressive preschoolers using observational methods. They found that, across the school year, the use of aggression decreased. They suggest that this is because children, when they first join a new class, are jostling for social position, and use aggressive means in some cases. The use of aggression was related to social dominance, and children who are socially dominant do not just use aggression more frequently than others, but also use it more effectively, switching between aggressive and affiliative strategies (much like Hawley's 'bistrategic controllers' (Hawley 2002, 2003)).

In this way, we can see that *some* children who make use of aggressive strategies in their interactions with peers are still popular. What is important, and highlighted by both Roseth *et al.* (2007) and Hawley (2003), is that these children are using aggressive tactics selectively and in a socially skilled way. Those who rely solely on aggressive strategies, rather than balancing them with prosocial behaviours, were found to be more disliked than others (Hawley, 2003).

Beyond the influence of sociometric status, other researchers have looked at loneliness and the friendships of children in relation to their behaviour with peers. Coplan *et al.* (2007) examined the correlates of loneliness among preschoolers and note that this is related to, but not identical to, social rejection. Loneliness was related to more anxiety, more aggression and increased peer exclusion. They suggest that lonely preschoolers may be a heterogeneous group, with some being anxious and lonely and others aggressive and lonely. Sebanc (2003) noted that preschool children (aged between three and five years) who had friends were more prosocial, more socially accepted and less socially rejected than those children who were friendless. In addition, when she examined the quality of these friendships, she found that these were related to children's social behaviour with peers more generally. Support within the friendship was positively correlated with prosocial behaviour and exclusivity/intimacy within the friendship was positively related to relational aggression and negatively related to social acceptance. Conflict within the friendship was related to both overt aggression and relational aggression, as well as higher levels of social rejection.

Overall, these findings indicate that the majority of preschool aggressors tend to be socially rejected by their classmates, but that some who use aggression selectively and in a socially skilled way may be socially dominant children who are popular with other children.

Victims and peer-relations In relation to peer-victimisation, it would be expected that social isolation may place a child at risk of peer-victimisation (as Hodges *et al.* (1997) have found among older groups that friends can have a protective function against victimisation) and that the experience of victimisation may lead to a child becoming further isolated. However, the low stability of victimisation at this age may mean that we might not be able to see any differences between victims and non-victims as most children may experience victimisation fleetingly. This was confirmed by the findings of Monks *et al.* (2002, 2005) with preschoolers in England and Spain, who found that peer-identified young victims tended to be of average sociometric status. However, Perren and Alsaker (2006) showed that teacher-nominated victims were of lower sociometric status. This difference in findings may highlight the differences between peer- and teacher-reports, as discussed earlier.

Social cognition

Much of the research exploring individual difference factors in relation to social behaviour, including aggressive and withdrawn behaviours, has focused on social-cognitive abilities, including theory of mind, understanding emotions and empathy. The preschool period (between three and six years) is an interesting age on which to focus as children are developing many of these skills rapidly during the preschool period.

Aggressors and social-cognitive abilities Hughes and Leekam (2004) note that theory of mind ability, often assessed by false belief (FB) tasks, may influence, and be influenced by, social relations. They note that theory of mind can have a positive, neutral or negative relationship to socially desirable behaviour. Hay *et al.* (2004) suggest that problems in social understanding, executive function and regulating emotion can lead to aggression and a lack of prosocial skills, which in turn lead to problems in peer-acceptance. Among older children, ringleader bullies have been shown to exhibit superior theory of mind abilities (e.g. Sutton *et al.*, 1999). It has been suggested that these skills may enable them to manipulate others, supported by the finding that social intelligence is positive correlated with indirect aggression (Kaukianen *et al.*, 1999).

Monks *et al.* (2005) examined the relationship between preschool aggressive behaviour towards peers and FB performance. They found that aggression was not related to superior performance on theory of mind and that, in fact, aggressive children tended to score slightly lower (although not significantly) than other children. They suggest that the disparity with the findings of Sutton *et al.* (1999) may reflect the developing nature of peer-victimisation during early childhood. Types of aggression used by young children tend to be direct in nature, and these forms of aggression are only weakly related to social cognition (e.g. Kaukiainen *et al.*, 1999). Additionally, the group nature of peer-victimisation appears to differ in preschool classes, with few children taking on the more peripheral roles of assistant to the bully and reinforcer. This may mean that peer-victimisation at this age is less reliant on good social-cognitive abilities, as it is not as important to be able to organise a gang of 'followers'. Monks *et al.* (2005) suggest a developmental change theory whereby children who are aggressive may develop their social skills through their aggressive interactions with peers, which could account for the advantage seen by older bullies. It is proposed that young aggressors may not be socially skilled initially, but, through their conflicts with other children, may develop skills in manipulating and deceiving others. Other researchers have found that exposure to social interactions (including conflict) is related to superior performance on tasks assessing social cognition (e.g. Foote and Holmes-Lonergan, 2003).

Diesendruck and Ben-Eliyahu (2006) looked at emotion understanding and theory of mind in relation to Israeli preschoolers' (aged four to six years) aggressive and prosocial behaviour. Here, aggressive children did not have poor FB understanding, but did perform poorly on tasks assessing emotion understanding in others. In contrast, prosocial children were found to perform highly on tasks assessing false belief and emotion understanding.

Strayer (2004) placed five-year-old children in small groups with peers they did not know and examined the link between children's aggressive and prosocial behaviour with their empathy. Strayer examined affective empathy, which involves feeling for the other individual and experiencing the same or a similar emotion in response. She found that empathy showed a negative relationship with aggressive behaviour and anger within the peer-settings, but it had a positive relation with prosocial behaviour. However, it is possible that this low level of empathy may enable children to behave aggressively without the negative feelings this may entail in others, or their limited social interactions may affect the development of empathy in aggressive children.

Victims and social cognition Research with older children has indicated that the victims of bullying have poorer theory of mind abilities (e.g. Sutton *et al.*, 1999), which may place children at risk of misreading others' intentions and therefore being more vulnerable to victimisation by aggressive peers. Research examining the characteristics of children victimised during preschool has found that, as a group, young victims do not fit this profile (Monks *et al.*, 2005). This, again, may be a reflection of the finding that few children are repeatedly victimised at this age and it may not be until children are older that aggressive children repeatedly target others who may be less capable of defending themselves.

Summary of chapter

The research reviewed in this chapter, based on work in a variety of developed countries worldwide, has indicated that some young preschool or kindergarten children behave aggressively towards their peers. However, it appears that peer-victimisation during early childhood differs from 'bullying' seen in later childhood, adolescence and adulthood. Although some children appear to behave aggressively towards their peers at this age, they do not appear to target the same few individuals repeatedly, but rather focus their aggression on a wide variety of class-mates. Additionally, unlike research with older children, it appears that peer-victimisation during preschool is less of a group process and more likely a dyadic interaction between aggressor and victim. Few children tend to be identified as 'supporting' (either actively or passively) the aggressive behaviour of others. Furthermore, the aggressive behaviours exhibited by young children tie in with previous research on develop-mental trends in aggression among older children. Overall, young chil-dren use a variety of different types of aggressive behaviour towards peers, including verbal, physical and relational, yet their aggression tends to take place in face-to-face encounters, rather than indirectly.

These findings indicate that a traditional definition of 'bullying' from a school or working context is not seen among preschool-aged children. However, the aggressive behaviour we see at this age may be the early development of this behaviour for some children. It may well be the case that, with age, these behaviours become more focused on those peers who are perceived as being more 'vulnerable', and that, with time, other children take on these roles which are more 'support-ive' of aggression.

The finding that aggressive individuals exhibit similar characteristics to older bullies (in terms of attachment, parenting styles and exposure to conflict) suggests that this group of aggressive children may contain some of those who go on to bully others later in school. Their harsher backgrounds may place them at risk for behaving aggressively as a result of social learning, implicit or explicit rewards from parents for aggressive behaviour or as a frustrated response to a difficult home-background. That aggressive preschoolers have poor emotion understanding and do not show any superiority of theory of mind, whereas older bullies show superior theory of mind abilities, suggests a developmental shift. Children may develop superior theory of mind and social understanding through these acts of aggression, so by middle childhood their higher levels of exposure to peer-related conflicts may have promoted the devel-opment of their social understanding (Monks *et al.*, 2005).

In general, preschool victims do not, as a group, appear to exhibit similar characteristics to older victims, such as insecure attachments, peer-rejection and poor social-cognitive abilities. However, this does appear to be related to the methodology employed to find out about this role (e.g. Monks *et al.*, 2010), with teacher-identified victims being more similar to older victims and peer- or self-identified victims tend-ing to be indistinguishable from others. This ties in with the finding from peer- and self-reports and observations that the role of victim during this period is less stable than among older groups.

Much research in this area has focused on the relationship between family factors and peer-aggression, indicating that the family environment may have an important impact on children's subsequent behaviour with peers. This has been postulated as working through a number of processes, such as attachment theory, coercion theory and social learning theory.

However, it is important to keep in mind the mainly correlational nature of the research reviewed above. It is possible that the characteristics highlighted in the literature place children at risk of becoming involved in peer-victimisation during the preschool period. However, it is also feasible in many of the cases that involvement in peer-victimisation may have an impact on these characteristics. For example, parenting and peer relations may influence and may be influenced by a child's behaviour. Furthermore, the development of social-cognitive abilities may influence children's behaviours but, additionally, children's behaviour may affect their opportunities to develop social-cognitive skills.

Implications for interventions and future research

Based on the findings reviewed within this chapter it is clear that intervention and prevention work to limit peer-victimisation needs to begin in preschool. Smith *et al.* (2004) concluded that intervention is required early, before these negative patterns of interaction are established. Additionally, the finding that family factors are implicated suggests that we need to involve families in this intervention and prevention work. There is a growing body of research on preschool peer-victimisation, but our knowledge in this area is still limited. In particular, carefully controlled longitudinal studies are needed to attempt to identify the risk factors for becoming a stable victim in order to inform the development of programmes to help children to avoid repeated victimisation. In addition, the finding that peer-victimisation does not appear to be a group process among younger children has implications for intervention work. Young children may be more amenable to intervention work and may have less invested in supporting peer-victimisation. Further research is required into this, in order to examine how, and at what point, the 'supporting' roles appear within peer-victimisation.

REFERENCES

Baldry, A.C. (2003). 'Bullying in schools and exposure to domestic violence'. *Child Abuse and Neglect*, 27: 713–32.
Bandura, A. (1973). *Aggression: A Social Learning Analysis*. Englewood Cliffs, NJ: Prentice Hall.

Baumrind, D. (1967). 'Child care practices anteceding three patterns of preschool behavior'. *Genetic Psychology Monographs*, 75: 43–88.

Björkqvist, K., Lagerspetz, K.M. and Kaukiainen, A. (1992). 'Do girls manipulate and boys fight? Developmental trends in regard to direct and indirect aggression'. *Aggressive Behavior*, 18: 117–27.

Bost, K.K., Vaughn, B.E., Newell-Washington, W., Ciclinski, K.L. and Bradbard, M.R. (1998). 'Social competence, social support, and attachment: demarcation of construct domains, measurement, and paths of influence for preschool children attending head start'. *Child Development*, 69: 192–218.

Bowlby, J. (1973). *Attachment and Loss,* vol. II, *Separation: Anxiety and Anger.* New York: Basic Books.

Braza, F., Braza, P., Carreras, M.R., Muñoz, J.M., Sánchez-Marín, J.R., Azurmendi, A., Sorozabal, A., García, A. and Cardas, J. (2007). 'Behavioral profiles of different types of social status in preschool children: an observational approach'. *Social Behavior and Personality*, 35: 195–212.

Casas, J.F., Weigel, S.M., Crick, N.R., Ostrov, J.M., Woods, K.E., Jansen Yeh, E.A. and Huddleston-Casas, C.A. (2006). 'Early parenting and children's relational and physical aggression in the preschool and home contexts'. *Applied Developmental Psychology*, 27: 209–27.

Coie, J.D., Dodge, K.A. and Coppotelli, H. (1982). 'Dimensions and types of social status: a cross-age perspective'. *Developmental Psychology*, 18: 557–70.

Coplan, R.J., Closson, L.M. and Arbeau, K.A. (2007). 'Gender differences in the behavioural associates of loneliness and social dissatisfaction in kindergarten'. *Journal of Child Psychology and Psychiatry*, 48: 988–95.

Crick, N.R. and Grotpeter, J.K. (1995). 'Relational aggression, gender and social-psychological adjustment'. *Child Development*, 66: 710–22.

Crick, N.R., Casas, J.F. and Ku, H. (1999). 'Relational and physical forms of peer victimization in preschool'. *Developmental Psychology*, 35: 376–85.

Crick, N.R., Casas, J.F. and Mosher, M. (1997). 'Relational and overt aggression in preschool'. *Developmental Psychology*, 33: 579–88.

Deater-Deckard, K. and Dodge, K.A. (1997). 'Externalising behaviour problems and discipline revisited: nonlinear effects and variation by culture, context and gender'. *Psychological Inquiry*, 8: 161–75.

Diesendruck, G. and Ben-Eliyahu, A. (2006). 'The relationships among social cognition, peer acceptance, and social behavior in Israeli kindergartners'. *International Journal of Behavioral Development*, 30: 137–47.

Dodge, K.A., Lansford, J.E., Salzer Burks, V., Bates, J.E., Pettit, G.S., Fontaine, R. and Price, J.M. (2003). 'Peer rejection and social information-processing factors in the development of aggressive behavior problems in children'. *Child Development*, 74: 374–93.

Farrington, D.P. (1993). 'Understanding and preventing bullying'. In M. Tonry and N. Morris (eds.), *Crime and Justice: An Annual Review of Research.* Chicago: University of Chicago Press.

Foote, R.C. and Holmes-Lonergan, H.A. (2003). 'Sibling conflict and theory of mind'. *British Journal of Developmental Psychology*, 21: 45–58.

Hanish L.D. and Guerra N.G. (2000). 'Predictors of peer-victimisation among urban youth'. *Social Development*, 9: 521–43.

Hawley, P.H. (2002). 'Social dominance and prosocial and coercive strategies of resource control in preschoolers'. *International Journal of Behavioral Development*, 26: 167–76.

—— (2003). 'Prosocial and coercive configurations of resource control in early adolescence: a case for the well-adapted Machiavellian'. *Merrill-Palmer Quarterly*, 49: 279–309.

Hay, D.F., Payne, A. and Chadwick, A. (2004). 'Peer relations in childhood'. *Journal of Child Psychology and Psychiatry*, 45: 84–108.

Hodges, E.V.E., Malone, M.J. and Perry, D.G. (1997). 'Individual risk and social risk as interacting determinants of victimisation in the peer group'. *Developmental Psychology*, 33: 1032–39.

Huesmann, L.R. and Guerra, N.G. (1997). 'Children's normative beliefs about aggression and aggressive behaviour'. *Journal of Personality and Social Psychology*, 72: 408–19.

Hughes, C. and Leekam, S. (2004). 'What are the links between theory of mind and social relations? Review, reflections and new directions of studies of typical and atypical development'. *Social Development*, 13: 590–619.

Kaukiainen, A., Björkqvist, K., Lagerspetz, K., Österman, K., Salmivalli, C., Rothberg, S. and Ahlbom, A. (1999). 'The relationship between social intelligence, empathy, and three types of aggression'. *Aggressive Behavior*, 25: 81–89.

Keane, S.P. and Calkins, S.D. (2004). 'Predicting kindergarten peer social status from toddler and preschool problem behaviour'. *Journal of Abnormal Child Psychology*, 32: 409–23.

Khaleque, A. and Rohner, R.P. (2002). 'Perceived parental acceptance–rejection and psychological adjustment: a meta-analysis of cross-cultural and intracultural studies'. *Journal of Marriage and Family*, 64: 54–64.

Kochenderfer, B.J. and Ladd, G.W. (1996). 'Peer victimization: cause or consequence of school maladjustment?' *Child Development*, 67: 1305–17.

Kochenderfer-Ladd, B.J. and Wardrop, J.L. (2001). 'Chronicity and instability of children's peer victimization experiences as predictors of loneliness and social satisfaction trajectories'. *Child Development*, 72: 134–51.

Ladd, G.W. (2006). 'Peer rejection, aggressive or withdrawn behaviour, and psychological maladjustment from ages 5 to 12: an examination of four predictive models'. *Child Development*, 77: 822–46.

Ladd, G.W. and Burgess, K.B. (1999). 'Charting the relationship trajectories of aggressive, withdrawn, and aggressive/withdrawn children during early grade school'. *Child Development*, 70: 910–29.

—— (1998). 'Parenting behaviours and parent–child relationship: correlates of peer victimization in kindergarten?' *Developmental Psychology*, 34: 1450–58.

—— (2001). 'Do relational risks and protective factors moderate the linkages between childhood aggression and early psychological and school adjustment?' *Child Development*, 72: 1579–601.

—— (2006). 'Identifying victims of peer aggression from early to middle childhood: analysis of cross-informant data for concordance, estimation of relational adjustment, prevalence of victimization, and characteristics of identified victims'. *Psychological Assessment*, 14: 74–96.

Lansford, J.E., Chang, L., Dodge, K.A., Malone, P.S., Oburu, P., Palmérus, K., Bacchini, D., Pastorelli, C., Bombi, A.S., Zelli, A., Tapanya, S., Chaudhary, N., Deater-Deckard, K., Manke, B. and Quinn, N. (2005). 'Physical discipline and children's adjustment: cultural normativeness as a moderator'. *Child Development*, 76: 1234–46.

Monks, C.P. and Smith, P.K. (2006). 'Definitions of "bullying": age differences in understanding of the term, and the role of experience'. *British Journal of Developmental Psychology*, 24: 801–21.

Monks, C.P., Ortega, R. and Torrado, E. (2002). 'Unjustified aggression in a Spanish pre-school'. *Aggressive Behavior*, 28: 458–76.

Monks, C.P., Smith, P.K. and Swettenham, J. (2003). 'Aggressors, victims and defenders in preschool: peer, self and teacher reports'. *Merrill-Palmer Quarterly*, 49: 453–69.

(2005). 'The psychological correlates of peer victimisation in preschool: social cognitive skills, executive function and attachment profiles'. *Aggressive Behavior*, 31: 571–88.

Monks, C.P., Palermiti, A., Ortega, R. and Costabile, A. (2010). 'Peer-victimisation in preschools: a cross-national comparison of England, Spain and Italy'. *Spanish Journal of Psychology*, 13 (2):

Moss, E., Parent, S., Gosselin, C., Rosseau, D. and St-Laurent, D. (1996). 'Attachment and teacher-reported behaviour problems during the pre-school and early school-age period'. *Development and Psychopathology*, 8: 511–25.

Nelson, D.A. and Crick, N.R. (2002). 'Parental psychological control: implications for childhood physical and relational aggression'. In B.K. Barber (ed.), *Intrusive Parenting: How Psychological Control Affects Children and Adolescents*. (pp. 168–89). Washington, DC: American Psychological Association.

Nelson, D.A., Hart, C.A., Yang, C., Olsen, J.A. and Jin, S. (2006). 'Aversive parenting in China: associations with child physical and relational aggression'. *Child Development*, 77: 554–72.

Ortega, R. and Monks, C.P. (2005). 'Agresividad injustificada entre preescolares: un estudio preliminary [Unjustified aggression between preschoolers: a preliminary study]'. *Psicothema*, 17: 453–58.

Ostrov, J.M. (2008). 'Forms of aggression and peer victimisation during early childhood: a short-term longitudinal study'. *Journal of Abnormal Child Psychology*, 36: 311–22.

Ostrov, J.M. and Bishop, C.M. (2008). 'Preschoolers' aggression and parent–child conflict: a multiinformant and multimethod study'. *Journal of Experimental Child Psychology*, 99: 309–22.

Ostrov, J.M. and Keating, C.F. (2004). 'Gender differences in preschool aggression during free play and structured interactions: an observational study'. *Social Development*, 13: 255–77.

Ostrov, J.M., Pilat, M.M. and Crick, N.R. (2006). 'Assertion strategies and aggression during early childhood: a short-term longitudinal study'. *Early Childhood Research Quarterly*, 21: 403–16.

Paterson, G. and Sanson, A. (1999). 'The association of behavioural adjustment to temperament, parenting and family characteristics among 5-year-old children'. *Social Development*, 8: 293–309.

Pellegrini, A.D. and Bartini, M. (2000). 'An empirical comparison of methods of sampling aggression and victimization in school settings'. *Journal of Educational Psychology*, 92: 360–66.

Perren, S. and Alsaker, F.D. (2006). 'Social behavior and peer relationships of victims, bully-victims, and bullies in kindergarten'. *Journal of Child Psychology and Psychiatry*, 47: 45–57.

Perry, D.G., Perry, L.C. and Boldizar, J.P. (1990). 'Learning of aggression'. In M. Lewis and S. Miller (eds.), *Handbook of Developmental Psychopathology* (pp. 135–46). New York: Plenum Press.

Persson, G.E.B. (2005). 'Young children's prosocial and aggressive behaviors and their experiences of being targeted for similar behaviors by peers'. *Social Development*, 14: 206–28.

Roseth, C.J., Pellegrini, A.D., Bohn, C.M., Van Ryzin, M. and Vance, N. (2007). 'Preschoolers' aggression, affiliation, and social dominance relationships: an observational, longitudinal study'. *Journal of School Psychology*, 45: 479–97.

Russell, A., Hart, C.H., Robinson, C.C. and Olsen, S.F. (2003). 'Children's sociable and aggressive behavior with peers: a comparison of the U.S. and Australia and contribution of temperament and parenting styles'. *International Journal of Behavioral Development*, 27: 74–86.

Salmivalli, C., Lagerspetz, K.M.J., Björkqvist, K., Österman, K. and Kaukiainen, A. (1996). 'Bullying as a group process: participant roles and their relations to social status within the group'. *Aggressive Behavior*, 22: 1–15.

Schäfer, M., Korn, S., Brodbeck, F., Wolke, D. and Schulz, H. (2005). 'Bullying roles in changing contexts: the stability of victim and bully roles from primary to secondary school'. *International Journal of Behavioral Development*, 29: 323–35.

Schwartz, D., Dodge, K.A., Pettit, G.S. and Bates, J.E. (1997). 'The early socialization of aggressive victims'. *Child Development*, 68: 665–75.

Schwartz, D., Pettit, G.S., Dodge, K.A. and Bates, J.E. (2000). 'Friendship as a moderating factor in the pathway between early harsh home environment and later victimization in the peer group'. *Developmental Psychology*, 36: 646–62.

Sebanc, A.M. (2003). 'The friendship features of preschool children: links with prosocial behavior and aggression'. *Social Development*, 12: 249–68.

Shahim, S. (2008). 'Sex differences in relational aggression in preschool children in Iran'. *Psychological Reports*, 102: 235–38.

Shaw, D.S., Owens, E.B., Vondra, J.I., Keenan, K. and Winslow, E.B. (1996). 'Early risk factors and pathways in the development of early disruptive behaviour problems'. *Development and Psychopathology*, 8: 679–99.

Shin, Y. and Kim, H.Y. (2008). 'Peer victimization in Korean preschool children: the effects of child characteristics, parenting behaviours and teacher–child relationships'. *School Psychology International*, 29: 590–605.

Slaughter, V., Dennis, M.J. and Pritchard, M. (2002). 'Theory of mind and peer acceptance in preschool children'. *British Journal of Developmental Psychology*, 20: 545–64.

Smith, P.K. and Levan, S. (1995). 'Perceptions and experiences of bullying in younger pupils'. *British Journal of Educational Psychology*, 65: 489–500.

Smith, P.K. and Monks, C.P. (2005). 'L'amicizia e il gioco tra coetanei in età prescolare'. In L. Genta (ed.), *La Socializzazione in Età Prescolare* [*Friendship and Play between Preschool Peers*] (pp. 57–77). Rome: Carocci.

—— (2008). 'Concepts of bullying: developmental and cultural aspects'. *International Journal of Adolescent Medicine and Health*, 20: 101–12.

Smith, P.K., Madsen, K.C. and Moody, J.C. (1999). 'What causes the age decline in reports of being bullied at school? Towards a developmental analysis of risks of being bullied'. *Educational Research*, 41: 267–85.

Smith, P.K., Pepler, D. and Rigby, K. (eds.) (2004). *Bullying in Schools: How Effective Can Interventions Be?* Cambridge: Cambridge University Press.

Snyder, J., Brooker, M., Patrick, R., Snyder, A., Schrepferman, L. and Stoolmiller, M. (2003). 'Observed peer victimization during early elementary school: continuity, growth, and relation to risk for child antisocial and depressive behavior'. *Child Development*, 74: 1881–98.

Stadelmann, S., Perren, S., von Wyl, A. and von Klitzing, K. (2007). 'Associations between family relationships and symptoms/strengths at kindergarten age: what is the role of children's parental representations?' *Journal of Child Psychology and Psychiatry*, 48: 996–1004.

Strayer, J. (2004). 'Empathy and observed anger and aggression in five-year-olds'. *Social Development*, 13: 1–13.

Sutton, J., Smith, P.K. and Swettenham, J. (1999). 'Bullying and "theory of mind": a critique of the "social skills deficit" view of anti-social behaviour'. *Social Development*, 8: 117–27.

Troy, M. and Sroufe, A.L. (1987). 'Victimisation among preschoolers: role of attachment relationships history'. *Journal of the American Academy of Child and Adolescent Psychiatry*, 26: 166–72.

UNICEF (2008). *The Childcare Transition: A League Table on Early Childhood Education and Care in Advanced Countries*. Florence: UNICEF Innocenti Research Centre, www.unicef-irc.org/publications/pdf/rc8_eng.pdf (accessed 20 January 2009).

Wood, J.J., Cowan, P.A. and Baker, B.L. (2002). 'Behavior problems and peer rejection in preschool boys and girls'. *Journal of Genetic Psychology*, 163: 72–88.

Wood, J.J., Emmerson, N.A. and Cowan, P.A. (2004). 'Is early attachment security carried forward into relationships with preschool peers?' *British Journal of Developmental Psychology*, 22: 245–53.

Ybarra, G.J., Wilkens, S.L. and Lieberman, A.F. (2007). 'The influence of domestic violence on preschooler behavior and functioning'. *Journal of Family Violence*, 22: 33–42.

3   Bullying in schools: thirty years of research

Peter K. Smith

Bullying in school has become a topic of international concern over the last 30 years. Starting with research in Scandinavia, Japan and the UK, there is now active research in most European countries, in Australia and New Zealand, Canada and the USA and Japan and South Korea (Jimerson *et al.*, 2010; Koo *et al.*, 2008; McGrath and Noble, 2006; Smith *et al.*, 1999b). In fact, the research on school bullying can be thought of as a research programme, in the sense of Lakatos (1970), with its core being the conception of bullying as a distinct category of aggressive behaviour. This programme has gone through four distinct waves or phases. In this chapter I will set the scene by outlining these four waves of research, and then follow the standard chapter format for this book in reviewing the research in more detail.

First wave of research: origins, 1970s–1988

Leaving aside one or two isolated earlier studies, the systematic study of bullying in schools can be dated from the 1970s, mainly in Scandinavia. A physician, Heinemann, published a book *Mobbning – Gruppvåld bland barn och vuxna* (*Mobbing – Group Aggression against Boys and Girls*) in 1972, which Olweus credits as first seriously raising awareness of the issue. In 1973, Olweus published *Forskning om skolmobbning*, translated into English as *Aggression in Schools: Bullies and Whipping Boys* (1978). This book was the first important scientific work on the topic, and thus justifies the assertion that there is now a 30-year tradition of research.

In this book, Olweus defined bullying or 'mobbing' in terms of physical and verbal behaviours, although he explicitly rejected the connotations of the 'mobbing' label (which implies group bullying), since much bullying appeared to be by one person. Through the 1980s Olweus developed a self-report questionnaire to assess bullying, an important tool in subsequent work. Also, in parallel with the first Norwegian National Anti-Bullying campaign, launched in 1983, he developed a school-based intervention programme. His evaluation of the original version of the Olweus Bullying Prevention Program (1983–85), with reports of reductions in bullying of around 50 per cent, encouraged researchers and inspired the next wave of research. A meeting in Stavanger in 1987 brought together a number of European researchers.

Second wave of research: establishing a research programme, 1989–mid 1990s

From around 1989, books and journal articles started to appear, and surveys in other countries beyond Scandinavia were beginning to be carried out. Besides self-report surveys, some studies started to use peer-nomination methodology. Also, some intervention campaigns took place, partly inspired by the Norwegian campaign; early large-scale interventions were in England (Smith and Sharp, 1994), Canada (Pepler et al., 1994) and Flanders (Stevens and Van Oost, 1995).

An important change in this period was a broadening of researchers' definitions of bullying, to include indirect and relational bullying (such as rumour-spreading, social exclusion); this followed the similar broadening of understanding of 'aggression', following the work of Bjorkqvist and colleagues in Finland and Crick and colleagues in the USA. Furthermore, work on bullying was becoming more international. Contacts were taking place with researchers in North America (for example, Pepler in Canada) and, towards the end of this period, with researchers in Japan. In fact, studies on *ijime* (the term closest to 'bullying') dated back at least to the 1980s, but this separate research tradition only made substantial contact with the Western research tradition following a Monbusho/UNESCO study in the latter 1990s (see Smith et al., 1999b).

Third wave of research: an established international research programme, mid 1990s–2004

During this period, research on 'traditional' bullying became an important international research programme. Many more publications appeared, and research on bullying featured substantially in European and international conferences. Surveys, and interventions, took place in many countries (see 21 country reports in Smith et al. (1999b) and 11 country reports on interventions in Smith et al. (2004a). A notable methodological step was the introduction of participant roles in bullying, from Salmivalli's work in Finland (Salmivalli et al., 1996). Researchers in the USA substantially developed research on victimisation and bullying during this period: see the edited collections by Juvonen and Graham (2001) and Espelage and Swearer (2004). Important work was also being undertaken in Australia and New Zealand: see Rigby (2002) and Sullivan *et al.* (2004).

Fourth wave of research: cyberbullying, 2004–present

A substantial shift and new impetus in the bullying research programme has been the advent of cyberbullying (see Rivers *et al.*, Chapter 10). Significant awareness of cyberbullying, and press reports, appear to date from around 2000–01. In England, for example, the DfES pack *Don't Suffer in Silence* (2000) did not mention cyberbullying; but a revision published in 2002 mentions 'sending malicious emails or text messages on mobile phones' (p. 9). Indeed, early forms of cyberbullying seem to have been mainly text messages or emails, at least judging from the extant research; for example, Noret and Rivers (2006) surveyed 11,000 English pupils from 2002 to 2005, asking about who had 'received nasty or threatening text messages or emails'. Starting from a small number of articles in the first few years of this century (although rather more on websites), academic publications in the cyberbullying area have increased rapidly in the last few years. Notable publications in the area are the book by Willard (2006), a special issue of the *Journal of Adolescent Health* (2007), the books by Shariff (2008), Kowalski *et al.* (2008) and Hinduja and Patchin (2008), a special issue of the *Zeitschrift für Psychologie/Journal of Psychology* (2009) and a book by Li *et al.* (in press).

Of course, work on traditional bullying continues in this latest wave of studies, but methodologies (such as questionnaires) have had to be adapted to include new forms of bullying. Cyberbullying also brings some new challenges and opportunities to the bullying research programme, notably greater disciplinary breadth, and a chance to extend the focus beyond just the school context, and beyond just the school age range (Smith, 2010).

Definitions of bullying

Although there is no universally agreed definition, there is some consensus in the Western research tradition that bullying refers to repeated aggressive acts against someone who cannot easily defend themselves (see Olweus, 1999; Ross, 2002). A similar definition, though perhaps with broader connotations, is that bullying is a 'systematic abuse of power' (Rigby, 2002; Smith and Sharp, 1994). Although the two criteria of repetition and power imbalance are not universally accepted, they are now widely used. It should be noted however that there are problems with extending this definition in a simple way to cyberbullying; both as regards repetition (a single act by an aggressor, such as posting a nasty website comment, may be seen, commented on and forwarded by many others) and as regards imbalance of power (clearly it does not refer to physical strength or numerical strength in this context). The distinction of 'bullying' from more general 'aggression' has been an important and widely accepted aspect of traditional bullying research, but may be on much less firm ground as regards cyberbullying and cyber-aggression (Dooley et al., 2009).

Taking the traditional definition of bullying, then the repetition and imbalance of power are likely to lead to particular outcomes, such as fear of telling by the victim, low self-esteem and depression. The relative defencelessness of the victim implies an obligation on others to intervene, if we take their democratic rights seriously. Olweus (1993) has argued that it is a 'fundamental democratic right' not to be bullied. The increase in international concern about school bullying appears to reflect an increase in concern for rights issues throughout the twentieth century (Greene, 2006), which has been evidenced by an awareness of, and legislation against, forms of discrimination on the basis of (for example) sex, race, age, religion, disability and sexual orientation – a process that is still continuing. Although bullying or victimisation generally refers to discrimination on a more individual basis, the term *bias bullying* has been used to refer to victimisation based on such group characteristics.

A number of European countries have developed legal requirements concerning bullying in schools, including Finland, France, Ireland, Luxembourg, Malta, Sweden and the UK; others (e.g. Belgium and Germany) have legal requirements concerning violence in schools (see Ananiadou and Smith, 2002).

What we know about school bullying

Given this history of research, as briefly sketched previously, what have we learnt? Here I focus on pupil–pupil bullying, which is by far the most extensively studied. In school, we can consider teacher–teacher (although this comes under workplace bullying), teacher–pupil, pupil–teacher, as well as pupil–pupil bullying (Terry, 1998). However, it is mainly pupil–pupil bullying which has been the focus of research up until now. I review the following topics: methods of study; incidence figures; types of bullying; roles in bullying; causes of bullying and correlates of bully and victim roles; structural features of bullying; contributions of theory; implications for intervention; and proposals for future research.

Methods of study

It is not immediately obvious how to study school bullying, as it generally is not something that bullies would want to be discovered doing. However, several methods have been developed and used to study the phenomenon.

A straightforward method is to get *teacher or parent reports*. Teachers, or parents, can usually give some information on whether their pupil, or son/daughter, is or has been involved as a bully or victim. Such information is easy to get, and teacher opinions are important in their own right. But it is generally of limited value in understanding pupils' experiences, as other data suggest that adults often know only a fraction of what is going on. As far as pupil–pupil bullying is concerned, it is the pupils themselves who are the expert witnesses. Teacher-reports may nevertheless be most useful for young children around four to five years of age (Monks *et al.*, 2003).

A widely used approach has been pupil self-report data in *questionnaires*, usually anonymous. Olweus (1996) developed this methodology, and other variants have been used, for example the Life in School questionnaire in the UK (Arora, 1994). Such a method is most suitable for large surveys, and indeed has no substitute in this respect. Of course, the information is limited to what is in a structured questionnaire, and if it is anonymous, individual bullies or victims cannot be identified. Generally, correlates of bully or victim (or bully/victim) status can only be made with one individual's questionnaire response – that is to say, it relies on one informant.

Peer nominations provide an alternative pupil-based approach. Here, pupils are asked to nominate classmates for involvement in roles such as bully or victim. Multiple informants can provide good reliability in identifying bullies or victims, and this method is suitable for class-based work. It is more time-consuming (involving individual interviews), and ethical issues are raised by asking pupils to identify others in this way. Two common instruments are those by Rigby and Slee (1991) and the Salmivalli Participant Role Scale (1996).

Direct observations can be made, for example by watching in the playground and making notes or discrete audio-taped observations (Boulton, 1995), or by using video and radio microphones (Pepler and Craig, 1995; Pepler *et al.*, 1998). Such methods are particularly difficult and time-consuming, and are not used widely. It may also be biased towards detecting physical bullying, rather than more subtle verbal and indirect forms. Nevertheless direct observations have a special validity, as all other methods are indirect, filtered through perceptions of individuals and the nature of reporting to the investigator.

Table 3.1. *Incidence of bullying and being bullied in US students (from Nansel et al., 2001)*

%	None	1 or 2 times	Sometimes	Weekly
Being bullied	58.9	24.2	8.5	8.4
Bullying others	55.7	25.0	10.6	8.8

Table 3.2. *Incidences of being a victim of bullying, with gender and age differences (10 to 14 years), in four countries (from Morita, 2001)*

Victim	Total	Girls	Boys	10	11	12	13	14
England	12.2	11.8	12.7	18.7	13.1	12.1	10.5	.6
Netherlands	13.9	13.1	14.8	14.7	16.6	14.2	10.3	.1
Norway	10.0	9.1	11.1	12.4	11.9	9.5	10.0	—
Japan	9.6	9.0	9.9	13.4	9.9	9.5	8.2	.5

More *qualitative methods* can be employed, such as focus groups, ethnographic observations and interviewing key informants. Important examples in this tradition have demonstrated the range of girls' bullying (Owens *et al.*, 2000) and of sexual bullying (Duncan, 1999). These do not exhaust the range of methodologies, as records kept by schools, such as incident reports of bullying, may also be useful.

Some studies have reported on correlations across different methodologies, typically for identifying bullies and victims. These are usually reasonable but no means high correlations, and reinforce the advantage of multi-method approaches (Monks *et al.*, 2003; Pellegrini and Bartini, 2000).

Incidence figures

All the above methods can provide information on the incidence of bullying and victimisation, although some are better suited to this, especially survey questionnaires. However the actual incidence figures obtained can vary very greatly, independent of the actual phenomenon. Two examples from large-scale surveys are given in Tables 3.1 and 3.2.

Nansel *et al.* (2001) reported a survey of over 15,000 students in US schools, in Grades 6 to 10 (ages 12 to 16). Their figures, summarised in Table 3.1, are based on a self-report questionnaire, and show frequency of being bullied/bullying others, in the last term.

Morita (2001) provided a report to Monbusho (Ministry of Education in Japan) on a cross-national study of bullying (or *ijime*). This used the same self-report questionnaire with 10- to 14-year-old school pupils in Japan, England, the Netherlands and Norway, with samples of several thousand in each country. Table 3.2 shows percentages of pupils who reported being bullied (victim) more than just once or twice in the last six months, based on a self-report questionnaire. Differences by sex and age are also shown.

Even considering just questionnaires, incidence figures will be influenced by: what time span is being asked about (e.g. last month, last term, last year, ever at school); what frequency is regarded as bullying (e.g. once/twice a term, once a month, once a week or more); what definition is used (e.g. whether it includes indirect as well as direct forms, and also cyberbullying). When the questionnaire is administered in the school or calendar year can also be important, if a short time span (last month or term) is taken.

All these issues often make it difficult to compare across different studies. It also means that absolute incidence figures are rather meaningless in isolation. Some broad generalisations can be made. It is clear that victims of bullying are a substantial minority (maybe around 5–20 per cent of pupils), and bullies (who take part in bullying others) are usually a smaller minority (maybe around 2–20 per cent). Those who are both bullies and victims, the bully/victims, vary greatly in incidence according to methodology and criteria.

Despite the difficulties associated with incidence figures, such information is important, for two main purposes. First, reports of incidence can be vitally important in awareness raising, and associated publicity, when concern about the topic of school bullying is lacking. In England, some early incidence figures led to wide publicity and nationally funded action, and this scenario has been repeated in various forms in several other countries (Smith *et al.*, 1999b). Second, incidence figures are necessary for monitoring and evaluating the effects of school-based interventions. When the same instrument and criteria are used at pre- and post-test (and by the same research team), then there can be reasonable confidence that the figures obtained are meaningful, at least in terms of registering a comparative increase or decrease in the phenomenon (although, even then, problems raised by increased awareness, and changed pupil definitions of bullying following the intervention, may contaminate the straightforward interpretation of the findings).

The media often portray bullying as a problem that is on the increase. In fact (with the probable exception of cyberbullying; see Rivers *et al.*, Chapter 10), it appears to be decreasing in England. For example, over the last few years, data gathered from some 16,000 pupils in Leicestershire schools (Pupil Attitude Survey 2005/2006) show that the proportion who say that they have ever been bullied in school this year more than just once or twice was 16.3 per cent in 2002/2003, 14.9 per cent in 2003/2004, 14.4 per cent in 2004/2005 and 13.9 per cent in 2005/2006. This slow but steady decline does suggest that anti-bullying work is having an effect, but also that much remains to be done.

Types of bullying

While a number of typologies of aggression and of bullying exist, the main types include:

- *Physical* – hitting, kicking, punching, taking or damaging belongings.
- *Verbal* – teasing, taunting, threatening.
- *Social exclusion* – systematically excluding someone from social groups ('You can't play with us').
- *Indirect and other relational* – spreading nasty rumours, telling others not to play with someone.
- *Cyber* – using new forms such as text message, email, website bullying.

A 14-country cross-national study of words for 'bullying' (Smith *et al.*, 2002), and the situations they are applied to, found considerable similarities across various countries in these types (though with some variations, particularly related to social exclusion situations). Boys and girls generally described bullying in the same way, even though their experiences may differ (see below). However there were noticeable age changes. Young pupils (e.g. up to about eight years) seem to mainly distinguish 'nice' and 'nasty' behaviours, so that bullying is not distinguished readily from other aggressive or unpleasant behaviours. Older pupils however distinguish bullying from fighting, and also distinguish the main forms as outlined above (Monks and Smith, 2006).

Bias bullying

Some bullying is based on (or justified by) the victim being a member of a particular group, often a marginalised or disadvantaged one, rather than on individual characteristics. Children can experience racist teasing and name-calling, and those of non-white ethnic origin have been shown to experience more racist name-calling (though not necessarily other forms of bullying) than white children of the same age and gender. Bullying can take place on the basis of a child's sex, or involve sexual harassment (Duncan, 1999). Mainly in secondary schools, children may be teased about their sexual orientation, and even physically assaulted or ridiculed about this by other pupils or teachers (Rivers, 1995).

Roles in bullying

The obvious roles obtained from questionnaires and from nomination data are those of bully and victim. It is usually these incidence figures that are reported. It is easy to calculate data for two other roles. Bully/victims are those who score on both bully and victim, and non-involved or control pupils are those who score on neither. However, this is only the bare bones of a more complicated dynamic.

Pikas (2002) and others had long distinguished two types of victim: the so-called passive victim, who has not directly provoked the bullying; and the provocative victim, who can be thought to have contributed to their being bullied by having acted in an annoying, provocative way to peers (thus, this group may overlap considerably with the bully/victims).

Salimivalli *et al.* (1996) took things further by splitting up the roles involved in bullying. Through peer nomination procedures she identified roles of *ringleader* bullies (who take the initiative), *follower* bullies (who then join in) and *reinforcers* (who encourage the bully or laugh at the victim). She also identified *defenders* (who help the victim) and *bystanders* (who stay out of things), as well as the victims themselves. Subsequently some investigators have distinguished between bystanders, who see the bullying but do not act in any way, and *outsiders*, who just have not seen what is happening.

Salmivalli's work was with young adolescents. Sutton and Smith (1999) adapted the participant roles methodology for 8–11-year-olds in England, and Monks *et al.* (2003) adapted it further for use with young children (four to six years), using cartoon pictures. The roles of bully (or aggressor), victim and defender can be identified with some reliability even at four to six years, but the other roles are not clearly understood until middle childhood (Sutton and Smith, 1999).

Causes of bullying and correlates of the bully and victim roles

Aggressive behaviour and inequalities of power are commonplace in human groups, including peer-groups in school, so bullying can be a temptation. We can envisage many levels of causation:

• *Society level* – tolerance of violence, bullying and abuse of power in society; portrayals in the mass media.

- *Community level* – neighbourhood levels of violence and safety; socio-economic conditions.
- *School level* – school climate and quality of teacher and pupil relationships; school policies on and sanctions against bullying; school physical environment.
- *Family level* – nature of parent–child and sibling relationships.
- *Interpersonal level* – attitudes of the main peer-groups in the school; nature and quality of friendships.
- *Individual level* – temperament and personality.

Most of the research on school bullying has been at the family, interpersonal and individual level. However, class-level factors can be important (e.g. Salmivalli and Voeten, 2004), as can community-level variables (Benbenishty and Astor, 2005). In Colombia, Chaux *et al.* (2009) found that high levels of community violence as well as some school variables were significant predictors of bullying rates.

Correlates of the victim role

Many studies have examined correlates of the victim role. Victims of bullying often experience anxiety and depression, low self-esteem, physical and psychosomatic complaints (Williams *et al.*, 1996). In extreme cases, they may commit suicide (Kaltiala-Heino *et al.*, 1999). Hawker and Boulton (2000), carrying out a meta-analysis of many studies, found that victimisation was most strongly related to depression, moderately associated for social and global self-esteem and less strongly associated with anxiety.

Hodges *et al.* (1997) found that having few friends, or friends who can not be trusted or who are of low status, and sociometric rejection (dislike by peers) are risk factors for being a victim. Some victims come from over-protective or enmeshed families (Smith and Myron-Wilson, 1998). Children who are both bullies and victims (aggressive victims) may come from particularly troubled or abusive families (Schwartz *et al.*, 1997).

Having a disability or special educational needs is another risk factor for being a victim. Children with special needs are two to three times more at risk of being bullied; they are also more at risk of taking part in bullying others (Knox and Conti-Ramsden, 2003; Nabuzoka, 2000). Possible reasons for this include: particular characteristics that may make them an obvious 'target'; in mainstream settings these children are usually less well integrated socially and lack the protection against bullying which friendship gives; and those with behavioural problems may act out in an aggressive way and become 'provocative victims'.

Correlates of the bully role

Personal correlates of the bullying role include temperamental factors (such as being hot-tempered; Olweus, 1993), readily attributing hostile motives and having defensive egotism (Salmivalli *et al.*, 1999); however ringleader bullies at least may have high social intelligence and theory of mind skills, although used for antisocial ends – they can be 'skilled manipulators' (Kaukiainen *et al.*, 1999; Sutton *et al.*, 1999).

At the interpersonal level, bullying children tend to be peer-rejected in infant/junior school but less so in secondary school; towards adolescence, some aggressive and bullying children can have quite high status in peer-groups (Pellegrini and Bartini, 2001).

Family factors have been commonly implicated as risk factors for children who persistently bully others. They are more likely to come from families lacking warmth, in which violence is common and discipline inconsistent. Fathers who were bullies at school are likely to have sons who were bullying at school (Farrington, 1993; Olweus, 1993).

Correlates of the defender role

Although less studied, the characteristics of those children who are prepared to actively defend victims, rather than be passive or even colluding bystanders, are of interest and importance. Some research suggests that defenders are more empathic (Nickerson *et al.*, 2008); however, other research suggests that empathy alone is not enough. In addition, defending is predicted by feelings of self-efficacy, and high sociometric standing, such that defenders can feel confident and empowered to defend, despite the strength and popularity of some bullying children (Caravita *et al.*, 2009).

Structural features of bullying

Characteristic age differences emerge from the self-report surveys. Self-reports of being a victim decline over 8 to 16 years (see Table 3.2 as an example), whereas self-reports of bullying others do not decline (Smith *et al.*, 1999a). There is also a shift with age away from physical bullying and towards indirect and relational bullying, as for aggression generally (Björkqvist *et al.*, 1992). Typical gender differences are also found. Boys are more numerous in the bully category, but the sexes are more equal in the victim category. Boys practise/experience more physical bullying; girls more indirect and relational bullying.

There has been considerable work on coping strategies used by pupils to deal with attempts to bully them. A consistent finding is that rates of telling a teacher are lower in older pupils and boys (Hunter and Boyle, 2004; Naylor *et al.*, 2001). Another study of 406 pupils aged 13–16 years in schools with peer-support systems found the five most frequent coping strategies were to talk to someone, ignore it, stick up for yourself, avoid/stay away from bullies and make more/different friends (Smith *et al.*, 2004b). Over a two-year period, those who had stopped being victims more often had talked to someone about it (67 per cent) than those who had stayed victims (46 per cent) or become victims (41 per cent). Coping strategies can be complex with outcomes dependent on many factors; telling teachers can be successful but needs a consistent and effective response from teaching staff.

Another finding relates to attitudes about bullying in the peer-group as a whole. Although most pupils say they do not like bullying, a significant minority do say they could join in bullying. Perhaps surprisingly, these 'pro-bullying' or 'anti-victim' attitudes increase with age up to 14–15 years (after which they start to decline). Such anti-victim attitudes are more marked in boys than girls – and especially for boys as regards boy victims (Olweus and Endresen, 1998).

Contribution of theory

One criticism sometimes made of the school bullying research programme is that there has not been much use made of theory (Smith, 2010). The majority of studies have been descriptive, making use of available instruments such as the Olweus questionnaire and the Salmivalli Participant Role Scale. There is certainly no one dominant theoretical approach, but there are a number of openings for theory.

Perhaps the most traditional approach has been from social-cognitive theory, and Crick and Dodge's (1994) Social Information Processing Model has been influential. They propose that distorted or deviant processing of social information may result in aggression, and specifically bullying (Crick and Dodge, 1999), and that these are maladaptive behaviours. However, Sutton *et al.* (1999) found that ringleader bullies (those who 'organise' the bullying) scored highly on tasks assessing theory of mind. They argued that some bullies, rather than lacking social skills, are socially skilled in the way they organise and carry out bullying behaviour.

An evolutionary approach to bullying behaviour has begun to be developed (Kolbert and Crothers, 2003). This too would oppose a simple 'maladaptive' view of bullying behaviour, as it would see bullying, like other common forms of aggressive behaviour (Hawley *et al.*, 2007), as having costs and benefits and as being in some circumstances adaptive for an individual doing the bullying (e.g. by gaining resources or defending sub-group identity), even if not beneficial for the victim or the wider community. This is consistent with, for example, Olweus' (1993) discussion of the opportunity structure, or costs and benefits of bullying, in particular settings, and the possible adaptiveness of bullying behaviour as a strategy to gain peer-group status (e.g. Pellegrini and Long, 2002). Gender differences in bullying (as in aggression generally) can be explained in terms of sexual selection theory and effective strategies for damaging the status or reputation of males or females, respectively (Pellegrini and Archer, 2005). This perspective does not in any sense defend the morality of bullying, and there are also evolutionary roots to reciprocity and fairness (Trivers, 1971).

One example of a specific theoretical approach was the proposal of a scapegoating theory of victimisation by Schuster (1999). This supposed that there was a group need to have a victim (as 'scapegoat') so that one could expect one victim in most school class groups. This was a good theoretical proposal, which could be falsified, and indeed has been falsified by studies in both English and Austrian schools; see Mahdavi and Smith (2007) and other articles in the special issue of the *European Journal of Developmental Psychology*, 4 (3), 2007.

A more mainstream social psychological approach has come from social identity theory. Social identity is a person's knowledge that he or she belongs to a social category or group, defined by dimensions such as ethnicity, race, religion, age and gender. From the perspective of social identity, people generally divide the social world into distinct categories, viewing other persons as belonging either to the in-group (their own group) or to the out-group (another group). Individuals in the 'in-group' are viewed in favourable terms whereas those in the 'out-group' are perceived more negatively (Nesdale and Flesser, 2001). There is also some pressure to conform to in-group norms of behaviour. For example Ojala and Nesdale (2004) found that children's attitudes towards bullying could be moderated by in-group norms and perceived threat to group distinctiveness. This and further studies in a similar vein (e.g. Nesdale *et al.*, 2008) have generally used artificial scenarios or group assignments, so can be criticised for not getting evidence from actual bullying behaviours, but they do throw some light on determinants of attitudes and the importance of group pressures.

Some theoretical approaches concerning individual development within the family may help to explain why some children become more likely to engage in bullying behaviour, or to be bullied. Such approaches include attachment theory, social learning theory, parenting styles, family systems theory, family relationship schemas, shame management theory and cognitive contextual theory (see Duncan, 2004; Smith, 2008).

For example, Ahmed and Braithwaite (2004) developed a shame management theory, in which shame acknowledgement plays a central role in maintaining adaptive personal relationships through effective acknowledgement, making amends and discharge of shame. Shame displacement is seen as maladaptive: debilitating feelings of persistent shame may lead to externalised hostility and scapegoating; and unidentified shame can lead to distancing from others and other-directed anger. They found that bullying others was predicted by shame displacement, lack of shame acknowledgment and parents stigmatising shaming, as well as family disharmony. Ttofi and Farrington (2008a) tested what they labelled as reintegrative shaming theory (RST), and found that mother (but not father) bonding to child related to reintegrative shaming and shame acknowledgement, and thus to reduced sibling bullying, though with some significant gender effects. Relatedly, they (Ttofi and Farrington, 2008b) suggest that these findings also fit with defiance theory (Sherman, 1993), whereby unfair or stigmatising sanctions (and failure to acknowledge shame from such sanctions) may actually increase rather than decrease subsequent misbehaviours (in this case, bullying).

Finally, some recent studies have found substantial heritability for bully and victim roles (e.g. Ball *et al.*, 2008). This is basically an empirical finding rather than a theoretical approach, but it does suggest some vulnerability for getting into these roles, perhaps depending on temperament and/or neurological factors, and perhaps interacting with environmental factors.

Implications for intervention

Over the last 20 years, there have been an appreciable number of large-scale intervention projects in schools. Before reviewing these, it is important to state clearly that some interventions would be beyond the scope of the school. These include parent training, dealing with parental stress, reducing community violence and moderating levels of gratuitous violence in the mass media: all of these could be important if not necessary steps in reducing bullying in schools. The intervention projects to be considered did not attempt such ambitious targets but limited themselves mainly or entirely to work within the school.

The main types of intervention have included whole-school policies or class-based rules; work with pupils in classrooms, through the curriculum, to raise awareness and discuss school policy or class rules; improving the school environment, especially design and supervision of play areas and play times, where much bullying can happen; introducing peer-support systems, to help encourage outsiders and bystanders to be defenders, helping victims and challenging bullies; providing assertiveness training and social skills training to those pupils who may be victims; and working with bullying children, perhaps using Pikas or Support Group Method (Pikas, 2002; Robinson and Maines, 2007) approaches. In addition, it is important for schools to liaise with and involve parents in anti-bullying policies and work (Smith *et al.*, 2003).

Interventions in Norway

The first large-scale, school-based intervention campaign (launched in 1983) was carried out at a nationwide level in Norway. There was a survey in schools, materials and videos for teachers, advice for parents and mass publicity, and two assessments of its impact have been reported. Olweus (1993) monitored 42 schools in Bergen. Using his self-report questionnaire, and comparing equivalent age groups, he found that, from 1983 to 1985, reported bullying fell by 50 per cent, for both boys and girls. There were also falls in reported antisocial behaviour and there was no increase in reported bullying outside school. This encouraging finding has been widely reported and has inspired much subsequent work. Roland (1993) monitored 37 schools in Stavanger. He found that, from 1983 to 1986, there was no clear decrease in victimisation, although there was a modest correlation of positive outcomes with active use of materials by the schools. The difference between these two reports may well be due to the difference in help given to schools – more support during the intervention was given in the Bergen study, while in Stavanger the researchers just returned after three years to administer the post-test questionnaires.

More recent work in Norway directed by Roland (2000) focuses on class climate and makes more use of pupils. Recent work by Olweus (2004) in the second Bergen project (1997–98) and the Oslo project (1999–2000) finds reductions in the range of 21–50 per cent in Grades 5 to 7 (though possibly less with older pupils).

Interventions in the UK

The largest intervention programme in the UK has been the DFE Sheffield project 1991–94 (Smith and Sharp, 1994). The team worked with 23 schools over four terms. Each school developed a whole-school policy and chose from a range of other interventions. There was approximately a 17 per cent reduction in being bullied for primary schools, and small reductions (around 3–5 per cent) in five of the seven secondary schools. In addition, there was a strong positive correlation between amount of effort (as assessed by both the research team and pupils) and outcomes achieved.

Other interventions

Other wide-scale interventions have taken place in many countries, including Australia, Belgium, Canada, Finland, Germany, Ireland, Italy, Spain, Switzerland and the USA. For an edited collection of intervention studies, see Smith *et al.* (2004a). The Olweus programme, although very successful in Norway, has not yet achieved the same levels of success in the USA (Bauer *et al.*, 2007; Limber *et al.*, 2004).

Meta-analyses of interventions

Amongst a number of reviews and meta-analyses of such studies, Farrington and Baldry (2007) found that, of 16 studies reviewed, outcomes were desirable in eight cases, mixed in two cases, non-significant in four cases and undesirable in two cases. In general, most interventions have some positive impact but with more modest effects than the 50 per cent reduction found in Olweus' work in Bergen. One that does report this level of success is a project in Andalucía (Ortega *et al.*, 2004), where a broad-based intervention was sustained over a four-year period. Reviews by Smith *et al.* (2003) and Ttofi *et al.* (2008) identified some factors related to success:

- *Nature of intervention* – an obvious possibility but in fact the evidence so far is that it is the effort and commitment that matters, rather than the details of what is done.
- *Support by researchers* – this may have explained the greater success in the Bergen compared to the Stavanger evaluations in Norway, but the evidence from the Flanders project in Belgium (Stevens *et al.*, 2004) is that its more general impact may be small.
- *Length of intervention* – probably important and may help explain the relative success of the SAVE intervention in Andalucía.
- *Ownership by school and effective implementation* – probably very important, as suggested by the school variations in the Sheffield project (Smith and Sharp, 1994).
- *Age of pupils* – several projects find reductions easier to obtain in primary than in secondary schools (although Ttofi *et al.* (2008) reported

an opposite finding, this appears to be due to their omission of studies such as those of Stevens *et al.* (2004) and is contrary to my own experience and that of Olweus).

- *Neighbourhood, community and societal context* – may be important but difficult to estimate (see Benbenishty and Astor (2005) for recent work on school violence, considering these levels).

Possible ways forward in research and practice

A number of suggestions can be made to try to improve the outcomes of anti-bullying interventions in schools. One is that we need to further design intervention materials and activities to target indirect bullying, and cyberbullying, as well as physical and direct bullying. Not all teachers and pupils recognise social exclusion and rumour-spreading as bullying (Boulton, 1997). Girls specialise more in these kinds of bullying, and there is some evidence that current anti-bullying interventions target boys more than girls (Eslea and Smith, 1998). We need to tackle girls' bullying too, and this presents its own challenges (Owens *et al.*, 2000). The recent rise of cyberbullying and its particular characteristics have presented a new set of challenges to anti-bullying work.

We need to consider the dynamics of bully–victim relationships and the different roles within them. We need to evaluate further the range of peer-support schemes that aim to change bystanders and outsiders to defenders (Cowie *et al.*, 2002). We also need to understand that some bullying children are socially skilled: they may need empathy training, but simple-minded social skills training could be misguided or even counterproductive.

It is probably important to start interventions early, in infant/primary schools, before bully and victim roles become more stable. Also, it is necessary to ensure maintenance of interventions over time. Anti-bullying work cannot be 'done' and then dropped; it is a continuing process that needs maintenance and periodic renewal. There needs to be an understanding of this and incentives (legal requirements, and parent pressure, can contribute to this). Training of teachers in anti-bullying work should be placed on a much more regular footing, preferably included in initial teacher training courses much more systematically and thoroughly than at present (Nicolaides *et al.*, 2002).

We need to monitor effects of different interventions carefully, using multi-methods where possible. Research has been very predominately quantitative so far, and there is a need for more qualitative studies too, perhaps detailed case studies of individual pupils or individual schools, to throw more light on perceptions of bullying, group dynamics, changes over time and processes contributing to change.

At a practical level, pressure on government from national organisations is likely to be important. In England, the Anti-Bullying Alliance (ABA) provides a useful exemplar. ABA was founded by two charitable organisations concerned with children, the NSPCC (National Society for the Prevention of Cruelty to Children) and the NCB (National Children's Bureau), in 2002. It brings together over 50 national organisations in England, from the voluntary and private sectors, local education authorities, professional associations and the research community, into one network to work together to reduce bullying and create safer environments for children and young people to live, grow, play and learn. With funding from the then DfES (Department for Education and Skills), and later DCSF (Department for Children, Schools and Families), it has supported regional seminars, the development of a portfolio of resources and the setting up of nine regional support networks throughout England. Anti-Bullying Weeks have been held annually since 2004.

We need to learn from both successes and failures in school-based interventions to reduce bullying. The results so far have been modestly encouraging. But we do also need to consider whether intervening in schools only is enough. Bullying does not only happen in schools, and schools are only part of the problem and part of the solution.

Conclusion

School bullying is a pervasive problem. It now has a research history spanning the last 30 years. During this period, a considerable amount of useful knowledge has been gained and this has fed into a range of intervention programmes. The large-scale, school-based interventions that have been properly evaluated have had modestly encouraging results, but these vary considerably. Some reasons for this, and ways forward, are considered. In sum, some important advances have been made in tackling this important social problem, but much remains to be done to reduce bullying appreciably and effectively.

REFERENCES

Ahmed, E. and Braithwaite, V. (2004). '"What, me ashamed?" Shame management and school bullying'. *Journal of Research in Crime and Delinquency*, 41: 245–69.

Ananiadou, K. and Smith, P.K. (2002). 'Legal requirements and nationally circulated materials against school bullying in European countries'. *Criminal Justice*, 2: 471–91.

Arora, T. (1994). 'Measuring bullying with the "Life in School" checklist'. *Pastoral Care in Education*, 12: 11–15.

Ball, H.A., Arsenault, L., Taylor, A., Maughan, B., Caspi, A. and Moffitt, T.E. (2008). 'Genetic and environmental influences on victims, bullies and bully-victims in childhood'. *Journal of Child Psychiatry and Psychiatry*, 49: 104–12.

Bauer, N.S., Lozano, P. and Rivara, F.P. (2007). 'The effectiveness of the Olweus bullying prevention program in public middle schools: a controlled trial'. *Journal of Adolescent Health*, 40: 266–74.

Benbenishty, R. and Astor, R.A. (2005). *School Violence in Context*. Oxford: Oxford University Press.

Björkqvist, K, Lagerspetz, K. and Kaukiainen, A. (1992). 'Do girls manipulate and boys fight? Developmental trends in regard to direct and indirect aggression'. *Aggressive Behavior*, 18: 117–27.

Boulton, M.J. (1995). 'Playground behaviour and peer interaction patterns of primary school boys classified as bullies, victims and not involved'. *British Journal of Educational Psychology*, 65: 165–77.

(1997). 'Teachers' views on bullying definitions, attitudes and ability to cope'. *British Journal of Educational Psychology*, 67: 223–33.

Caravita, S., DiBlasio, P. and Salmivalli, C. (2009). 'Unique and interactive effects of empathy and social status on involvement in bullying'. *Social Development*, 18: 140–63.

Chaux, E., Molano, A. and Podlesky, P. (2009). 'Socio-economic, socio-political and socio-emotional variables explaining school bullying: a country-wide multilevel analysis'. *Aggressive Behavior*, 35: 520–29.

Cowie, H., Naylor, P., Talamelli, L., Chauhan, P. and Smith, P.K. (2002). 'Knowledge, use of and attitudes towards peer support'. *Journal of Adolescence*, 25: 453–67.

Crick, N.R. and Dodge, K.A. (1994). 'A review and reformulation of social information-processing mechanisms in children's social adjustment'. *Psychological Bulletin*, 115: 74–101.

(1999). '"Superiority" is in the eye of the beholder: a comment on Sutton, Smith and Swettenham'. *Social Development*, 8: 128–31.

Dooley, J.J., Pyżalski, J. and Cross, D. (2009). 'Cyberbullying versus face-to-face bullying: a theoretical and conceptual review'. *Zeitschrift für Psychologie* [*Journal of Psychology*], 217: 182–88.

Duncan, N. (1999). *Sexual Bullying*. London and New York: Routledge.

Duncan, R.D. (2004). 'The impact of family relationships on school bullies and their victims'. In D.L. Espelage and S.M. Swearer (eds.), *Bullying in American Schools* (pp. 227–44). Mahwah, NJ: Lawrence Erlbaum.

Eslea, M. and Smith, P.K. (1998). 'The long-term effectiveness of anti-bullying work in primary schools'. *Educational Research*, 40: 203–18.

Espelage, D.L. and Swearer, S.M. (eds.) (2004). *Bullying in American Schools: A Socio-ecological Perspective on Prevention and Intervention*. Mahwah, NJ and London: Lawrence Erlbaum.

Farrington, D. (1993). 'Understanding and preventing bullying'. In M. Tonry (ed.), *Crime and Justice: A Review of Research,* vol. 17 (pp. 381–458). Chicago: University of Chicago Press.

Farrington, D. and Baldry, A. (2007). 'Effectiveness of programs to prevent school bullying'. *Victims and Offenders*, 2: 183–204.

Greene, M.B. (2006). 'Bullying in schools: a plea for a measure of human rights'. *Journal of Social Issues*, 62: 63–79.

Hawker, D.S.J. and Boulton, M.J. (2000). 'Twenty years' research on peer victimization and psychosocial maladjustment: a meta-analytic review of cross-sectional studies'. *Journal of Child Psychiatry and Psychiatry*, 41: 441–55.

Hawley, P., Little, T.D. and Rodkin, P. (eds.) (2007). *Aggression and Adaptation*. Mahwah, NJ: Lawrence Erlbaum.

Hinduja, S. and Patchin, J.W. (2008). *Bullying beyond the Schoolyard: Preventing and Responding to Cyberbullying*. Thousand Oaks, CA: Corwin Press.

Hodges, E.V.E., Malone, M.J. and Perry, D.G. (1997). 'Individual risk and social risk as interacting determinants of victimisation in the peer group'. *Developmental Psychology*, 33: 1032–39.

Hunter, S.C. and Boyle, J.M.E. (2004). 'Appraisal and coping strategy use of victims of school bullying'. *British Journal of Educational Psychology*, 74: 83–107.

Jimerson, S.R., Swearer, S. and Espelage, D.L. (eds.) (2010). *Handbook of Bullying in Schools: An International Perspective*. New York: Routledge.

Juvonen, J. and Graham, S. (eds.) (2001). *Peer Harassment in School: The Plight of the Vulnerable and Victimized*. New York: Guilford Press.

Kaltiala-Heino, R., Rimpela, M., Marttunen, M., Rimpela, A. and Rantenan, P. (1999). 'Bullying, depression, and suicidal ideation in Finnish adolescents: school survey'. *British Medical Journal*, 319: 348–51.

Kaukiainen, A., Björkqvist, K., Lagerspetz, K., Österman, K., Salmivalli, C., Forsblom, S. and Ahlbom, A. (1999). 'The relationships between social intelligence, empathy, and three types of aggression'. *Aggressive Behavior*, 25: 81–89.

Knox, E. and Conti-Ramsden, G. (2003). 'Bullying risks of 11-year-old children with specific language impairment (SLI): does school placement matter?' *International Journal of Language and Communication Disorders*, 38: 1–12.

Kolbert, J.B. and Crothers, L.M. (2003). 'Bullying and evolutionary psychology: the dominance hierarchy among students and implications for school personnel'. *Journal of School Violence*, 2: 73–91.

Koo, H., Kwak, K. and Smith, P.K. (2008). 'Victimization in Korean schools: the nature, incidence and distinctive features of Korean bullying or wang-ta'. *Journal of School Violence*, 7: 119–39.

Kowalski, R.M., Limber, S.P. and Agatston, P.W. (2008). *Cyber Bullying: Bullying in the Digital Age*. Malden, MA: Blackwell.

Lakatos, I. (1970). 'Falsification and the methodology of scientific research programmes'. In I. Lakatos and A. Musgrave (eds.), *Criticism and the Growth of Knowledge* (pp. 91–196). Cambridge: Cambridge University Press.

Li, Q., Cross, D. and Smith, P.K. (in press). *Bullying Goes to the Global Village: Research on Cyberbullying from an International Perspective*. Chichester: Wiley-Blackwell.

Limber, S.P., Nation, M., Tracy, A.J., Melton, G.B. and Flerx, V. (2004). 'Implementation of the Olweus Bullying Prevention Programme in the Southeastern United States'. In P. K. Smith, D. Pepler and K. Rigby (eds), *Bullying in Schools: How Successful Can Interventions Be?* (pp. 55–79). Cambridge: Cambridge University Press.

Mahdavi, J. and Smith, P.K. (2007). 'Individual risk factors or group dynamics? An investigation of the scapegoat hypothesis of victimization in school classes'. *European Journal of Developmental Psychology*, 4: 353–71.

McGrath, H. and Noble, T. (2006). *Bullying Solutions: Evidence-based Approaches to Bullying in Australian schools*. Frenchs Forest, NSW: Pearson Education Australia.

Monks, C.P. and Smith, P.K. (2006). 'Definitions of "bullying": age differences in understanding of the term, and the role of experience'. *British Journal of Developmental Psychology*, 24: 801–21.

Monks, C., Smith, P.K. and Swettenham, J. (2003). 'Aggressors, victims and defenders in preschool: peer, self and teacher reports'. *Merrill-Palmer Quarterly*, 49: 453–69.

Morita, Y. (2001). *Ijime no kokusai hikaku kenkyu* [*Cross-national Comparative Study Of Bullying*]. Tokyo: Kaneko Shobo.

Morita, Y., Soeda, H., Soeda, K. and Taki, M. (1999). 'Japan'. In P. K. Smith, Y. Morita, J. Junger-Tas, D. Olweus, R. Catalano and P. Slee (eds), *The Nature of School Bullying: A Cross-national Perspective* (pp. 309–23). London and New York: Routledge.

Nabuzoka, D. (2000). *Children with Learning Difficulties: Social Understanding and Adjustment*. Blackwell: BPS Books.

Nansel, T.R., Overpeck, M.D., Pilla, R.S., Ruan, W.J., Simons-Morton, B. and Scheidt, P.C. (2001). 'Bullying behaviors among US youth: prevalence and association with psychosocial adjustment'. *Journal of the American Medical Association*, 285: 2094–100.

Naylor, P., Cowie, H. and del Rey, R. (2001). 'Coping strategies of secondary school children in response to being bullied'. *Child Psychology and Psychiatry Review*, 6: 114–20.

Nesdale, D., and Flesser, D. (2001). 'Social identity and the development of children's group attitudes'. *Child Development*, 72: 506–17.

Nesdale, D., Durkin, K., Maass, A., Kiesner, J. and Griffiths, J.A. (2008). 'Effects of group norms on children's intentions to bully'. *Social Development*, 17: 889–907.

Nickerson, A.B., Mele, D. and Princiotta, D. (2008). 'Attachment and empathy as predictors of roles as defenders or outsiders in bullying interactions'. *Journal of School Psychology*, 46: 687–703.

Nicolaides, S., Toda, Y. and Smith, P.K. (2002). 'Knowledge and attitudes about school bullying in trainee teachers'. *British Journal of Educational Psychology*, 72: 105–18.

Noret, N. and Rivers, I. (2006). 'The prevalence of bullying by text message or email: results of a four year study'. Poster presented at British Psychological Society Annual Conference, Cardiff, April.

Ojala, K. and Nesdale, D. (2004). 'Bullying and social identity: the effects of group norms and distinctiveness threat on attitudes towards bullying'. *British Journal of Developmental Psychology*, 22: 19–35.

Olweus, D. (1978). *Aggression in Schools: Bullies and Whipping Boys*. Washington, DC: Hemisphere.

(1993). *Bullying at School: What We Know and What We Can Do*. Oxford: Blackwell.

(1996). *The Revised Olweus Bully/Victim Questionnaire*. HEMIL, University of Bergen, Norway.

(1999). 'Sweden'. In P.K. Smith, Y. Morita, J. Junger-Tas, D. Olweus, R. Catalano and P. Slee (eds.), *The Nature of School Bullying: A Cross-national Perspective* (pp. 7–27). London and New York: Routledge.

(2004). 'The Olweus Bullying Prevention Programme: design and implementation issues and a new national initiative in Norway'. In P.K. Smith, D. Pepler and K. Rigby (eds.), *Bullying in Schools: How Successful Can Interventions Be?* (pp. 13–36). Cambridge: Cambridge University Press.

Olweus, D. and Endresen, I.M. (1998). 'The importance of sex-of-stimulus object: age trends and sex differences in empathic responsiveness'. *Social Development*, 3: 370–88.

Ortega, R., del Rey, R. and Mora-Merchan, J. (2004). 'SAVE model: an anti-bullying intervention in Spain'. In P.K. Smith, D. Pepler and K. Rigby (eds.), *Bullying in Schools: How Successful Can Interventions Be?* (pp. 167–85). Cambridge: Cambridge University Press.

Owens, L., Shute, R. and Slee, P. (2000). '"Guess what I just heard! "': indirect aggression among teenage girls in Australia'. *Aggressive Behavior*, 26: 67–83.

Pellegrini, A.D. and Archer, J. (2005). 'Sex differences in competitive and aggressive behaviour'. In B. J. Ellis and D. F. Bjorklund (eds.), *Origins of the Social Mind* (pp. 219–44). New York: Guilford Press.

Pellegrini, A.D. and Bartini, M. (2000). 'An empirical comparison of methods of sampling aggression and victimization in school settings'. *Journal of Educational Psychology*, 92: 360–66.

(2001). 'Dominance in early adolescent boys: affiliative and aggressive dimensions and possible functions'. *Merrill-Palmer Quarterly*, 47: 142–63.

Pellegrini, A.D. and Long, J.D. (2002). 'A longitudinal study of bullying, dominance, and victimization during the transition from primary school through secondary school'. *British Journal of Developmental Psychology*, 20: 259–80.

Pepler, D.J. and Craig, W.M. (1995). 'A peek behind the fence: naturalistic observations of aggressive children with remote audiovisual recording'. *Developmental Psychology*, 31: 548–53.

Pepler, D.J., Craig, W.M. and Roberts, W.L. (1998). 'Observations of aggressive and nonaggressive children on the school playground'. *Merrill-Palmer Quarterly*, 44: 55–76.

Pepler, D.J., Craig, W., Zeigler, S. and Charach, A. (1994). 'An evaluation of an anti-bullying intervention in Toronto schools'. *Canadian Journal of Community Mental Health*, 13: 95–110.

Pikas, A. (2002). 'New developments of the Shared Concern Method'. *School Psychology International*, 23: 307–26.

Pupil Attitude Survey (2005/06). Leicestershire County Council, MIS, Statistics and Information Unit.

Rigby, K. (2002). *New Perspectives on Bullying*. London and Philadelphia, PA: Jessica Kingsley.

Rigby, K. and Slee, P.T. (1991). 'Bullying among Australian schoolchildren: reported behavior and attitudes to victims'. *Journal of Social Psychology*, 131: 615–27.

Rivers, I. (1995). 'Mental health issues among young lesbians and gay men bullied in school'. *Health and Social Care in the Community*, 3: 380–83.

Robinson, B. and Maines, G. (2007). *Bullying: A Complete Guide to the Support Group Method*. London: Sage.

Roland, E. (1993). 'Bullying: a developing tradition of research and management'. In D. Tattum (ed.), *Understanding and Managing Bullying* (pp. 15–30). Oxford: Heinemann Educational.

(2000). 'Bullying in school: three national innovations in Norwegian schools in 15 years'. *Aggressive Behavior*, 26: 135–43.

Ross, D.M. (2002). *Childhood Bullying and Teasing. What School Personnel, Other Professionals, and Parents Can Do*, 2nd edn. Alexandria, VA: American Counseling Association.

Salmivalli, C. and Voeten, M. (2004). 'Connections between attitudes, group norms, and behaviors associated with bullying in schools'. *International Journal of Behavioral Development*, 28: 246–58.

Salmivalli, C., Kaukiainen, A., Kaistaniemi, L. and Lagerspetz, K. (1999). 'Self-evaluated self-esteem, peer-evaluated self-esteem and defensive egotism as predictors of adolescents' participation in bullying situations'. *Personality and Social Psychology Bulletin*, 25: 1268–78.

Salmivalli, C., Lagerspetz, K., Björkqvist, K., Österman, K. and Kaukiainen, A. (1996). 'Bullying as a group process: participant roles and their relations to social status within the group'. *Aggressive Behavior*, 22: 1–15.

Schuster, B. (1999) 'Outsiders at school: the prevalence of bullying and its relation with social status'. *Group Processes and Intergroup Relations*, 2: 175–90.

Schwartz, D., Dodge, K.A., Pettit, G.S. and Bates, J.E. (1997). 'The early socialization of aggressive victims of bullying'. *Child Development*, 68: 665–75.

Shariff, S. (2008). *Cyber-bullying: Issues and Solutions for the School, the Classroom and the Home*. London and New York: Routledge.

Sherman, L.W. (1993). 'Defiance, deterrence and irrelevance: a theory of the criminal sanction'. *Journal of Research in Crime and Delinquency*, 30: 445–73.

Smith, P.K. (2008). 'Family dynamics related to bullying and victimisation'. *Japanese Journal of Family Psychology*, 22: 167–83.

(2010). 'Cyberbullying: the European perspective'. In J. Mora-Merchan and T. Jäger (eds.), *Cyberbullying: A Cross-national Comparison*. Landau: Verlag Emprische Pädagogik.

Smith, P.K. and Myron-Wilson, R. (1998). 'Parenting and school bullying'. *Clinical Child Psychology and Psychiatry*, 3: 405–17.

Smith, P.K. and Sharp, S. (eds.) (1994). *School Bullying: Insights and Perspectives.* London: Routledge.

Smith, P.K., Ananiadou, K. and Cowie, H. (2003). 'Interventions to reduce school bullying'. *Canadian Journal of Psychiatry*, 48: 591–99.

Smith, P.K., Cowie, H., Olafsson, R. and Liefooghe, A.P.D. (2002). 'Definitions of bullying: a comparison of terms used, and age and sex differences, in a 14-country international comparison'. *Child Development*, 73: 1119–33.

Smith, P.K., Madsen, K. and Moody, J. (1999a). 'What causes the age decline in reports of being bullied in school? Towards a developmental analysis of risks of being bullied'. *Educational Research*, 41: 267–85.

Smith, P.K., Pepler, D.J. and Rigby, K. (eds.) (2004a). *Bullying in Schools: How Successful Can Interventions Be?* Cambridge: Cambridge University Press.

Smith, P.K., Talamelli, L., Cowie, H., Naylor, P. and Chauhan, P. (2004b). 'Profiles of non-victims, escaped victims, continuing victims and new victims of school bullying'. *British Journal of Educational Psychology*, 74: 565–81.

Smith, P.K., Morita, Y., Junger-Tas, J., Olweus, D., Catalano, R. and Slee, P. (eds.) (1999b). *The Nature of School Bullying: A Cross-national Perspective.* London and New York: Routledge.

Stevens, P. and van Oost, P. (1995). 'Pesten op school: Een actieprogramma [Bullying in school: an action programme]'. In *Handboek leerlingbegeleiding. Probleeemgedrag aanpakken* [*Manual for Pupil Guidance: Tackling Problem Behaviour*] (pp. 93–100). Amsterdam: Kluwer.

Stevens, V., Van Oost, P. and De Bourdeauhuij, I. (2004). 'Interventions against bullying in Flemish schools: programme development and evaluation'. In P.K. Smith, D. Pepler and K. Rigby (eds.), *Bullying in Schools: How Successful Can Interventions Be?* (pp. 141–65). Cambridge: Cambridge University Press.

Sullivan, K., Cleary, M. and Sullivan, G. (2004). *Bullying in Secondary Schools.* London: Paul Chapman.

Sutton, J. and Smith, P.K. (1999). 'Bullying as a group process: an adaptation of the participant role approach'. *Aggressive Behavior*, 25: 97–111.

Sutton, J., Smith, P.K. and Swettenham, J. (1999). 'Social cognition and bullying: social inadequacy or skilled manipulation?' *British Journal of Developmental Psychology*, 17: 435–50.

Terry, A.A. (1998). 'Teachers as targets of bullying by their pupils: a study to investigate incidence'. *British Journal of Educational Psychology*, 68: 255–68.

Trivers, R.L. (1971). 'The evolution of reciprocal altruism'. *Quarterly Review of Biology*, 46: 35–37.

Ttofi, M. and Farrington, D. (2008a). 'RST, moral emotions, and bullying'. *Aggressive Behavior*, 34: 352–68.

(2008b). 'Bullying: short-term and long-term effects, and the importance of defiance theory in explanation and prevention'. *Victims and Offenders*, 3: 313–36.

Ttofi, M., Farrington, D. and Baldry, A. (2008). *Effectiveness of Programmes to Reduce School Bullying.* Stockholm: Swedish Council for Crime Prevention.

60   *Peter K. Smith*

Willard, N.E. (2006). *Cyberbullying and Cyberthreats*. Eugene, OR: Center for Safe and Responsible Internet Use.

Williams, K., Chambers, M., Logan, S. and Robinson, D. (1996). 'Association of common health symptoms with bullying in primary school children'. *British Medical Journal*, 313: 17–19.

4 Peer violence in residential children's homes: a unique experience

Christine Barter

Until recently, the issue of peer violence in residential children's homes has been largely absent from the official, professional and academic agenda. This is despite the fact that young people in care have consistently highlighted it as one of their overriding concerns. This chapter seeks to provide insights into the incidence and nature of peer violence in residential children's homes. Initially the international research evidence on peer violence in residential welfare settings will be considered. Following this, research undertaken by the current author and colleagues will be presented, which is, as far as we are aware, the first study to focus exclusively on the problem of peer violence within residential children's homes. Based on in-depth interviews with over 140 young people and professionals from 14 different residential settings, the research was able to capture the impact that peer violence had on young people's residential lives. Patterns of peer violence unique to this environment are documented. In conclusion, a range of residential policy and practice responses, based on empirical findings, are presented.

Background

It is difficult to provide an accurate account of how many children and young people experience living in a children's home. Neither the UK nor, for example, the USA, can provide systematic information on the number of children in residential care (Little *et al.*, 2005). In March 2007, there were some 65,000 children and young people looked after in the UK; 10,000 were in residential care on any one day. However, the actual number of young people accommodated over a 12-month period will be considerably greater as a result of the short-term nature of many placements. Chipenda-Dansokho *et al.* (2003) estimate that each night in the USA around 100,000 children are in a variety of residential settings purchased or provided by child welfare agencies. Thus a significant number of children, predominantly those aged over 13 years old, will experience living in a children's home, at least for some of their childhood. The UK residential welfare sector is now mainly used to accommodate adolescents with complex and demanding backgrounds. Most young people in residential homes share histories of child abuse and neglect, or exhibit antisocial behaviour, and many have mental health problems (van Beinum *et al.*, 2001; Kendrick *et al.*, 2004; Sinclair and Gibbs, 1998).

Terminology and definitions

Before we proceed it is important to reflect on terminology. Caveats associated with the use of the term 'bullying' have been raised (Barter *et al.*, 2004). A central concern is the wide-ranging nature of the definition, whereby distinct forms of behaviour become merged under a single homogenous category. This all-inclusive categorisation can obscure the differential power dynamics which underpin different forms of intimidation and violence, for example sexual violence. However, not all research has used the concept of bullying in this way. Some studies routinely delimitate between different forms of bullying and produce complex typologies of behaviour and risk.

In addition, the problem of bullying has often been studied in isolation from wider peer behaviour and cultures. It is important to recognise how negative peer cultures underpin and shape young people's experiences of intimidation and violence. For example, sexual swearing or use of the term 'gay' to refer to something in a derogatory manner is not necessarily aimed at any specific person, but nevertheless can provide the context in which intimidation and violence, including 'bullying', can increase (Kendrick and Mair, 2002).

For these reasons this chapter will use the term bullying only where an author applies this concept without any further clarification. Otherwise, the wider term peer violence, as a broader category which includes all forms of physical, emotional and sexual intimidation and violence, will be used.

Theoretical standpoint

Much of the research on residential child care in the UK has been undertaken from a sociological or social work perspective. This is in contrast to the majority of contributions in this collection, which predominantly adopt a psychological standpoint. However, the need to adopt a more multidisciplinary approach to understanding social issues, including peer violence and bullying, is now widely acknowledged (Layder, 1998). By combining different perspectives and theoretical frameworks from sociology, psychology, social welfare, education and related disciplines, a more powerful and comprehensive understanding can be achieved.

Over the past decade researchers, policy makers and practitioners have recognised that the specific position of children and young people needs to be acknowledged through an examination of their views and experiences. This view is also clearly articulated in the numerous inquiries and reviews into the institutional abuse of children. It is no longer acceptable to view children as the passive recipients of research and knowledge. In contrast, children and young people should be viewed as actors in their own right, both constrained by social structures and as agents acting within and upon them (James et al., 1998; Mullender et al., 2002). This standpoint will be adopted in this chapter.

Peer violence in residential children's care

Compared to other areas, research on peer violence in residential child welfare settings is in its infancy. This is particularly surprising given that young people in residential care constitute some of the most damaged children and young people in society. Previous research has consistently shown the high degree of difficulties young people in residential care face in their lives. Most young people accommodated in residential provision share histories of child maltreatment and disputed family situations. Sinclair and Gibbs (1998) showed that child abuse was a common experience and that fewer than one in six of residents had families where both natural parents lived together. In addition, the same study goes on to show the extent of their behavioural problems: seven out of ten had been excluded from school; six out of ten had some involvement in delinquency; just under half had been violent to adults or other children; running away or putting themselves at risk of sexual exploitation was also common. Worryingly, a third had attempted to commit suicide or self-harmed.

A substantial body of research has demonstrated an association between domestic violence, child abuse and peer violence, which may or may not constitute bullying (see Barter and Berridge, 2010). Recent UK research, reflecting other international findings, showed that family violence and aggressive friendship networks were associated with teenagers' experiences of partner violence in their intimate relationships (Barter et al., 2009; also see Ortega and Sánchez, Chapter 6).

In the light of these findings, and taking into account the high incidence rate for child abuse in the residential population, it is worrying that so little research has addressed the issue of peer violence in residential settings, either in the UK or internationally (Barter *et al.*, 2004; Freundlich *et al.*, 2007). This is perhaps especially disconcerting given the high number of institutional child abuse scandals in the UK. From the early 1970s through to the 1990s, a horrific legacy of abuse, predominately sexual, but also physical and emotional, has been exposed (Brannan *et al.*, 1993; Colton, 2002; Committee of Inquiry into Children's Homes and Hostels, 1986; Kirkwood, 1993; Wolmar, 2000). Sexual, physical and emotional forms of child abuse are similar in nature to familial abuse. However, a form of abuse unique to institutional settings is programme abuse. This consists of an institution's regime or treatment programme, which, although often accepted as legitimate by staff, to an external observer would be viewed as abusive. The UK 'pindown' scandal (Levy and Kahan, 1991) is an example of such a situation, where physical assaults took place under the pretext of restraint and where children were placed in isolation for weeks, and sometimes months, with inadequate clothing and food, and denied external contact.

In response, numerous inquiries and reviews have been undertaken which have provided an array of safeguards to more effectively protect children and young people living away from home. Research seems to confirm that thanks, at least in part, to these enhanced safeguards, children are now significantly less likely to experience abuse by staff and other professionals (Sinclair and Gibbs, 1998). Although abuse by adults in residential children's homes has hit the headlines, on account of its appalling nature and persistence over many years, much of the available evidence has indicated that residents are most often at risk of violence from *other young people* within residential settings (see Barter, 1997; Gibbs and Sinclair, 2000). Nevertheless, the factors which enabled such wide-scale abuse by residential staff, managers and other professionals to go undetected provide important implications for understanding all forms of institutional violence, including peer violence. Inquiry reports have produced a range of recommendations aimed at providing better safeguarding for children in care.

Residential safeguards have included: better vetting of residential staff; more defined aims and objectives of residential homes and placements; and a greater openness of residential settings, including increased external scrutiny of residential practices. However, commentators have argued that one of the main reasons for the widespread abuse to have gone on for so long was the negative perceptions of children in care (Moss *et al.*, 1990; Safe and Sound Group and NPCC, 1995). Some of the children and young people who were abused disclosed their experiences at the time; however, their allegations were either not taken seriously or ignored by those in authority. It is argued that the very negative perception of children's residential provision as the 'dumping' ground of last resort for troubled and troublesome children meant that the catalogue of abuse suffered by children and young people at the hands of residential staff, and others in authority, went unheeded. Numerous inquiries have placed considerable weight on the low status of residential provision within the social work profession. Residential workers were often unqualified, under-trained, low-paid, lacked consistent supervision from managers and had little external professional support. These factors, alongside others, including the numerous scandals, contributed to the low morale of the sector and hindered the introduction and retention of qualified and experienced professionals.

Thus historically the most damaged and vulnerable children in society were placed in settings where few safeguards existed, external scrutiny was minimal and residential workers, and in some cases managers, lacked basic understanding of children's complex needs. That this position has now changed is undeniable, although the low status of residential social work as a profession still prevails. Nonetheless, the legacy of the scandals continues, and young people still experience residential placements as potentially stigmatising. This is demonstrated in recent research which showed that children in residential and foster care experience a higher rate of bullying at school than children in their families (Morgan, 2008). Consequently, children's experiences of residential care should not be viewed in isolation, as they have implications for their welfare whilst in the residential placement as well as in the wider community.

Incidence rates of peer violence in residential children's homes

Unlike school settings, no systematic evidence exists on the incidence or prevalence of peer violence, including bullying, in the residential child care sector. Most of the accounts described below address the issue of peer violence in children's homes as part of research on, or inquiries into, broader aspects of residential care. However, some insights can be gained.

Young people's own accounts provide some detail of the frequency and nature of peer violence, indicating that it constitutes a major problem in many residential settings (Paterson et al., 2003). Morris and Wheatley (1994) investigated calls to a dedicated phone line set up by ChildLine for children in care. In the first six months of its operation, 250 calls were received; three-quarters of callers were girls. The most common problems related to bullying or other forms of violence from peers in the home. The behaviour included teasing, name-calling or being picked on and physically assaulted by peers. Predominantly, assailants were male residents. Most callers stated that they had told a staff member but felt that their concerns had not been properly addressed. Young people reported that residential workers seemed reluctant to act on allegations when the violence had not been directly observed by a staff member. However, as most violence occurred away from staff supervision, this was problematic.

Other studies use data derived from official investigations. It is important to recognise that the findings from such studies are limited to cases which have been reported to an authority and have been evaluated as serious enough to warrant further inquiry. Two UK studies have focused on reported allegations of institutional abuse. Westcott and Clement (1992) looked at all cases of institutional abuse reported to the NSPCC (National Society for the Prevention of Cruelty to Children), over a period of 12 months. Information was provided on 84 children abused in 43 residential settings. Four-fifths of the cases involved some kind of sexual abuse and a fifth involved physical abuse (not mutually exclusive). Half occurred in children's homes, and half of the perpetrators were peers, usually male. The report highlighted the particular vulnerability of disabled children to institutional abuse: over a third of those abused were reported to have a learning difficulty. In the second study, Barter (1998) examined NSPCC independent investigations of abuse in residential settings over a two-year period. This revealed 36 investigations concerning allegations made by 67 children against 50 abusers. A fifth of these involved abuse by other residents, mainly boys. Over a quarter of allegations of sexual abuse involved peers. A further two US studies provide some international context. Rosenthal *et al.* (1991) looked at 261 reported incidents of institutional abuse. Overall, 16 per cent of the 325 perpetrators were peers in residence. However, Spencer and Knudsen (1992) found much higher levels of peer instigators of abuse, with 70 per cent of perpetrators of sexual abuse in residential children's homes being other children and young people.

Evidence presented to the major UK reviews of residential services, set up in response to a series of scandals, also indicated high levels of violence from young people. Members of the Children's Safeguards Review team covering England and Wales held meetings with young people from 20 local authorities and reported that the danger most often identified was that from other children, especially bullying, physical abuse and theft (Utting, 1997). Indeed, the report estimated that 'possibly half the total of abuse reported in institutions is peer abuse' (p. 99).

Other studies have found incidence rates for being bullied or bullying in residential care range from one in six young people (Triseliotis *et al.*, 1995) to as high as one in two (Farmer and Pollock, 1998; Gibbs and Sinclair, 2000). O'Neill's (2001) study of 10 secure units found that nearly all the young people had been bullied. In all of the above studies, the bullying had frequently occurred over a prolonged period of time without being detected by residential staff or external welfare professionals.

Gibbs and Sinclair (2000) provide some of the most systematic findings on the incidence and effect of bullying in UK children's homes. The researchers surveyed 223 children from 48 children's homes. Participants were asked, amongst other things, about *attempts at bullying* in the home by other residents – an experience which the authors note 'is likely to be highly uncomfortable' but that is recognised as a subjective definition, which, they continue, 'rel[ies] on the respondents' account of their experience' (Gibbs and Sinclair, 2000, p. 249). A great deal of literature testifies to the validity of self-reports of bullying (Connell and Farrington, 1996), although Barter *et al.* (2004) found discrepancies in some participants' self-identification of bullying, which will be addressed later in this chapter. Gibbs and Sinclair discovered that other residents, rather than staff, were the main instigators of bullying. Nearly half of participants stated that they had experienced an attempt at being 'bullied' during their stay at the home.

Overall levels of 'bullying' in residential children's homes seem comparable to, and indeed often substantially higher than, those in other non-residential settings, such as schools. Incidence rates varied considerably between different residential settings depending on the type of home, management structure and institutional cultures; these important issues will be pursued later in this chapter. Thus, the available research seems to indicate, perhaps unsurprisingly given the resident population, that peer violence, including bullying, is a substantial problem for residential child-care settings.

Nature of peer violence in residential settings

Most of the above research uses the all-inclusive term 'bullying' and thus provides little insight into the actual nature of the behaviour involved. In contrast, the work of Barter and colleagues (2004) seeks to explore in depth the nature of peer violence in residential child welfare settings and it is therefore on this research that the rest of this chapter will primarily focus. This study is the only one in the UK focused exclusively on this form of violence in residential children's care. The aim of the research was not to measure the incidence of peer violence, but to clarify the context in which particular types of violence occurred and their meanings to those involved, and to produce messages for prevention and intervention. To fulfil these aims a qualitative methodology was used that combined a discussion of personal experiences through semi-structured interviews with the use of vignettes (short case studies of actual situations involving different forms of peer violence) to facilitate abstract evaluations (see Barter and Renold, 2000). Observations of peer interactions were also undertaken in the sample homes.

The research took place in 14 English children's homes. The majority were run by local authorities; three, however, were in the private sector and two were managed by voluntary agencies. We interviewed 71 young people between the ages of 8 and 17 years. Slightly more boys (45) than girls (27) participated and almost a quarter were from minority ethnic groups. Seventy-one staff also participated, including residential social workers, seniors and managers. From young people's and workers' accounts, four different forms of peer violence were derived:

- *Direct physical assault* – examples from young people's accounts included 'punching', 'grabbing hair', 'fist fights', 'leathering', 'beatings', 'slapping'.
- *Physical 'non-contact' attacks* – these harmed young people emotionally rather than physically; for example, destruction of personal belongings, invasion of personal space and intimidation via looks or gestures.
- *Verbal abuse* – generally name-calling concerning sexual reputations, family, appearance or ethnicity.
- *Unwelcome sexual behaviours* – these were experienced as both sexual and abusive by young people, including 'flashing', grabbing a girl's breast, inappropriate touching, unwanted sexual gestures and remarks, and rape.

In Barter *et al.*'s (2004) study, young people described differential levels of impact. *Low-level* attacks were viewed as having little impact; they were infrequent, did not involve a severe use of force and were often a spontaneous response to an isolated event. *High-level* attacks were when force was severe, and they were frequent and part of a wider power structure. Young people viewed the impact as significant, often couched in terms of 'fear' and 'vulnerability'. It is important to note that most young people who described their experiences as bullying also self-defined this as high impact.

Physical violence

Well, there are little fights like but they are minor in my eyes ... never anything proper serious. (Female resident, age 16)

Overall, nearly all the young people reported some form of physical violence towards themselves, either as instigators or as bystanders. One of the most interesting findings was the lack of gender differences, with both boys and girls reporting physical violence as both victims and instigators equally. However there was a gender variation in how different types of physical violence were perpetrated and experienced by young people, particularly in terms of impact and the social context in which the violence was embedded.

Half of the girls' experiences of violence, and a third of the boys', were restricted to *low-level* physical violence. In young people's evaluations low-level forms of violence occurred mainly in the 'safe' context of friendship groups. Boys used this form of violence to publically present a particular kind of 'macho' or 'hard' masculinity to their (male) peers. Such 'attacks' occurred only when staff were present, thus providing a safe arena in which boys could be seen as the 'aggressor' and thereby confirm their masculinity to others, in the full knowledge that staff would intervene to stop any injury to themselves or others. In contrast, girls often reported isolated and sporadic attacks in response to a specific trigger. This form of physical violence was often infrequent and quickly resolved. It was often a response to being 'wound up' by young people. Crucially to young people's evaluations, as both recipients and instigators of low-level violence, no wider power dynamics appeared present. However, this was not the case in respect to high-level physical violence:

I thought they were going to bully me, like do what happened in my past like ... and I thought the kids here were going to do it [suffocate him with a pillow]. (Male resident, age 13)

Nearly three-quarters of young people, proportionally more boys than girls, experienced *high-level* physical violence. As the above quotation illustrates, often young people's experiences of peer violence did not originate in the residential home, reinforcing previous research on the continuity of peer violence and bullying for individuals across settings (e.g. Gibbs and Sinclair, 2000).

Barter *et al.* (2004) found that most high-impact incidents took place within, rather than between, groups of boys and girls. Incidents ranged from knife attacks to severe beatings resulting in broken bones and concussion. For a minority, these attacks were isolated incidents; however more commonly the violence and intimidation was habitual, reflecting the wider power dynamics involved. According to the assailants, these attacks were often premeditated, with the severest attacks happening in bedrooms and at night, when staff surveillance was minimal. Nearly all instigators justified their violence as an appropriate response to an alleged provocation. Girls provided a range of reasons for using high-level violence; mostly these focused on violence as self-defence, either for themselves or to protect another young person from physical attack. Boys' accounts of their use of violence were often framed in terms of *uncontrolled masculinity*, in which they described their use of physical violence almost as a natural male instinct; as one male interviewee said, 'boys will be boys and that's it'. The use of high-level violence by boys also sent messages to other residents that they were 'not to be messed with'. Indeed, in over half of incidents other residents were involved either as active contributors or passive bystanders. Thus high-level physical violence, which some but not all young people said constituted bullying, appeared to be a group phenomenon rather than one-to-one intimidation.

Non-contact violence

I've had my room trashed twice by them [other residents], all my stuff thrown out the window and ruined ... like even my bedroom isn't mine in here. (Female resident, age 13)

Non-contact violence included physical behaviour that did not cause physical injury but psychological pain. Examples included *control* mechanisms such as intimidation via looks, gestures or tone of voice, where a young person exercised some form of control over another. Sometimes this was underpinned by physical violence, although this was not always the case. Non-contact forms of violence also included damage to property, including defecating on young people's beds and clothes, and theft and invasion of personal space, such as bedrooms.

Almost half of participants experienced this form of intimidation, and most young people described non-contact violence as 'bullying'. However, and unlike physical forms of violence, very few young people were prepared to report acting in this way. Generally, young people experienced this as part of a wider cycle of peer violence; consequently two-thirds viewed these attacks as high-level. The most frequently experienced incidents involved the destruction of personal belongings from the victims' bedrooms – known as 'trashing'. More girls than boys experienced this form of intimidation, and girls generally viewed it as having a greater negative impact on their welfare than boys (McRobbie,

1990). Further, young people stated that even when they were not in the home their targeting continued.

Other incidents included threats of physical injury, psychological control mechanisms that affected a young person's freedom or imposed an aggressor's will upon them or non-verbal forms of aggression. Intimidation by other residents found in over half of the sample homes resulted in young people's movements or activities being restricted, including being unable to enter certain communal spaces for fear of repercussions and an inability to speak freely at meetings or to choose group activities or outings.

Verbal violence

It can really hurt what they say to you, especially if they say something bad about your mum; that really hurts. (Male resident, age 11)

Barter et al. (2004) identified that low-level verbal insults seemed to be a common, taken-for-granted aspect of residential life, which went mainly unchallenged by staff. However, high-level verbal attacks contravened boundaries of acceptability. Girls most often relied on tarnishing the sexual reputation of their (female) victims to cause harm. Boys were more likely to insult (female) family members, especially through 'mother cussing'. This was particularly upsetting for boys, who often felt that, because of male codes of honour, their role was to protect female family members and particularly their sexual reputations. In many instances young people had very conflicting relationships with their families, often involving abuse or rejection; negative references to their families were thus often very difficult for young people to cope with. Consequently, the impact of verbal attacks should not be underestimated. Over a third of young people who suffered repeated attacks stated that the long-lasting emotional harm caused was more damaging than some forms of high-level physical attacks, echoing previous findings (Tomison and Tucci, 1997).

Sexual violence

This lad [another resident] came in one night stoned out of his head and thought he could do what he wanted and took advantage [sexual assault] ... it was horrible. (Female resident, age 14)

In Barter et al.'s (2004) study, accounts of peer sexual violence were the lowest of all forms of violence. Girls were three times more likely to report this than boys, and most saw it as being high-level. Girls spoke to us about a range of sexually harmful behaviours they had experienced in their current or past placements, up to and including one rape. Most perpetrators were male. All incidents involved some degree of coercion. The majority of attacks occurred in the victim's bedroom. Over half of young people had not informed staff, although they had told other young people.

Other studies have also highlighted the high rate of sexual violence inflicted by other residents (Lunn, 1990; Morris and Wheatley, 1994; O'Neill, 2001). O'Neill argues that the lack of confidentiality in the units studied meant that most of the young people were aware of the reasons for admission, which meant that some of the girls who had been sexually abused or worked as prostitutes were subject to negative labels based on sexuality and were subject to verbal, physical and sexual assaults. Sinclair and Gibbs (1998) found that over a third of female residents but only one in nine males reported that unwanted sexual advances had occurred prior to admission. Nearly a quarter of females and 7 per cent of males said such incidents had happened post-admission. Farmer and Pollock (1998) discovered that children who had been abused at home were more likely to be placed in residential care, whereas those who had abused others mostly went to foster homes, where it was assumed they would be less of a risk. However, half the sexually abused children in the sample went on to abuse others, mostly involving peers in residential and foster placements.

Encouragingly, these research findings indicate that residential care can offer some young people protection against sexual violence, as a proportion of young people had experienced victimisation only prior to their admission. Unfortunately this also meant that some young people were not protected.

Perceptions of bullying

Research has also indicated that both young people and residential workers do not view all 'victims' as being equally deserving (Barter _et al._, 2004). Residents who were viewed as 'winding up' other residents were perceived as a 'justified' target for retaliation, often physical, from other young people. Workers did not necessarily recognise a young person's inability to control their behaviour, which made them a target for peer violence, to be an indication of their wider unmet needs. Some residential workers in Barter _et al._'s research allowed peer retaliations to take place, within certain boundaries of harm, when their own efforts to stop the behaviour had failed. Similarly in O'Neill's (2001) study, a victim-blaming approach from staff emerged, in which staff argued that some bullied young people were responsible for their own victimisation.

Barter *et al*. (2004) also identified certain discrepancies in how some young people self-defined bullying. In interviews some young participants stated they had been bullied, when researchers could not identify any abuse of power or use of intimidation.

Wider cultural contexts

The culture of the institution is influential in the occurrence of violence. Where young people feel valued there is less likelihood of peer violence, but where the institution fails to take the issue seriously, and where staff use intimidation to control young people, intimidation and violence frequently occur (Land and Tattum, 1989). It is therefore important to locate peer violence in wider power structures (Green, 2005; Kendrick, 2008; O'Neill, 2008), which may be intensified in the residential context. From the literature three main mechanisms were influential in mediating peer violence in young people's cultures: peer-group hierarchies, gender and racism.

Peer-group hierarchies

The existence of pecking orders and 'top dog' networks has been highlighted in previous literature (Brannan *et al*., 1993; Parkin and Green, 1997). Parkin and Green (1997) stated that 'top dog' networks existed in many of the homes they investigated, whereby one or two children exercised considerable power and influence over others as a result of actual or perceived physical strength and manipulation. They continued that this enabled young people to boost their reputations, or to diminish those of others, and to gain influence with staff. O'Neill (2001) discovered that many of the staff in secure units appeared to condone bullying through the 'pecking order', suggesting it was inherent in the system and that young people had to be prepared for it.

Barter *et al*. (2004) also found that peer-group hierarchies or 'pecking orders' were a central context in which young people experienced violence. Nearly all of the 14 homes in their sample had a resident hierarchy, which was often linked with abuses of power, including violence. Young people viewed the hierarchy as an inevitable, but not necessarily a natural, aspect of residential life. Many of the 'lower-status' young people described their experience of the hierarchy as one of intimidation and exploitation. Staff, in contrast, often saw it as benign, even helpful in controlling young people in their care by utilising the power that 'top dogs' had over other residents. As James *et al.* (1998, p. 77) argue, 'the peer-group culture partly emerges out of the temporal demands laid on children and young people by the institution structures through which their growing up is regulated and controlled.'

Young residents were often in very close proximity, for long periods of time, with other young people they may or may not know. Often, many of these young people had experienced disrupted and abusive families, whilst others were accommodated because of their perceived delinquency (which may or may not be associated with family neglect or maltreatment). It is perhaps unsurprising, given such a milieu, that peer-group hierarchies based on intimidation predominated, especially if left unchallenged by workers.

Peer-group dynamics were seen as being most problematic when they were in flux: when a new resident had to find their position or when a resident from the top of the hierarchy left and their position thus became vacant. Sinclair and Gibbs (1998) acknowledge in their study that a number of the heads of homes commented on the importance of the 'pecking order' and of the struggles to adjust it as a result of the admission of a new resident. Workers stated they sometimes left young people to 'sort it out' themselves as long as it didn't 'get out of hand'. Unfortunately most of the violence which occurred at these times was hidden from staff, and strong disincentives were present in many homes to stop young people telling or 'grassing'. Overall, most young people wanted staff to be more proactive in challenging this hierarchy.

However, the peer-group hierarchy was experienced differently in relation to a young person's reason for entering care. Half of the young people in Gibbs and Sinclair's (2000) study whose primary reason for being placed in care was previous abuse, but only a third of those whose reason for being accommodated was delinquency, were victimised through the peer hierarchy. The authors conclude that many of the homes contained a context where older, more delinquent young people established a hierarchy to humiliate or bully younger, less 'street-wise' residents. Similarly, Dishon *et al.* (1999) argue that grouping troubled young people together can make their problems worse. In particular, their research indicates that antisocial boys frequently reinforce each other's aggressive behaviour in group settings. This finding resonates with other findings from locked facilities for children and young people, where incident rates for all forms of violence are especially high and reciprocal (Edgar and O'Donnell, 1997).

However, the peer-group context, if situated in a placement which meets children's needs, can act as a positive resource, where 'the group operates to monitor and secure residents' safety and acts as a means of maintaining group culture' (Emond, 2003, p. 334). However, it is unlikely that a beneficial peer culture, as described above, will thrive if the institution fails to meet the complex, and often conflicting, needs of its resident group. The importance of the management of residential homes in relation to peer violence will be returned to later in the chapter.

Gender

Throughout this chapter the importance of gender in understanding peer violence has been highlighted. Studies such as Barter *et al.* (2004) and Parkin and Green (1997) position gender as a central theoretical framework for understanding how violence is experienced but also conceptualised by both young people and residential workers. Both groups' perceptions of violence, including bullying, were influenced by the gendered stereotyping of 'normal' behaviour. Behaviour that was expected and tolerated as an expression of youthful masculinity was not accepted when exhibited by girls. Young people and staff felt that male physical violence was a normal, although uncontrolled, aspect of boys' behaviour and a natural expression of their developing masculinity. Similarly, girls saw sexual aggression from boys as a common, if unwelcome, feature of male sexuality. Residents and workers often regarded sexually provocative behaviour from girls as a trigger for sexual assaults by boys. Thus the female target was blamed for the violence while the boy's responsibility for his actions was minimised as a result of his being unfairly 'led on'.

Racism

The research found less racist behaviour in homes than might be expected given children's and young people's accounts of racism in other contexts (see Barter, 1997). Racism was an area where residential workers were proactive and where clear agency policies and practices were in place. Young people generally provided an anti-racist perspective, although certain 'outsider' groups, specifically South Asians, were at greater risk of racial victimisation. Such groups were not ascribed the 'street credentials' of wider youth cultures with which many of the young people engaged (Majors, 1989; Sewell, 1997). More recent research on young care leavers from different ethnic groups shows that white young people are experiencing the worst outcomes (Barn *et al.*, 2005), indicating that children from some minority groups are, in some areas, having their needs more successfully met.

Children's and young people's protective strategies

Most young people advocated retaliation as their main response to a perceived attack (Barter *et al.*, 2004). High-level attacks generally were thought to justify targeted and planned retaliation. Nearly all accounts used narratives of revenge, prevention, protection of honour and similar justifications. In most homes young people used peers rather than staff as a source of emotional support (Emond, 2002). Peers were the first port of call in all incidents later disclosed to staff. Reasons given by young people included: feeling that staff would be unable to solve or might even exacerbate the problem; lack of trust/empathy; and to avoid 'getting into trouble' themselves through violating non-disclosure cultures ('grassing'). In homes where young people stated they had positive relationships with workers, residents more often approached staff for help and support. In homes with positive staff and child relationships young people perceived interventions as being more successful than in homes where relationships were viewed less favourably.

O'Neill (2001) found that, although some young people in the secure units thought staff were in control, the majority view was that staff did not realise the extent or seriousness of the bullying or deal with it adequately. This left young people feeling unsafe and resulted in them having to find ways to protect themselves, often through the use of physical force. This often led staff to punish young people when they acted to protect themselves through the use of violence.

Staff understanding and response

Consistency of staff intervention has been shown to differ both between and within homes (Barter *et al.*, 2004; O'Neill, 2001). For example, O'Neill (2001) reports that some degree of staff acknowledgement existed in relation to the occurrence of bullying and intimidation in the secure units, although a rather complacent attitude from staff minimised its extent and importance. However, O'Neill reports that different attitudes were evident between staff in the units; in some cases residential workers had expressed their concerns about the level and impact of bullying to senior staff members but these concerns were not acted upon or were ignored.

Barter *et al.* (2004) reports that responses to physical violence produced the most consistent accounts, indicating it was routine for workers to intervene in physical violence, up to and including restraint if conciliatory methods were unsuccessful. However, workers report being confused and concerned about their ability to physically restrain young people when necessary (Berridge and Brodie, 1996). Non-contact violence was unanimously considered the most difficult to identify and intercept, thanks to its hidden nature, rooted in the group's power dynamics. Staff described its covert nature as 'undertone', 'undercurrent' and 'backdoor' violence (Barter et al., 2004). Barter et al. found that residential workers were often reluctant to talk about sexual violence, although managers appeared more confident. Many felt unsure about what constituted 'inappropriate' sexual behaviour and how best to respond; some felt they had failed to challenge 'relationships' which they felt contained some degree of coercion. Workers also diminished the importance of verbal abuse, especially sexual insult, thinking it too ingrained in the young people's everyday language for them to have any significant impact for change. They did recognise that verbal violence based around 'mother cussing' had a significant effect, but primarily were preoccupied with children's physical safety. Only two homes routinely challenged such language, reflecting their managers' and residential workers' high expectations of children's behaviour generally; in both homes all forms of violence were low. Work by Kendrick and Mair (2002), in a unit for sexually aggressive young men, found that when the use of swearing and sexualised language was systematically challenged a marked difference was observed in bullying levels.

Barter et al. report that the main method of securing young people's safety was through direct supervision. Restriction of young people's movements, for example to certain parts of the building, especially bedrooms, was a key mechanism to increase surveillance. Overall, strategies appeared reactive rather than proactive. For example, many homes widely used negative sanctions for disruptive behaviour, but few systematic rewards for positive behaviour or achievements were in evidence. Only a minority undertook any form of proactive group work with young people. Indeed, staff stated that they lacked the confidence and ability to undertake group work. This was despite the fact that the researchers observed some of the same workers 'informally' discussing very sensitive matters with young people to significant effect. Over half of the homes had access to an independent advocacy service; however, most young people viewed this as helping with practical problems, such as placement difficulties, rather than being a source of emotional support, and few had discussed issues of violence.

Residential context

The triggers for peer violence and the negative residential peer cultures which underpinned it show some similarity to those described in other youth group contexts, such as schools, youth clubs and custodial institutions (Cawson *et al.*, 2000; Frosh *et al.*, 2002; Kendrick, 1997; Pitts *et al.*, 2000; Virdee *et al.*, 1999). However, when these dynamics are transferred to children's residential care they acquire a dimension not present in day-school settings: the enforced closeness of everyday living with strangers, creating round-the-clock vulnerability to the peer-group. Children and young people in residential settings are particularly sensitive to triggers for violence as a result of previous experiences of abuse. Children's homes, with their small, mixed-gender groups and daily access to the community, also differ from custodial settings. Any of these characteristics could be found singly in other settings. Only in children's homes do they come together as a unique experience.

The dual role of residential care as both a 'home' and a setting for social welfare intervention can be conflicting. The position of children's residential care as a quasi-domestic setting for daily life can create unique vulnerabilities thanks to the combination of public and private spheres. Although violence between young people in children's homes shows many similarities to that found in other contexts, its operation throughout all areas of young people's lives, particularly the likelihood of invasion of personal space and attacks at night, can make its impact much greater. Ward (2004), in recognition of this dilemma, argues for the need to contain ordinary caring practices found in family contexts whilst at the same time acknowledge that many of the children in placement, including those who experience peer violence, may need specialist assistance. Ward argues that it is imperative that, whilst more specialist residential services need to be provided, these cannot be at the expense of disrupting the ordinariness of everyday living. This is not an easy balance for homes to achieve.

Responding to peer violence in residential settings

Research clearly demonstrates that the type and management of child-care placements directly influence the incidence of residential violence. Gibbs and Sinclair (2000) found that in general the average level of reported bullying was higher in homes which also scored high on other aspects of 'deviant behaviour'. This finding illustrates how important it is to consider all aspects of children's and young people's experiences rather than any specific form of behaviour or violence in isolation.

Reducing violence requires a planned, proactive approach. Clear and agreed definitions and descriptions of the unacceptable behaviour and its consequences are a prerequisite. Training needs to enable staff to both recognise the signs of peer violence and to use possible intervention techniques. Young people's experiences and insights need to inform and shape this process through direct consultation. Responses need to acknowledge the harm caused by verbal attacks, and how this provides the context for physical and sexual violence. Cultures that support violence as a 'natural' or 'normal' aspect of peer-relations, whether through peer-group hierarchies, derogatory language or gender, need to be challenged.

Research shows that children's homes with similar resident groups in terms of past experience of violence and abuse exhibit very different incidence rates for violence and bullying (Barter *et al.*, 2004). In their study, Gibbs and Sinclair (2000) report that the lowest rates for bullying were associated with smaller homes, where staff shared a common philosophy, adopted a similar approach and heads of homes had a clear vision, a feasible remit and were able to act upon their own initiative. Similarly, Brown *et al.* (1998) emphasise the beneficial effect of placing children in settings where there is congruence between structure and culture. Others have stressed the need to minimise inappropriate placements in homes, particularly in relation to placing instigators and those with a history of victimisation together (Brogi and Bagley, 1998; Kendrick, 2004).

These findings confirm that, although individual characteristics may make some young people more or less susceptible to peer violence, the management and structure of the setting can have a greater influencing factor in mediating young people's exposure to violence. Residential care can mediate the potentially negative effect of group living, through behavioural treatments, community-like settings, positive relationships with adult providers, positive attention, praise and careful monitoring/supervision of young people (Handwerk *et al.*, 2000).

Many residential homes have now developed specific policies around peer violence, although systematic evaluations of these strategies are still largely absent. One area where evaluations have begun to emerge is restorative justice. In the UK, a growing interest has emerged in the use of a restorative justice approach to work with children and young people and particularly in dealing with issues of conflict and bullying (Littlechild and Sender, 2006; Willmott, 2007). Restorative justice is a term used to describe the processes that aim to address the harm caused by a criminal offence or a non-criminal incident. At the heart of restorative justice is the principle that, via a method of structured communication, victims and perpetrators can discuss how they were affected by the incident and can explore what needs to happen to repair the harm caused (Willmott, 2007; Youth Justice Board, 2004).

Littlechild and Sender (2006) and Willmott (2007), amongst others, have identified that restorative justice approaches may be usefully applied in children's residential care settings. Willmott provides a 'snapshot' of its use in residential settings rather than a representative account, identifying ten residential children's homes where approaches based on restorative justice were being used. The main reasons for introducing this approach in the sample homes were mainly assaults on staff and other residents, bullying between residents and disagreements between peers.

Overall the research found that the use of restorative justice approaches within residential settings had a positive impact for both the residential staff and the residents themselves. Many described the approach as empowering for all parties involved, helping all sides in a conflict or dispute to have their say on what had happened and giving them a stake in how the situation might best be resolved. Evidence from some sites showed that young people themselves sometimes used restorative justice approaches in sorting out their own disagreements with other residents.

The only study to undertake a formal evaluation of this approach raised a number of issues regarding its effectiveness in responding to bullying (Littlechild, 2003). Overall, Littlechild concluded that the introduction of restorative justice had been successful in the residential unit studied. Staff generally felt that the restorative justice training they had received provided them with better ways of dealing with conflicts in the unit; it had changed the way in which most staff dealt with conflict, including bullying; and it was seen as a valuable tool in helping young people to think about their behaviour and take responsibility for their actions. However, the evaluation also found that issues concerning bullying (as opposed to other behaviour) were the most difficult to resolve. Staff felt that the approach best applied to individual conflicts or disagreements where a 'solution' could be identified. As bullying involved sets of relationships between residents, based on wider power dynamics, rather than a specific incident, reaching an 'agreement' was more challenging. In addition, there could be negative repercussions for the victim as a result of reporting the bullying to staff. Encouragingly, the evaluation noted that the general level of conflict between young people declined, creating a more positive residential culture, which is crucial in safeguarding young people from peer intimidation and violence.

Identifying and adapting strategies that may work

As we have seen, peer violence is a complex phenomenon and one where a multi-level approach is more likely to be effective in the long term than isolated or narrowly focused initiatives. Research has identified that no simple solutions exist to combat peer violence and bullying. Rather than ask 'what works?', evidence indicates it is more realistic to ask 'what might work' in a particular setting (Oliver and Candappa, 2003). A range of possible approaches emerging from school bullying interventions that may be developed for the residential context have been suggested by Barter (2008); these include:

- *Friendship support* – enhancing friendship skills can act as an important protective factor (Besag, 1989), and programmes that incorporate this approach, for example circle of friends, have shown promising results (Ginsberg *et al.*, 1986).
- *Mentoring* – mentoring schemes in which older, more confident non-aggressive young people are matched with younger and more isolated ones have been attempted.
- *Peer-group initiatives* – Frost (1991) claims that peer-group pressure offers the most effective deterrent to bullying. School-based responses have highlighted the importance of working with individuals and groups. Approaches have included peer support and mediation, including peer counselling and 'listener' schemes, group education and discussion (Cowie and Sharpe, 1994; Department for Education and Skills, 2002; Eslea and Smith, 1998; Smith and Sharp, 1994).
- *Confidential support* – the provision of confidential support and confidential reporting systems, independent from staff, has been associated with positive outcomes in some settings.
- *Positive reward system* – my research found a reliance on controlling behaviour through negative sanctions. However, homes that accompany this with a reward system for positive behaviour or achievements showed some promising results.

Conclusion

The building blocks of a more comprehensive approach to addressing peer violence in children's residential care do exist. Research into peer violence and bullying in different settings provides some important insights and strategies for developing prevention and intervention. Residential managers, working alongside young people and residential staff, need to explore how such initiatives can be used, as well as develop a range of strategies specific to the residential context.

However, and as this chapter has demonstrated, the residential context, including the mix of young people, many of whom have complex and often conflicting needs, provides a unique setting that calls for distinct policy and practice responses. Young people need to be consulted to ensure their experiences and evaluations shape safeguarding responses. Ultimately any initiative or policy will be less effective if the wider management structure fails to provide clear aims and objectives for children's care placements. A referral system which takes into account the current mix of young people in a placement and their needs is essential. Residential workers and young people need to implement high thresholds for appropriate behaviour and not tolerate behaviour which, outside the residential context, would be viewed as unacceptable. Research suggests that peer violence and bullying in children's homes is a significant problem for young people's welfare. However, the same research also clearly demonstrates that children's homes with very similar resident groups exhibit disparate rates of peer violence. It is these findings which provide the evidence that such violence is not an integral aspect of the residential experience but an aberration which can be safeguarded against.

REFERENCES

Barn, R., Andrew, L. and Mantovani N. (2005). *Life after Care: A Study of the Experiences of Young People from Different Ethnic Groups.* York and Bristol: Joseph Rowntree Foundation/Policy Press.

Barter, C. (1997). 'Who's to blame: conceptualising institutional abuse by children'. *Early Child Development and Care*, 133: 101–04.

(1998). *Investigating Institutional Abuse of Children: An Exploration of the NSPCC Experience.* London: NSPCC.

(2008). 'Prioritising young people's concerns in residential care: responding to peer violence'. In A. Kendrick (ed.), *Residential Child Care: Prospects and Challenges.* London: Jessica Kingsley.

Barter, C. and Berridge, D. (eds.) (2010). *Children Behaving Badly? Violence between Children and Young People.* Chichester: Wiley.

Barter, C. and Renold, E. (2000). 'I wanna tell you a story: the application of vignettes in qualitative research with young people'. *Social Research Methodology, Theory and Practice*, 3: 307–23.

Barter, C., McCarry, M., Berridge, D. and Evans, K. (2009). *Partner Exploitation and Violence in Teenage Intimate Relationships.* London: NSPCC.

Barter, C., Renold, E., Berridge, D. and Cawson, P. (2004). *Peer Violence in Children's Residential Care.* Basingstoke: Palgrave.

Beinum, M. van, Marin, A. and Bonnett, C. (2001). 'Catching children as they fall: mental health promotion in residential child care in East Dunbartonshire'. *Scottish Journal of Residential Child Care*, 1: 14–22.

Berridge, D. and Barter, C. (forthcoming). 'Conclusion'. In C. Barter and D. Berridge (eds.), *Children Behaving Badly? Violence between Children and Young People.* Chichester: Wiley.

Berridge, D. and Brodie, I. (1996). 'Residential child care in England and Wales: the inquiries and after'. In M. Hill and J. Aldgate (eds.), *Child*

Welfare Services: Developments in Law, Policy, Practice and Research. London: Jessica Kingsley.

Besag, V.E. (1989). *Bullies and Victims in Schools: A Guide to Understanding and Management.* Milton Keynes: Open University Press.

Brannan, C., Jones, J.R. and Murch, J.D. (1993). 'Lessons from a residential special school enquiry: reflections on the Castle Hill Report'. *Child Abuse Review,* 2: 271–75.

Brogi, L. and Bagley, C. (1998). 'Abusing victims: detention of child sexual abuse victims in secure accommodation'. *Child Abuse Review,* 7: 315–29.

Brown, E., Bullock, R., Hobson, C. and Little, M. (1998). *Making Residential Care Work: Structure and Culture in Children's Homes.* Aldershot: Ashgate.

Cawson, P., Wattam, C., Brooker, S. and Kelly, G. (2000). *Child Maltreatment in the United Kingdom: A Study of the Prevalence of Child Abuse and Neglect.* London: NSPCC.

Chipenda-Dansokho, S., Little, M. and Thomas, B. (2003). 'Residential services for children: definitions, numbers and classifications'. Chicago: Chapin Hall Center for Children.

Colton, M. (2002). 'Factors associated with abuse in residential child care institutions'. *Children and Society,* 6: 33–44.

Committee of Inquiry into Children's Homes and Hostels (1986). *Report of the Committee of Inquiry into Children's Homes and Hostels (Kincora Inquiry).* London: HMSO.

Connell, A. and Farrington, D. (1996). 'Bullying amongst incarcerated young prisoners: developing an interview schedule and some preliminary results'. *Journal of Adolescence,* 19: 75–93.

Cowie, H. and Sharp, S. (1994). 'Tackling bullying through the curriculum'. In P.K. Smith and S. Sharp (eds.), *School Bullying: Insights and Perspectives.* London: Routledge.

Department for Education and Skills (2002). *Bullying: Don't Suffer in Silence.* London: Department for Education and Skills, www.dfes.gov.uk/bullying/ (accessed 26 May 2009).

Dishon, D., McCord, J. and Poulan, F. (1999). 'When interventions harm: peer groups and problem behaviour'. *American Psychologist,* 54: 755–64.

Edgar, K. and O'Donnell, I. (1997). 'Responding to victimisation'. *Prison Service Journal,* 109: 15–19.

Emond, R. (2002). 'Understanding the resident group'. *Scottish Journal of Residential Child Care,* 1: 30–40.

    (2003). 'Putting the care into residential care: the role of young people'. *Journal of Social Work,* 3: 321–37.

Eslea, M. and Smith, P.K. (1998). 'The long-term effectiveness of anti-bullying work in primary schools'. *Education Research,* 40: 203–18.

Farmer, E. and Pollock, S. (1998). *Sexually Abused and Abusing Children in Substitute Care.* Chichester: Wiley.

Freundlich, M., Avery, R. and Padgett, D. (2007). 'Care or scare? The safety of youth in congregate care in New York City'. *Child Abuse and Neglect,* 31: 173–86.

Frosh S., Phoenix A. and Pattman R. (2002). *Young Masculinities: Understanding Boys in Contemporary Society.* Basingstoke: Palgrave.

Frost, L. (1991). 'A primary school approach: what can be done about the bully?' In M. Elliot (ed.), *Bullying: A Practical Guide to Coping for Schools* (pp. 40–49). Harlow: Longman.

Gibbs, I. and Sinclair, I. (2000). 'Bullying, sexual harassment and happiness in residential children's homes'. *Child Abuse Review*, 9: 247–56.

Ginsberg, D., Gottman, J. and Parker, J. (1986). 'The importance of friendship'. In J.M. Gottman and J.G. Parker (eds.), *Conversations of Friends*. Cambridge: Cambridge University Press.

Green, L. (2005). 'Theorizing sexuality, sexual abuse and residential children's homes: adding gender to the equation'. *British Journal of Social Work*, 35: 453–81.

Handwerk, M.L., Field, C.A. and Friman, P.C. (2000). 'The iatrogenic effects of group intervention for antisocial youth: premature extrapolations?' *Journal of Behavioral Education*, 10: 223–38.

James, A., Jenks, C. and Prout, A. (1998). *Theorizing Childhood*. Cambridge: Polity Press.

Kendrick, A. (1997). 'Safeguarding children living away from home: a literature review'. In R. Kent (ed.), *Children's Safeguards Review for the Scottish Office*. Edinburgh: The Stationery Office.

    (2004). 'Managing children and young people who are sexually aggressive'. In H. Kemshall and G. McIvor (eds.), *Managing Sex Offender Risk* (pp. 165–86). London: Jessica Kingsley.

Kendrick, A. (ed.) (2008). *Residential Child Care: Prospects and Challenges*. London: Jessica Kingsley.

Kendrick, A. and Mair, R. (2002). 'Developing focused care: a residential unit for sexually aggressive young men'. In M. Calder (ed.), *Young People Who Sexually Abuse: Building the Evidence Base for Your Practice*. Lyme Regis: Russell House Publishing.

Kirkwood, A. (1993). *The Leicestershire Inquiry 1992*. Leicester: Leicestershire County Council.

Land, D.A. and Tattum, D.P. (1989). *Supporting the Child in School*. Milton Keynes: Open University Press.

Layder, D. (1998). *Sociological Practice: Linking Theory and Social Research*. London: Sage.

Levy, A. and Kahan, B. (1991). *The Pindown Experience and the Protection of Children*. Stafford: Staffordshire County Council.

Little, M., Kohm, A. and Thompson, R. (2005). 'The impact of residential placement on child development: research and policy implications'. *International Journal of Social Welfare*, 14: 200–09.

Littlechild, B. (2003). *An Evaluation of the Implementation of a Restorative Justice Approach in a Residential Unit for Young People in Hertfordshire: Final Report*. Hatfield: University of Hertfordshire, Department of Health and Social Care.

Littlechild, B. and Sender, H. (2006). 'Young people's residential units: restorative justice and relational conflict resolution'. *Childright*, 227: 2–14.

Lunn, T. (1990). 'Pioneers of abuse control'. *Social Work Today*, 22: 9.

Majors, R. (1989). 'Cool pose: the proud signature of black survival'. In: M.S. Kimmel and M.A. Messner (eds.), *Men's Lives*. New York: Macmillan.

McRobbie, A. (1990). *Feminism and Youth Culture from 'Jackie' to 'Just Seventeen'*. London: Macmillan.

Morgan, R. (2008). *Children on Bullying: A Report by the Children's Rights Director of England*. London: Ofsted.

Morris, S. and Wheatley, H. (1994). *Time to Listen: The Experience of Young People in Foster and Residential Care*. London: ChildLine.

Moss, M., Sharpe, S. and Fay, C. (1990). *Abuse in the Care System: A Pilot Study by the National Association of Young People in Care*. London: NAYPIC.

Mullender, A., Hague, G.M., Imam, I., Kelly, L., Malos, E.M. and Regan, L. (2002). *Children's Perspectives on Domestic Violence*. London, Sage.

Oliver, C. and Candappa, M. (2003). *Tackling Bullying: Listening to the Views of Children and Young People. Summary Report for ChildLine*. London: Department for Education and Skills.

O'Neill, T. (2001). *Children in Secure Accommodation: A Gendered Exploration of Locked Institutional Care for Children in Trouble*. London: Jessica Kingsley.

(2008). 'Gender matters in residential child care'. In A. Kendrick (ed.), *Residential Child Care: Prospects and Challenges*. London: Jessica Kingsley.

Parkin, W. and Green, L. (1997). 'Cultures of abuse within residential child care'. *Early Child Development and Care*, 133: 73–86.

Paterson, S., Watson, D. and Whiteford, J. (2003). *Let's Face It! Care 2003: Young People Tell It How It Is*. Glasgow: Who Cares? Scotland.

Pitts, J., Marlow, A., Porteous, D. and Toon, I. (2000). *Inter-group and Inter-racial Violence and the Victimisation of School Students in a London Neighbourhood*. Funded by the Economic and Social Research Council and Violence Research Programme, University of Luton, www.regard.ac.uk.

Rosenthal, J., Motz, J., Edmondson, D. and Groze, V. (1991). 'A descriptive study of abuse and neglect in out-of-home placement'. *Child Abuse and Neglect*, 15: 249–60.

Safe and Sound Group and National Society for the Prevention of Cruelty to Children (1995). *So Who Are We Meant to Trust Now? Responding to Abuse in Care: The Experiences of Young People*. London: NSPCC.

Sewell, T. (1997). *Black Masculinities and Schooling: How Do Black Boys Survive Modern School?* Stoke-on-Trent: Trent Books.

Sinclair, I. and Gibbs, I. (1998). *Children's Homes: A Study in Diversity*. Chichester: Wiley.

Smith, P.K. and Sharp, S. (eds.) (1994). *School Bullying: Insights and Perspectives*. London: Routledge.

Spencer, J.W. and Knudsen, D.D. (1992). 'Out-of-home maltreatment – an analysis of risk in various settings for children'. *Children and Youth Services Review*, 14: 485–92.

Tomison, A.M. and Tucci, J. (1997). 'Emotional abuse: the hidden form of maltreatment'. *Issues in Child Abuse Prevention*, 8: 16.

Triseliotis, J., Borland, M., Hill, M. and Lambert, L. (1995). *Teenagers and Social Work Services*. London: HMSO.

Utting, W. (1997). *People like Us: The Report on the Review of Safeguards for Children Living Away from Home*. London: The Stationery Office.

Virdee, S., Modood, T., Newburn, T. and Shaw, C. (1999). *Understanding Racial Harassment in Schools*. Funded by the ESRC. Universities of Strathclyde and Bristol, www.regard.ac.uk.

Ward, A. (2004). 'Towards a theory of the everyday: the ordinary and the special in daily living in residential care'. *Child and Youth Care Forum*, 33: 209–25.

Westcott, H. and Clement, M. (1992). *NSPCC Experience of Child Abuse in Residential Care and Educational Placements: Results of a Survey*. London: NSPCC.

Willmott, N. (2007). *A Review of the Use of Restorative Justice in Children's Residential Care*. London: National Children's Bureau.

Wolmar, C. (2000). *Forgotten Children: The Scandals in Britain's Children's Homes*. London: Vision.

Youth Justice Board (2004). *Key Elements of Effective Practice: Restorative Justice*. London: Youth Justice Board.

5   Domestic violence: bullying in the home

Paul B. Naylor, Laurie Petch and Parveen Azam Ali

In this chapter we consider domestic violence, including physical and psychological abuse, harm, bodily injury, assault and the infliction of fear between family or household members in the home. We suggest that almost all domestic violence constitutes bullying since it involves the 'systematic abuse of power' (Smith and Sharp, 1994, p. 2), which relies on the aggressor's and target's unequal access to power (Farrington, 1993). First, we consider the prevalence of abuse that occurs between adults in intimate relationships; the abuse of children and adolescents by adults; and abuse that occurs between child and adolescent siblings. This is followed by the correlates and impact of each of these types of abuse. We acknowledge that children and adolescents abuse their parents and carers and that this should not be minimised, but because studies of these topics are very sparse we do not consider them here. We then consider theoretical accounts of domestic violence where we feel that they cast light on the phenomenon. Finally, we conclude with implications, as we see them, for policy and professional practice, and with suggestions for further research in the field.

Nature and prevalence of domestic violence

Abuse between adults

The term domestic violence is often used to refer to men as perpetrators of violence in heterosexual relationships. A large proportion of domestic violence between adults consists of intimate partner violence (IPV). The World Health Organization (WHO, 1997) defined IPV in terms of what male intimate partners do to adult and adolescent women. More recently, the WHO (2002) acknowledged that women can also be violent towards their male partners and there is no reason why the term cannot be applied to IPV in gay and lesbian relationships.

While acknowledging that female-on-male IPV exists, the number of women reporting abuse by men is far greater than the converse (e.g. Coker *et al.* (2002) reported a prevalence of 29 per cent). Empirical findings on the prevalence of IPV in heterosexual and homosexual relationships have been found to be similar, at 25–35 per cent (Gunther and Jennings, 1999). Other prevalence studies, however, suggest that IPV by men on women is higher, at 33–54 per cent (Abbott *et al.*, 1995; Ernst *et al.*, 1997), and the number of women reporting physical injury arising from IPV is greater than it is for men (Phelan *et al.*, 2005).

IPV probably exists in all countries, cultures and societies, but estimating the prevalence across cultures is difficult as a result of inconsistencies in definition, under-reporting and a lack of epidemiological studies (Bradley *et al.*, 2002). Nonetheless, data suggest that around one in three women worldwide experience IPV at some point in their lives (WHO, 1997). Cross-sectional population surveying is often considered to be the most accurate method for determining the prevalence of IPV. For instance, a review of 48 population-based surveys from around the world revealed that between 10 and 50 per cent of women report experiencing IPV at some point in their lives, with 10–30 per cent experiencing sexual violence by an intimate partner (WHO, 2002).

Reviews suggest that prevalence rates vary both between countries and between studies. This variance may be due to inconsistencies in how IPV is defined, and cultural contexts may play a role here. In order to confront these issues and to assess the extent of the problem, the WHO sponsored a multi-country study on women's health to determine the prevalence of physical and sexual IPV (Heise *et al.*, 1999). The study spanned 10 countries and used standardised population-based household surveys. The findings showed a reported lifetime prevalence of physical and sexual violence that ranged from 15–71 per cent for women aged 15–49 years (*n* = 2,097). Specifically, the proportion of women who had ever experienced physical violence ranged from 13 per cent in Japan to 61 per cent in Peru, with a very similar pattern for sexual violence (6 per cent in Japan; 59 per cent in Peru) (Garcia-Moreno *et al.*, 2006).

Children's exposure to IPV between adults

Children's vicarious witnessing of violence (Domestic Violence Exposure – DVE) between adults in the home, most commonly spouses or partners, represents a second, important dimension of domestic bullying. The methodological problems involved in assessing the proportion of children exposed to DVE are well summarised by Osofsky (2003). Nevertheless, the papers that Osofsky reviews indicate prevalence levels of between 16 and 25 per cent in non-clinical populations. Fusco and Fantuzzo conclude that about 40 per cent of investigated domestic violence incidents in the USA, according to their definition, involve children. The subtypes of DVE discovered included: direct sensory exposure (75 per cent), physical involvement of the child (37 per cent), participation of the child in the precipitating event (35 per cent) and occasions when the child called for help (28 per cent).

Abuse of children and adolescents by adults

When researchers define adult-on-child domestic violence they typically seek to differentiate abuse from harm, that is, ill-treatment from its effects (Fakunmoju, 2009). One recent definition of child abuse refers to 'acts of commission or omission which directly or indirectly result in harm to the child and prevent a normal development into healthy adulthood' (Mok, 2008, p. 979). US investigations of reported abuse among 889,000 children suggest that about 40 in 1,000 children experience some form of abuse by adults while living with parents or guardians (Donohue, 2004; Wells, 2008). In order of prevalence, based on UK statistics for children and young people involved with child protection services (Department for Children, Schools and Families (DCSF), 2008), such abuse is typically divided into: neglect, emotional abuse, physical abuse, mixed abuse and sexual abuse.

Neglect or emotional maltreatment is experienced by 16 per cent of children known to child protection services in the USA (Wells, 2008), and about 44 per cent of their English counterparts (DCSF, 2008). Emotional abuse comprises persistent acts 'which are considered potentially psychologically damaging, by conveying to children that they are worthless, flawed, unloved, unwanted, endangered, or of value only in meeting another's needs' (Jones, 2000, Section 9.3.1). This category includes allowing a child to experience the maltreatment of another person (Mok, 2008). During the years 2004–08, about 23 per cent of children subject to child protection measures in the UK had experienced emotional abuse (DCSF, 2008).

Child physical abuse (CPA) consists of non-accidental events including: battering, shaking (DiScala et al., 2000), close confinement such as tying or binding of arms or legs, locking in a cupboard and refusal to allow needed treatment for a professionally diagnosed medical problem (Wells, 2008). Government sources estimate the prevalence of CPA at 5.7 per 1,000 children in the USA and about 0.8 per 1,000 children in England (Department of Health, 2000; Sedlak and Broadhurst, 1996). In contrast, a larger proportion (7 per cent) of respondents to a population-based retrospective survey of 18–33-year-olds in the UK reported having experienced serious physical abuse while growing up

(Brooker *et al.*, 2001). A school-based survey study in China placed prevalence levels of severe and very severe physical punishment at 15.1 per cent and 2.8 per cent, respectively (Leung *et al.*, 2008).

Adult-on-child sexual abuse (CSA) is defined by the presence of two elements: (1) contact and non-contact (e.g. exhibitionism) sexual activities, and (2) the abusive condition (Jones, 2000, Section 9.3.1). The second criterion is founded on the premise that sexual interaction between minors and adults always involves coercion, because of the power differential between the parties involved (Jones, 2000). Approximately 8 per cent of the cases involving child protection in England for 2004–08 involved CSA (DCSF, 2008). In contrast, Gorey and Leslie's (1997) integrative review combined data from 16 studies of non-clinical, North American samples and found levels of 14.5 per cent for female and 7.2 per cent for male children. Since some studies reported on girls only, an overall prevalence level across genders was not given. As a result of methodological differences, these results are considerably lower than the 27 per cent for females and 14 per cent for males cited in a contentious meta-analysis by Rind and colleagues (1998).

Abuse between child and adolescent siblings

'Sibling' refers to brothers and sisters who are genetically related (full- and half-siblings), or not genetically related (step-siblings), but who share the same home for most of the time. This last criterion is particularly important as it provides familiarity and makes opportunities for abuse available. Bullying and violence between siblings may be emotional (e.g. persistent verbal attacks), as well as physical or sexual. Wiehe (1997, p. 33) says that emotional abuse:

> ... refers to rejection; to coercive, punitive, and erratic discipline; to scapegoating, ridiculing, and denigration; to unrealistic behavioural expectations ... or the use of excessive threats in an attempt to control a [person].

Physical abuse includes hitting, punching, pulling, pushing, shoving or throwing things at the other (Goodwin and Roscoe, 1990). Sexual abuse includes acts of physical contact and those involving intended or unintended non-contact (such as indecent exposure and exposure to pornography). Sibling incest involves specific intentional sexual contact, including inappropriate fondling, oral sex, digital penetration and attempted or completed sexual intercourse. It may be true that incest can occur consensually, where partners provide nurture and safety to one another in abusive and painful family conditions (Canavan *et al.*, 1992). Such incest would be non-abusive if the partners had equal access to resources of power. Typically, however, the picture regarding the issue of consensual sexual abuse and incest is mixed. In Hardy's (2001) community sample, only 3 of the 14 undergraduates reporting this behaviour said that it was non-consensual. However for clinical samples the picture is different, since most perpetrators deny using threats to maintain secrecy while most of their targets report having been threatened or bribed to remain silent (e.g. Adler and Schutz, 1995; Laviola, 1992). As Christensen (1990) notes, it seems that most sibling incest involves coercion and repeated abuse.

The little we know about the prevalence of physical, verbal and emotional abuse in community samples comes from a US study (Hardy, 2001). Perhaps surprisingly, almost half of the 203 undergraduate participants reported that they had been physically abused during childhood by an older sibling, with 11 per cent saying that this happened on a daily basis. Compared with the number of studies of bullying amongst schoolchildren and adults in the workplace, studies of sibling bullying are few in number. In fact, only Duncan's (1999) US-based study of sibling (and peer) bullying amongst roughly equal numbers of male and female adolescents (n = 336 with at least one sibling) gives any indication as to its prevalence in the general population. Of these participants, about a third reported having been frequently bullied by siblings, with slightly more boys than girls affirming such abuse. About two-fifths of equal proportions of boys and girls also reported that they bullied their siblings.

Hardy (2001) also found that 14 women and 1 man said that they had been incestuously abused as children. Clinical and forensic samples, however, give some indication of the prevalence of different types of sexual abuse. Almost 90 per cent of abusers in two studies (Pierce and Pierce, 1987) attempted or completed some form of intercourse (vaginal, anal or oral penetration). In stark contrast, this was only true for one fifth of Gilbert's 14 cases (1992). It is probable that at least some of the disparity in these findings is explained by differences in the operational definitions of types of abuse and sampling methods used by these investigators.

Correlates and impact of domestic violence

Domestic violence between adults

Domestic violence often has extensive physical and psychological consequences for its victims, some of which are life-threatening. Physical effects include injuries ranging from cuts and bruises, skin punctures and bites, to more severe injuries leading to chronic conditions such as loss of hearing, sexually transmitted diseases (STDs), miscarriage, gynae-cological problems, chronic pelvic pain and irritable bowel syndrome (Campbell, 2002; Casique and Furegato, 2006). Effects on mental health include fear, depression, low self-esteem, anxiety disorders, headaches, obsessive-compulsive disorder, post-traumatic stress dis-order (PTSD), sexual dysfunction and eating problems (Romito *et al.*, 2005). Women experiencing physical and sexual violence report higher rates of poor health, decreased ability to walk, vaginal discharge, pain, loss of memory and dizziness (Ellsberg *et al.*, 2008; Vung *et al.*, 2009). For many women the only avenue of escape may seem to be suicide (Krug *et al.*, 2002). Male victims of female IPV report being kicked, bitten, punched or choked (Archer, 2002; Mechem *et al.*, 1999) and stabbed and burned (Vasquez and Falcone, 1997). Commonly reported effects of IPV in same-sex relationships include anxiety, depression, low self-esteem, disassociation, sleep disorders, shame, guilt, self-mu-tilation, suicidal ideation and attempts, drug and alcohol abuse, eating disorders and PTSD (Sloan and Edmond, 1996). In addition to the direct impact of IPV on adults, several studies indicate that witnessing this violence can have profound negative effects on children.

Exposure of children and adolescents to IPV

Some of the correlates of domestic violence exposure are similar to those of physical abuse (Fusco and Fantuzzo, 2009; Hiilamo, 2009). Age cor-relates with domestic violence exposure in that most of those exposed (52 per cent) in Fusco and Fantuzzo's (2009) community-based study were less than six years old (mean age of 4.8 years). Although the prevalence by family ethnicity ranged from 45 per cent among African-Americans to 4 per cent among Asians, ethnicity had no impact on the likelihood of domestic violence exposure when other factors such as poverty were con-trolled for (Fusco and Fantuzzo, 2009). The same study also found that children were more likely to be exposed to violence if the perpetrator and target were both parents of the child concerned. IPV exposure was also more common in single-parent households in which the carer had a lower educational level (Fantuzzo *et al.*, 1997). A recent French study found that chronic parental illness, housing problems and unemployment cor-related with exposure (Roustit *et al.*, 2009). In contrast to physical abuse, no correlation was found in Fantuzzo and colleagues' studies between parental substance abuse and domestic violence exposure among chil-dren, though Roustit's group did find such an association.

Studies have indicated the increased likelihood of internalising (e.g. depression, anxiety) and externalising (conduct problems such as bullying) symptoms for children who witness domestic violence and bullying. Evans *et al.* (2008) showed a small to medium mean effect size for DVE on internalising problems and noted a similar effect size for externalising. Further analysis suggested that boys who witness violence at home are significantly more likely to develop challenging behaviour than girls in similar situations, while gender differences for internalising symptoms were *not* noted. In contrast, narrative reviews have concluded that girls seem to be more at risk for internalising problems (Buka *et al.*, 2001). These difficulties include a likelihood of post-traumatic reactions such as hyper-vigilance, flashbacks and diminished concentration in school, which may, in turn, lead to depression, substance abuse, suicidal ideation, anxiety, eating disorders (Wonderlich *et al.*, 1997), weight problems and poor performance in school. Externalising outcomes may include aggression (Kolko, 1998).

The experience of witnessing abuse between adults also perpetuates the cycle of violence in other ways. For example, Roustit *et al.* (2009) found that participants who had witnessed inter-parental violence as children were significantly more likely to become involved in intimate partner violence or to perpetrate child abuse across the lifespan. In addition, studies have indicated a link between exposure to domestic violence and a propensity to become involved in aggressive interactions with peers (Anooshian, 2005).

Furthermore, DVE as a child is associated with adult difficulties in parent–child relationships, parental separation and divorce, imprisonment, depression, alcoholism (Roustit *et al.*, 2009) and other mental health problems, including suicide attempts (UNICEF, 2000). These effects appear to be exaggerated when compensatory, supportive adult–child relationships are lacking; the child's parents suffer from mental health problems; children experience the violence more directly; children are more closely related to the adults involved; or violence is more overt or longstanding (Osofsky, 2003; Roustit *et al.*, 2009). Roustit and colleagues also suggest that girls who witness IPV are more likely to go on to become depressed as adults, while boys are more likely to become physically abusive or dependent on alcohol.

Abuse of children and adolescents by adults in the home

The volume and diversity of literature on the subject means that, for the sake of integration, this section follows from left to right the developmental and ecological model of Jones (2000), which is reproduced here as Figure 5.1.

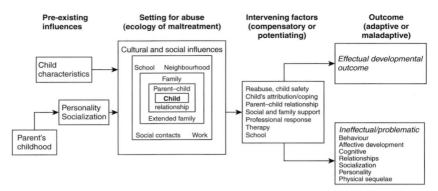

Figure 5.1 A developmental and ecological perspective on child maltreatment (Jones, 2000, p. 1825). By permission of Oxford University Press.

Parental precursors of neglect and physical abuse may include genetic susceptibility and childhood experiences, including prior abuse, leading to weak self-efficacy, depression and other mental health difficulties, high stress levels, anger-control problems, substance abuse, smoking and social isolation, including employment difficulties and also involvement in criminality (Anooshian, 2005; Donohue, 2004; Mok, 2008; Paz *et al.*, 2005; Stith *et al.*, 2009; Vostanis, 2004). Child predictive factors include the child's age (girls may be at more risk of sexual abuse between 8 and 14 years and boys between 8 and 12-years; Dhaliwal *et al.*, 1996). Children with conditions such as conduct disorder and learning difficulties/ intellectual disabilities appear to be particularly at risk for all forms of abuse, while those with cerebral palsy appear to be at risk for physical maltreatment and neglect only (Govindshenoy and Spencer, 2007).

Within Jones' (2000) 'ecology of maltreatment' itself, the filial relationships of parents who neglect their children and also abuse substances tend to be characterised by unwanted pregnancies, inapt developmental expectations, problem-solving deficits in child care, uncontrolled expressions of anger, erratic discipline, lack of maternal warmth and responsiveness and, consequently, poor parent–child attachments (Donohue, 2004; Wilson *et al.*, 1996). The ecology of physical abuse includes, like that of neglect, inconsistent discipline, prior child abuse by the mother's partner, poor relationships between the mother and her own parents, overly punitive punishment, low levels of supervision and a dearth of warmth in parental–child interactions, leading to weak attachments (Anooshian, 2005; Wilson *et al.*, 1996).

Moving to family context beyond the immediate parent–child relationship, it is critical to note that, of all the forms of maltreatment, neglect is most strongly associated with parental substance abuse (Donohue, 2004). More specifically, the drugs used most frequently by mothers identified as neglectful are, in order: cocaine (67 per cent), mixed drugs (24 per cent), alcohol and illegal drugs (14 per cent), opiates (10 per cent) and heroin (9 per cent) (Kienberger Jaudes et al., 1995). Hines et al. (2004) argue, however, that the link between substance abuse and child maltreatment is best explained by reference to common contextual factors such as deprivation, parental psychiatric difficulties, IPV and parental imprisonment. Second, it is also noteworthy that physical abuse overlaps with IPV in 45–70 per cent of families where it is found (Holt et al., 2008). Child physical abuse also co-occurs with general high levels of family conflict (Stith et al., 2009). Holt and colleagues' review found less consistent findings for the overlap of IPV and child sexual abuse, with estimates ranging from 4 to 77 per cent of families, depending on definition and study design. Children in larger families may also be more at risk of maltreatment than others, as may those of unmarried parents (Paz et al., 2005). In general, individual factors clearly interact with the context to increase the risks of abuse for children from ethnic minorities.

Furthermore, in cases where the family is homeless, a reciprocal relationship between social isolation and aggression within and outside the family is more likely to arise (Anooshian, 2005). Nevertheless, as Anooshian points out, it can be difficult to discriminate between effects of the family environment and neighbourhood effects in deprived areas (Paz et al., 2005), particularly those in which violence is frequent and normalised (Buka et al., 2001). The mother's attendance at or lack of access to antenatal classes is also associated with the abuse of young children (Wilson et al., 1996).

The recurrence of abuse, which, in general, may occur in between 3.5 to 22.2 per cent of cases within six months, clearly plays a role in moderating the impact of maltreatment (Hindley et al., 2006). DePanfilis and Zuravin's review (1998) found that a majority of studies indicated that neglect was more likely to recur than other forms of abuse, while the first month or two following an initial child protection report may be a particularly risky period for recurrence of all forms of abuse, with the hazard rate declining over time. Contrary to widespread opinion, in more than half of US families where abuse recurs, this happens only once.

A child's attributions about the abuse may also moderate its impact (Vostanis, 2004). Dhaliwal et al. (1996) and Rind et al. (1998) found that men tended to view childhood sexual abuse in a less negative light than women, and this difference appeared to reduce the impact for men. Rind *et al.* (1998) also found that, when males perceived partial consent with CSA, this factor was also positively correlated with better adjustment in young adulthood. It should be noted here that Rind and colleagues' findings have been challenged by later researchers and by policy makers. For both genders, the use of force in CSA is particularly associated with adverse outcomes (Rind *et al.*, 1998). Dhaliwal *et al.* (1996) concluded that boys are more likely to use avoidance coping strategies (including aggression), whereas girls are more likely to employ emotion-focused coping (such as focusing on the feelings experienced). Adult internal working models and social information processing are also believed to mediate the effects of maltreatment (Paz *et al.*, 2005). Lastly, parent–child relationships appear to play a critical role in mediating the impact of physical abuse on children (Anooshian, 2005).

Geeraert *et al.*'s (2004) meta-analysis of early selective interventions to protect at-risk children during the prenatal period to age three years from physical abuse and neglect found a small to moderate effect size, which was nonetheless significant and positive. Their results did not suggest that one intervention approach was more powerful than another, but the common elements in many of the programmes studied included the use of home visits, pre- or neonatal onset of the programme, services to support the parent, work on parent–child interaction and psycho-educational sessions concerning child development while, at the same time, enhancing social networks. Nevertheless, these elements may be more effective in combination than, for example, home visiting alone (Mok, 2008). For those children whose families do not respond to such intervention, foster care and adoption may seem the most plausible option, though Glaser (2000) cautions that desirable outcomes are more likely for younger children than for those who are older. In addition, preliminary data suggest that children who are placed with members of the extended family in 'kinship care' tend to achieve better outcomes than those placed with non-relatives (Winokaur *et al.*, 2009). As a result of institutional racism, disadvantaged ethnic groups such as African-Americans in the USA and aboriginal children in Canada may be more likely to enter and remain in the child-protection system (Hines *et al.*, 2004). Hines and colleagues also argue that policy changes may hinder ethnic minority parents from reuniting with their children to a disproportionate extent. For older children, universal school-based educational programmes may help to improve children's capacity to avoid sexual abuse through practising 'protective behaviours' (Zwi *et al.*, 2007). For those children who have already been abused, cognitive behavioural therapy (CBT) may help to ameliorate the consequences, although studies to date on the effectiveness of CBT have failed to achieve statistical significance (Macdonald *et al.*, 2006).

In terms of immediate impact, the injuries that children sustain during physical abuse, compared to accidents, are more likely to include damage to the thorax or abdomen, including rib fractures (71 per cent chance of abuse), or to numerous areas of the body (DiScala *et al.*, 2000). Abused children were also more likely to experience severe injuries, including brain damage, than those with accidental wounds to the head (Discala *et al.*, 2000). Changes in brain structure may also occur as a result of acute or chronic stress responses (Glaser, 2000). Physical abuse victims are therefore more likely to be admitted to an intensive care unit than accident patients, resulting in more extended hospital stays and an increased likelihood of multiple long-term impairments necessitating follow-up care, such as rehabilitative therapy. Children who have been sexually abused are clearly at risk of contracting STDs, though many common STDs may also be acquired through means other than sexual contact (Hammerschlag, 1998).

Abuse survivors in general are less likely to achieve necessary levels of academic achievement at school-leaving age than their peers, although these effects may be explained by factors within the child's developmental context rather than the abuse itself (Boden *et al.*, 2007). Children who have been neglected face significant difficulties in developing appropriately into adulthood (Hildyard and Wolfe, 2002). In comparison with those who have been physically abused, neglected children are more likely to display cognitive, language (Donohue, 2004; Paz *et al.*, 2005) and achievement difficulties, interpersonal isolation, poor acceptance by peers and internalising (rather than externalising) problems. Donohue (2004), however, argues that neglected children are particularly at risk of conduct problems. This discrepancy may be explained through different genotypes responding to the same stressor in different ways (Paz *et al.*, 2005), though such a hypothesis has been questioned (in relation to one gene at least) by recent work (Risch *et al.*, 2009). Furthermore, following changes in the brain, in the longer term, children who have been physically abused are prone to developing internalising and externalising psychological symptoms (Anooshian, 2005). In most studies, sexual abuse has been seen as a 'special destroyer of mental health' (Seligman, 1994, p. 232), with children who have been sexually abused appearing prone to emotional instability, eating disorders, depression and suicidality but not, surprisingly, addiction, at least as far as males are concerned (Dhaliwal *et al.*, 1996; Wonderlich *et al.*, 1997). Such findings were questioned by Rind *et al.* (1998), who stated that the deleterious effects of CSA had been exaggerated through over-reliance on clinical samples. The evidence linking CSA to sexual offending appears to be robust, but a connection between physical abuse as a child and adult sexual offending is not borne out by the literature (Jespersen *et al.*, 2009).

Domestic violence between child and adolescent siblings

Some studies suggest that during early and middle childhood, first-born children are more likely to be physically aggressive than their younger siblings (Felson and Rosso, 1988; Howe *et al.*, 2002), supporting the idea that bullying is associated with an imbalance of power. Howe *et al.* also found that, by comparison with boys, girls are more submissive in arriving at the resolution of physical aggression. This may suggest a power imbalance in favour of boys. In a rare longitudinal study in this field, Updegraff *et al.* (2002) studied 179 pairs of 13-year-old (second-born) and 15-year-old (first-born) adolescent siblings' 'domineering control' of peers and siblings. Findings showed that irrespective of gender, first-borns were more controlling of their siblings than they were of their best friend and that over the three years of the study there was a decline in the amount of control exhibited.

Most studies report that older brothers are perpetrators of sexual abuse and younger sisters are their targets (e. g. Adler and Schutz, 1995; Laviola, 1992). However, some studies report brother–brother incest (e.g. Becker *et al.*, 1986; Gilbert, 1992) and some sister–sister incest (e.g. Pierce and Pierce, 1987; Smith and Israel, 1987). There is also some evidence suggesting that step-siblings are particularly at risk of sibling sexual abuse and incest (Gilbert, 1992; Pierce and Pierce, 1987).

Although none of the reviewed studies provides any causal evidence for physical, verbal and emotional abuse between siblings, a number of correlates are suggested. For example, many sibling physical abusers have been physically abused or neglected by their parents or carers (Rosenthal and Doherty, 1984). Other studies suggest a link between discord in adults in families and inter-sibling aggression (e.g. Bush and Ehrenberg, 2003). In contrast, Hardy (2001) could find no link between inter-sibling physical abuse and other types of domestic violence. Rosenthal and Doherty found that levels of physical health and emotional well-being tended to be lower in sibling abusers when compared to non-abusers. Furthermore, significant differences were found between abusive and non-abusive groups on parent-report measures assessing sadness, unhappiness, helplessness and the degree of medical illness experienced by the child.

There is also a lack of causal evidence for sibling sexual abuse and incest, although the literature does suggest correlates that indicate some causal factors. For example, Pierce and Pierce (1987) found that 63 per cent of perpetrators had experienced long-term parental physical and verbal abuse. However, this was true for only around one-fifth of the perpetrators studied by Kaplan *et al.* (1988) and by Becker *et al.* (1986). Smith and Israel (1987) and Worling (1995) have found that most adolescent sibling sexual abusers have been sexually exploited by adults, most often within the context of the family. Kaplan *et al.* (1988), however, found that only 15 per cent of their sexual abusers reported having been sexually abused. Nevertheless, we conclude that the likelihood of sibling sexual abusers having been incestuously abused themselves is high.

Other correlates of sibling sexual abuse and incest have been found. These include marital discord between parents (e.g. Canavan *et al.*, 1992; Hardy, 2001); sexual dysfunction of mothers (Kaplan *et al.*, 1990); other contemporaneous incestuous relationships of fathers and grandfathers; and children witnessing their parents or other adults engaging in sexual activity (Pierce and Pierce, 1987). On the other hand, repressive parental attitudes to sex have also been found to be linked to sibling sexual abuse and incest (Smith and Israel, 1987), and other studies (e.g. Adler and Schutz, 1995; Kaplan *et al.*, 1988) have found that parents typically either deny that sibling sexual abuse has occurred or downplay its importance.

Most of the evidence concerning the short- and long-term impact of sibling maltreatment stems from studies of sexual abuse. Laviola's (1992) study of 17 women incestuously abused in childhood found that long-term effects included mistrust of men and women, sexual response problems and intrusive thoughts concerning the incest. Similarly, Canavan *et al.* (1992) reported that four women sexually abused by their older brothers in childhood all had low self-esteem.

Theoretical accounts of IPV and bullying

Over the years many theories have been proposed to account for domestic violence between adults and to distinguish abusive or violent personalities from those of non-violent and non-abusive people. Broadly, these theories can be classed as biological, psychological, psycho-social and/ or ecological.

The biological perspective on IPV studies the roles of genetic factors (Saudino and Hines, 2007), brain injury, brain infections and illnesses and structural or functional changes in the brain secondary to trauma in the development of violent and aggressive behaviour (Cunningham *et al.*, 1998) and neurotransmitters such as testosterone and serotonin (Soler *et al.*, 2000; Young and Leyton, 2002). However, very little evidence is presented to support the relationship of these factors with domestic violence and further research is needed to establish the links between biological factors.

The psychological perspective explores the role in IPV of various psychological and psychiatric problems. Some evidence suggests that perpetrators of IPV are more likely to suffer from a history of disturbed attachment needs in childhood (Stith *et al.*, 2004), aggressiveness (Baron *et al.*, 2007), substance and alcohol abuse (Stith *et al.*, 2004; Thompson and Kingree, 2006), lower self-esteem (Papadakaki *et al.*, 2009) and a lack of assertiveness, communication and problem-solving skills (Toro-Alfonso and Rodríguez-Madera, 2004; Schumacher *et al.*, 2001). A major difficulty is that accounting for violent and aggressive behaviour in terms of psychological or psychiatric issues may in some way be seen as excusing or justifying the abuser's behaviour, and may not help the victim to any real extent. It is also important to note here that none of the factors has been identified as the sole cause, as the findings of the studies are typically inconsistent.

The psycho-social perspective examines factors such as societal norms and broadly held attitudes towards violence (Erchak and Rosenfield, 1994). Various theories offered under this perspective include social learning theory (Bandura, 1977), resource theory (Blood and Wolfe, 1960), exchange theory (Homans, 1974), conflict theory (Quinney 1970) and stress theory (Jasinski, 2001). In general, these theories suggest that men's violence towards women arises from the behavioural models they were presented with when they were children, that is, fathers being violent towards mothers and mothers seemingly putting up with the abuse. This suggests that families play an important role in not only exposing children to violent behaviour, but also in inculcating in them an acceptance and approval of the use of such behaviour.

Blood and Wolfe (1960) proposed that, in marital or intimate relationships, the person who has more resources in terms of income, occupational status and education may have more power in the relationship. This so-called resource theory maintains that the root cause of IPV is not men's lack of absolute resources but lack of resources relative to their wives. There is some empirical confirmation of this theory. For example, employed women with unemployed husbands are more likely to be abused than when the converse is true (Macmillan and Gartner, 1999), and women who earn higher incomes than their husbands are at greater risk of experiencing IPV than where the converse is true (e.g. Melzer, 2002). A major problem with these psycho-social theories is the variation in the definition of terms such as what constitutes witnessing violence as a child. Moreover, resource theory contradicts those theories which suggest that the further empowerment of women through, for example, education and improving their employment opportunities, is key to tackling IPV against women.

Another perspective, based on the feminist paradigm, concerns the issues of power and control. Scholars believed that abusers use violence as a means of controlling their partner (e.g. Bograd, 1988). This idea led to the development of 'the power and control wheel' in 1980–81 as the outcome of a US Domestic Abuse Intervention Project (DAIP). This model attempts to explain the tactics used by an abuser to keep the victim in a submissive position and to maintain his or her power and control. Further, this model maintains that the responsibility for abusive control rests with the abuser and not the abused. Believers in structural patriarchal ideology tend to view IPV against women as acceptable, necessary, beneficial and justified by blaming women for what men perceive as their punishable behaviour (e.g. Haj-Yahia and Schiff, 2007; WHO, 2005). Structural patriarchy is characterised by cultural and personal values and beliefs that seek to justify male dominance. However, Dutton (1994) rejects the idea that there are causal relationships between structural patriarchy and IPV and concludes that IPV is more common in lesbian than in heterosexual relationships.

Walker (1979) developed the cycle of violence model with the aim of elucidating how and why women remain in abusive relationships. The cycle of violence is often predictable and consists of three phases: tension building; abuse or explosion; and honeymoon or forgiveness. In the first phase tension builds up between the couple and the abuser becomes frustrated, which he takes out on his female partner by acting violently. Violence may be exhibited in a variety of forms that may last from seconds to days. Following the violent attack the abuser feels relieved and calm and may express remorse to his partner. The couple then enjoys a honeymoon period in which the abused person thinks the abuser will change and will never become violent again. In some cases, the intensity of violence decreases and may stop for some time until the cycle is repeated (Walker, 2006). Constant exposure to the cycle typically results in the abused feeling helpless and fearful (Walker, 2006), blaming herself for the abuse and trying to avoid situations that may precipitate violence. This theory has also been applied to explain IPV in same-sex intimate relationships (Chesley et al., 1998; McClennen et al., 2002).

Finally, the ecological perspective is one of the most widely used frameworks. This perspective attempts to offer a comprehensive view of

IPV by looking at how personal, situational and socio-cultural factors interact (Heise, 1998). This model suggests that behaviour is shaped through interaction between individuals and their social surroundings (Dasgupta, 2001). The framework uses four domains of analysis: the individual; the interpersonal, the group or community; and the societal. The individual domain covers the biological and personal factors which influence individual behaviour such as age, gender, education, income, psychological difficulties and substance abuse. The interpersonal domain includes what happens in the family, between intimate partners and close friends and in the workplace. This domain attempts to explain the role of these relationships in contributing to the risk of perpetuating or accepting violence. The group domain investigates the role of the community in which the person lives and it considers factors such as the role of friends, school-mates and work colleagues that may increase a person's vulnerability to commiting or sustaining violent acts. Finally, the societal domain considers the broader structures and systems in which the person lives, such as parental roles and responsibilities, societal norms and the social and health structures affecting people's lives. Altogether, the model suggests that, in order to reduce IPV, factors in each domain of analysis need to be considered and dealt with simultaneously.

Implications for policy and professional practice

Domestic violence and children/adolescents

Fusco and Fantuzzo (2009) conclude that it would be judicious for policy makers to develop a surveillance system that would serve both to identify children exposed to domestic violence and also to connect protective agencies, including the police and social services. In bringing to light the high levels of child involvement in domestic violence, both as victims and by exposure, these authors envisage an extended role for police officers as 'public health sentinels' (Fusco and Fantuzzo, 2009, p. 255). Within this role, when attending to an incident of domestic violence, police would gather data on the demographic characteristics of the abused partner, the type of incident and whether any children live in the home, and enter these details into a database shared with child protection agencies. For such agencies themselves, the evidence reviewed here suggests the need to develop an ecological harm model that determines the type and extent of injury and trauma experienced and that considers the circumstances in which any incident(s) took place, as well as the events themselves (Fakunmoju, 2009). Moreover, in drawing links between the studies described here, practitioners should bear in mind that IPV is indicated as a risk factor for child abuse (Hiilamo, 2009).

For psychotherapists and counsellors who work with recovering victims of physical abuse or domestic violence exposure, the notion of the therapeutic value of recovered memory (Ladd, 1991) is questioned by some analogue studies which have shown that intentional forgetting plays a lesser role in post-traumatic responses than previously believed (Cloitre, 1998). Approaches to therapy for physically abusive parents and carers include behavioural models, which emphasise reinforcement and social learning (Kolko, 1998); systemic models, which examine and seek to alter child, parent and family variables that maintain cycles of violent interaction; and parent–child interaction therapy (Eisenstadt *et al.*, 1993), which incorporates both behavioural and systemic perspectives. For children who have been exposed to domestic violence, the models with the best indications appear to be group counselling (Kolko, 1998), which incorporates psycho-education about the nature and causes of domestic violence together with cognitive behavioural elements such as social skills development and training in relaxation and causal attribution. However, such technical approaches to therapy should also take into account that domestic violence represents a disturbance of lived experience (Langdridge, 2007), including the dimension of time. It is therefore important to elicit appreciative attitudes toward the present (Ladd, 1991), while working from current achievements and planning goals and projects that allow for transcendence of the abusive situation (van Deurzen, 2002). The impact of such interventions and of placements for fostered and adopted children who have experienced domestic violence should be assessed from the child's perspective.

Proposals for further research

There are a number of methodology and method issues that future research into domestic violence might attempt to address. Most studies so far conducted have relied on self-reports in the absence of any attempt at independent verification of the victims' claims. We recognise, however, that there may well be ethical limitations to obtaining such verification data. Further, wherever possible, data from a number of measures (e.g. self-report questionnaires and semi-structured interviews) should be triangulated to give more complete and robust profiles of targets, perpetrators and their families. We suggest that future studies should also strive to operationalise concepts of abuse and violence more stringently. Specifically, in some existing studies the measures used do not relate closely enough to at least one of the concepts of abuse as we have defined them here. We also suggest that, in order to unravel the causal mechanisms of domestic violence, there is need for greater use of longitudinal research. A lack of case-control and experimental designs to establish the efficacy and effectiveness of interventions also characterises the research reviewed here.

Much of the research on domestic violence is highly context specific and we feel that we need to know the extent to which existing findings generalise to other contexts. With the exception of studies of IPV, most of the research so far conducted has used small clinical samples from which it is difficult to generalise and so, for example, we know little about the prevalence of the many types of abuse in the general population. General population or community prevalence studies are urgently needed to inform policy makers and practitioners about the scale of problems. Further, we suspect that cross-cultural studies on the prevalence of sibling abuse would be illuminative regarding the qualitatively differential impacts on domestic violence of, for example, political and religious ideology; cultural values, beliefs, attitudes, social representations and discursive practices; education; and socioeconomic wealth.

Acknowledgements

We are grateful to Digby Tantam and Emmy van Deurzen for their expertise in and advice on the area of sibling abuse.

REFERENCES

Abbott, J., Johnson, R., Koziol-McLain, J. and Lowenstein, S.R. (1995). 'Domestic violence against women: incidence and prevalence in an emergency department population'. *Journal of the American Medical Association*, 273: 1763–67.

Adler, N.A. and Schutz, J. (1995). 'Sibling incest offenders'. *Child Abuse and Neglect*, 19: 811–19.

Anooshian, L.J. (2005). 'Violence and aggression in the lives of homeless children: a review'. *Aggression and Violent Behavior*, 10: 129–52.

Archer, J. (2002). 'Sex differences in physically aggressive acts between heterosexual partners: a meta-analytic review'. *Aggression and Violent Behavior*, 7: 213–351.

Bandura, A. (1977). *Social Learning Theory*. New York: General Learning Press.

Baron, K.G., Smith, T.W., Butner, J., Nealey-Moore, J., Hawkins, M.W. and Uchino, B.N. (2007). 'Hostility, anger, and marital adjustment: concurrent and prospective associations with psychosocial vulnerability'. *Journal of Behavioral Medicine*, 30: 1–10.

Becker, J.V., Kaplan, M.S., Cunningham-Rathner, B.A. and Kavoussi, R. (1986). 'Characteristics of adolescent incest sexual perpetrators'. *Journal of Family Violence*, 1: 85–87.

Blood, R.O. and Wolfe, D.M. (1960). *Husbands and Wives*. New York: Free Press.

Boden, J.M., Horwood, L.J. and Fergusson, D.M. (2007). 'Exposure to childhood sexual and physical abuse and subsequent educational outcomes'. *Child Abuse and Neglect*, 31: 1101–14.

Bograd, M. (1988). 'Feminist perspectives on wife abuse: an introduction'. In K. Yllö and M. Bograd (eds.), *Feminist Perspectives on Wife Abuse* (pp. 11–26). Beverly Hills, CA: Sage.

Bradley, F., Smith, M., Long, J. and O'Dowd, T. (2002). 'Reported frequency of domestic violence: cross-sectional survey of women attending general practice'. *British Medical Journal*, 324: 271.

Brooker, S., Cawson, P., Kelly, G. and Wattman, C. (2001). 'The prevalence of child abuse and neglect: a survey of young people'. *International Journal of Market Research*, 43: 249–89.

Buka, S.L., Stichick, T.L., Birdthistle, I. and Earls, F J. (2001). 'Youth exposure to violence: prevalence, risks and consequences'. *American Journal of Orthopsychiatry*, 71: 298–310.

Bush, J.E. and Ehrenberg, M.F. (2003). 'Young persons' perspectives on the influence of family transitions on sibling relationships: a qualitative exploration'. *Journal of Divorce and Remarriage*, 39: 1–35.

Campbell, J.C. (2002). 'Health consequences of intimate partner violence'. *The Lancet*, 359: 1331–36.

Canavan, M.C., Meyer, W.J. and Higgs, D.C. (1992). 'The female experience of sibling incest'. *Journal of Marital and Family Therapy*, 18: 129–42.

Casique, L.C. and Furegato, A.R.F. (2006). 'Violence against women: theoretical reflections'. *Revista Latino-Americana de Enfermagem*, 14: 950–56.

Chesley, L., MacAuley, D., Ristick, J. and Stewart, C. (1998). *Abuse in Lesbian Relationships: Information and Resources*. Ontario: Health Canada.

Christensen, C.W. (1990). 'A case of sibling incest: a balancing act'. *Journal of Strategic and Systemic Therapies*, 9: 1–5.

Cloitre, M. (1998). 'Intentional forgetting and clinical disorders'. In J.M. Golding and C.M. MacLeod (eds.), *Intentional Forgetting: Interdisciplinary Approaches*. Mahwah, NJ: Lawrence Erlbaum.

Coker, A.L., Davis, K.E., Arias, I., Desai, S., Sanderson, M., Brandt, H.M. and Smith, P.H. (2002). 'Physical and mental health effects of intimate partner violence for men and women'. *American Journal of Preventive Medicine*, 2: 260–68.

Cunningham, A., Jaffe, P.G., Baker, L., Dick, T., Malla, S., Mazaheri, N. and Poisson, S. (1998). *Theory-derived Explanations of Male Violence against Female Partners: Literature Update and Related Implications for Treatment and Evaluation*. London: Family Court Clinic, www.lfcc.on.ca/maleviolence.pdf (accessed 8 April 2009).

Dasgupta, S. (2001). *Towards an Understanding of Women's Use of Non-lethal Violence in Intimate Heterosexual Relationships*. Harrisburg, PA: VAWnet,

a project of the National Resource Center on Domestic Violence/
Pennsylvania Coalition against Domestic Violence, http://new.vawnet.org/
Assoc_Files_VAWnet/AR_womviol.pdf (8 April 2009).

DePanfilis, D. and Zuravin, S. J. (1998). 'Rates, patterns and frequency of
child maltreatment recurrences among families known to CPS'. *Child
Maltreatment*, 3: 27–42.

Department for Children, Schools and Families (2008). *Referrals, Assessments
and Children and Young People Who Are the Subject of a Child Protection Plan,
England, Year Ending March 2008*. London: The Stationery Office.

Department of Health (2000). *Health and Personal Social Services Statistics for
England* (1999 edn). London: HMSO.

Deurzen, E. van (2002). *Existential Counselling and Psychotherapy in Practice*,
2nd edn. London: Sage.

Dhaliwal, G.K., Gauzas, L., Antonowicz, D.H. and Ross, R.R. (1996). 'Adult
male survivors of childhood sexual abuse: prevalence, sexual abuse characteristics and long-term effects'. *Clinical Psychology Review*, 16: 619–39.

DiScala, C., Sege, R., Li, G.H. and Reece, R.M. (2000). 'Child abuse and
unintentional injuries: a 10-year retrospective'. *Archives of Pediatrics and
Adolescent Medicine*, 154: 16–22.

Donohue, B. (2004). 'Coexisting child neglect and drug abuse in young mothers: specific recommendations for treatment based on a review of the outcome literature'. *Behavior Modification*, 28: 206–33.

Dutton, D.G. (1994). 'Patriarchy and wife assault: the ecological fallacy'.
Violence and Victims, 9: 167–82.

Duncan, R. (1999). 'Peer and sibling aggression: an investigation of intra- and
extra-familial bullying'. *Journal of Interpersonal Violence*, 14: 871–86.

Ehrensaft, M.K., Cohen, P. and Johnson, J.G. (2006). 'Development of personality disorder symptoms and the risk for partner violence'. *Journal of
Abnormal Psychology*, 115: 474–83.

Eisenstadt, T.H., Eyberg, S., McNeil, C.B., Newcomb, K. and Funderbuck,
B. (1993). 'Parent–child interaction therapy with behavior problem chil-
dren: relative effectiveness of two stages and overall treatment outcome'.
Journal of Clinical Child Psychology, 22: 42–51.

Ellsberg, M., Jansen, H.A.F.M., Heise, L. et al. (2008). 'Intimate partner violence and women's physical and mental health in the WHO multi-country
study on women's health and domestic violence: an observational study'.
The Lancet, 371: 1165–72.

Erchak, G. and Rosenfield, R. (1994). 'Societal isolation, violent norms, and
gender relations: a re-examination of Levinson's model of wife beating'.
Cross-cultural Research, 28: 111–13.

Evans, S.E., Davies, C. and DiLillo, D. (2008). 'Exposure to domestic violence: a meta-analysis of child and adolescent outcomes'. *Aggression and
Violent Behavior*, 13: 131–40.

Ernst, A.A., Nick, T.G., Weiss, S.J., Houry, D. and Mills, T. (1997). 'Domestic
violence in an inner-city ED'. *Annals of Emergency Medicine*, 30: 190–97.

Fakunmoju, S.B. (2009). 'Contested cases of physical abuse: evidentiary characteristics of modified and overturned outcomes'. *Children and Youth
Services Review*, 31: 199–205.

Fantuzzo, J., Boruch, R., Beriama, A., Atkins, M. and Marcus, S. (1997). 'Domestic violence and children: prevalence and risk in five major U.S. cities'. *Journal of the American Academy of Child and Adolescent Psychiatry*, 36: 116–22.

Farrington, D. (1993). 'Understanding and preventing bullying'. In M. Tonry (ed.), *Crime and Justice: A Review of Research* (pp. 381–458). Chicago: University of Chicago Press.

Felson, R.B. and Rosso, N. (1988). 'Parental punishment and sibling aggression'. *Social Psychology Quarterly*, 51: 1–18.

Fusco, R.A. and Fantuzzo, J.W. (2009). 'Domestic violence crimes and children: a population-based investigation of direct sensory exposure and the nature of involvement'. *Children and Youth Services Review*, 31: 249–56.

Garcia-Moreno, C., Jansen, H., Ellsberg, M., Heise, L. and Watts, C. (2006). 'Prevalence of intimate partner violence: findings from the WHO multi-country study on women's health and domestic violence'. *The Lancet*, 368: 1260–69.

Geeraert, L., Van den Noortgate, W., Grietens, H. and Onghena, P. (2004). 'The effects of early prevention programs for families with young children at risk for physical child abuse and neglect: a meta-analysis'. *Child Maltreatment*, 9: 277–91.

Gilbert, C.M. (1992). 'Sibling incest: a descriptive study of family dynamics'. *Journal of Child and Adolescent Psychiatric and Mental Health Nursing*, 5: 5–9.

Glaser, D. (2000). 'Child abuse and neglect and the brain – a review'. *Journal of Child Psychology and Psychiatry and Allied Disciplines*, 41: 97–116.

Goodwin, M.P. and Roscoe, B. (1990). 'Sibling violence and agonistic interactions among middle adolescents'. *Adolescence*, 25: 451–67.

Gorey, K.M. and Leslie, D.P. (1997). 'The prevalence of child sexual abuse: integrative review adjustment for potential response and measurement biases'. *Child Abuse and Neglect*, 21: 391–98.

Govindshenoy, M. and Spencer, N. (2007). 'Abuse of the disabled child: a systematic review of population-based studies'. *Child Care, Health and Development*, 33: 552–58.

Gunther, J. and Jennings, M.A. (1999). 'Sociocultural and institutional violence and their impact on same-gender partner abuse'. In J.C. McClennen and J. Gunther (eds.), *A Professional Guide to Understanding Gay and Lesbian Violence in Relationships: Understanding Practice Interventions* (pp. 29–34). Lewiston, NY: Edwin Mellen Press.

Haj-Yahia, M.M. and Schiff, M. (2007). 'Definitions and beliefs about wife abuse among undergraduate students of social work'. *International Journal of Offender Therapy and Comparative Criminology*, 51: 170–90.

Hammerschlag, M.R. (1998). 'Sexually transmitted diseases in sexually abused children: medical and legal implications'. *Sexually Transmitted Infections*, 74: 167–74.

Hardy, M.S. (2001). 'Physical aggression and sexual behavior among siblings: a retrospective study'. *Journal of Family Violence*, 16: 255–68.

Heise L.L. (1998). 'Violence against women: an integrated, ecological framework'. *Violence Against Women*, 4: 262–90.

Heise, L.L., Ellsberg, M. and Gottemoeller, M. (1999). 'Ending violence against women'. *Population Reports*, Series L, No. 11. Baltimore: Johns Hopkins University School of Public Health, Population Information Program.

Hiilamo, H. (2009). 'What could explain the dramatic rise in out-of-home placement in Finland in the 1990s and early 2000s?' *Children and Youth Services Review*, 31: 177–84.

Hildyard, K.L. and Wolfe, D.A. (2002). 'Child neglect: developmental issues and outcomes'. *Child Abuse and Neglect*, 26: 679–95.

Hindley, N., Ramchandani, P.G. and Jones, D.P.H. (2006). 'Risk factors for recurrence of maltreatment: a systematic review'. *Archives of Disease in Childhood*, 91: 744–52.

Hines, A.M., Lemon, K., Wyatt, P. and Merdinger, J. (2004). 'Factors related to the disproportionate involvement of children of color in the child welfare system: a review and emerging themes'. *Children and Youth Services Review*, 26: 507–27.

Holt, S., Buckley, H. and Whelan, S. (2008). 'The impact of exposure to domestic violence on children and young people: a review of the literature'. *Child Abuse and Neglect*, 32: 797–810.

Homans, G.C. (1974). *Social Behavior: Its Elementary Forms*, rev. edn New York: Harcourt, Brace, Jovanovich.

Howe, N., Rinaldi, C.M., Jennings, M. and Petrakos, H. (2002). '"No! The lambs can stay out because they got cozies": constructive and destructive sibling conflict, pretend play, and social understanding'. *Child Development*, 73: 1460–73.

Jasinski, J.L. (2001). 'Theoretical explanations for violence against women'. In C.M. Renzetti, J.L. Edleson and R.K. Bergen (eds.), *The Sourcebook on Violence against Women* (pp. 5–22). Thousand Oaks, CA: Sage.

Jespersen, A.F., Lalumiere, M.L. and Seto, M.C. (2009). 'Sexual abuse history among adult sex offenders and non-sex offenders: a meta-analysis'. *Child Abuse and Neglect*, 33: 179–92.

Jones, D.P.H. (2000). 'Situations affecting child mental health'. In M.G. Gelder, J.J. Lopez-Ibor and N. Andreasen (eds.), *New Oxford Textbook of Psychiatry*. Oxford: Oxford University Press.

Kaplan, M.S., Becker, J.V. and Cunningham-Rathner, J. (1988). 'Characteristics of parents of adolescent incest perpetrators: preliminary findings'. *Journal of Family Violence*, 3: 183–91.

Kaplan, M.S., Becker, J.V. and Martinez, D.F. (1990). 'A comparison of mothers of adolescent incest vs. non-incest perpetrators'. *Journal of Family Violence*, 5: 209–14.

Kienberger Jaudes, P., Ekwo, E. and Voorhis, J.V. van (1995). 'Association of drug abuse and child abuse'. *Child Abuse and Neglect*, 19: 1065–75.

Kolko, D. (1998). 'Treatment and intervention for child victims of violence'. In P.K. Trickett and C.J. Schellenbach (eds.), *Violence against Children in the Family and the Community* (pp. 213–49). Washington, DC: American Psychological Association.

Krug, E.G., Dahlberg, L.L., Mercy, J.A., Zwi, A.B. and Lozano, R. (2002). *World Report on Violence and Health*. Geneva: WHO.

Ladd, J. (1991). 'Logotherapy's place for the ritually abused'. *International Forum for Logotherapy*, 14: 82–86.

Langdridge, D. (2007). *Phenomenological Psychology: Theory, Research and Method*. London: Pearson Education.

Laviola, M. (1992). 'Effects of older brother–younger sister incest: a study of the dynamics of 17 cases'. *Child Abuse and Neglect*, 16: 406–21.

Leung, P.W.S., Wong, W.C.W., Chen, W.Q. and Tang, C.S.K. (2008). 'Prevalence and determinants of child maltreatment among high school students in Southern China: a large scale school-based survey'. *Child and Adolescent Psychiatry and Mental Health*, 2, September, ArtID 27.

Lillenfeld, S.O. (2002). 'When worlds collide: social science, politics and the Rind *et al.* (1998) child sexual abuse meta-analysis'. *American Psychologist*, 57: 176–88.

Macdonald, G., Higgins, J.P.T. and Ramchandani, P. (2006). 'Cognitive-behavioural interventions for children who have been sexually abused'. *Cochrane Database of Systematic Reviews*, 4. DOI: 10.1002/14651858. CD001930.pub2.

Macmillan, R. and Gartner, R. (1999). 'When she brings home the bacon: labor-force participation and the risk of spousal violence against women'. *Journal of Marriage and the Family*, 61: 947–58.

McClennen, J.C., Summers, A.B. and Vaughan, C. (2002). 'Gay men's violence in relationships: dynamics, help-seeking behaviours, and correlates'. *Journal of Gay and Lesbian Social Services: Issues in Practice, Policy and Research*, 14: 23–49.

Mechem, C.C., Shofer, F.S., Reinhard, S.S., Hornig, S. and Datner, E. (1999). 'History of domestic violence among male patients presenting to an urban emergency department'. *Academic Emergency Medicine*, 6: 786–91.

Melzer, S.A. (2002). 'Gender, work and intimate violence: men's occupational violence spillover and compensatory violence'. *Journal of Marriage and Family*, 64: 820–32.

Mok, J.Y.Q. (2008). 'Non-accidental injury in children: an update'. *Injury: International Journal of the Care of the Injured*, 39: 978–85.

Osofsky, J.D. (2003). 'Prevalence of children's exposure to domestic violence and child maltreatment: implications for prevention and intervention'. *Clinical Child and Family Psychology Review*, 6: 161–70.

Paz, I., Jones, D. and Byrne, G. (2005). 'Child maltreatment, child protection and mental health'. *Current Opinion in Psychiatry*, 18: 411–21.

Papadakaki, M., Tzamalouka, G.S., Chatzifotiou, S. and Chliaoutakis, J. (2009). 'Seeking for risk factors of intimate partner violence (IPV) in a Greek national sample: the role of self-esteem'. *Journal of Interpersonal Violence*, 24: 732–50.

Phelan, M.B., Hamberger, L.K., Guse, C.E., Edwards, S., Walczak, S. and Zosel, A. (2005). 'Domestic violence among male and female patients seeking emergency medical services'. *Violence and Victims*, 20: 187–206.

Pierce, L.H. and Pierce, R.L. (1987). 'Incestuous victimization by juvenile sex offenders'. *Journal of Family Violence*, 2: 351–64.

Plichta, S.B. and Falik, M. (2001). 'Prevalence of violence and its implications for women's health'. *Women's Health Issues*, 11: 244–58.

Prosser, L.A. and Corso, P.S. (2007). 'Measuring health-related quality of life for child maltreatment: a systematic literature review'. *Health and Quality of Life Outcomes*, 5 (42). DOI:10.1186/1477–7525–5–42.

Quinney, R. (1970). *The Social Reality of Crime*. Boston: Little, Brown.

Rind, B., Tromovitch, P. and Bauserman, R. (1998). 'A meta-analytic examination of assumed properties of child sexual abuse college samples'. *Psychological Bulletin*, 124: 22–53.

Risch, N., Herrell, R., Lehner, T., Liang, K.Y., Eaves, L., Hoh, J. et al. (2009). 'Interaction between the serotonin transporter gene (5-HTTLPR), stressful life events, and risk of depression: a meta-analysis'. *Journal of the American Medical Association*, 301: 2462–71.

Romito, P., Molzan, T.J. and De Marchi, M. (2005). 'The impact of current and past interpersonal violence on women's mental health'. *Social Sciences and Medicine*, 60: 1717–27.

Rosenthal, P.A. and Doherty, M.B. (1984). 'Serious sibling abuse by preschool children'. *Journal of the American Academy of Child Psychiatry*, 23: 186–90.

Roustit, C., Renahy, E., Guernec, G., Lesieur, S., Parizot, I. and Chauvin, P. (2009). 'Exposure to interparental violence and psychosocial maladjustment in the adult life course: advocacy for early prevention'. *Journal of Epidemiology and Community Health*, 63: 1–6.

Saudino, K.J. and Hines, D.A. (2007). 'Etiological similarities between psychological and physical aggression in intimate relationships: a behavioral genetic exploration'. *Journal of Family Violence*, 22: 121–29.

Schumacher, J.A., Feldbau-Kohn, S.R., Slep, A.M. and Heyman, R.E. (2001). 'Risk factors for male-to-female partner physical abuse'. *Aggression and Violent Behavior*, 6: 281–352.

Sedlak, A.J. and Broadhurst, D.D. (1996). *The Third National Incidence Study of Child Abuse and Neglect (NIS-3)*. Washington, DC: United States' Department of Health and Human Services.

Seligman, M.E.P. (1994). *What You Can Change and What You Can't*. New York: Knopf.

Sloan, L. and Edmond, T. (1996). 'Shifting the focus: recognising the needs of lesbian and gay survivors of sexual violence'. *Journal of Lesbian and Gay Social Services*, 5: 33–52.

Smith, H. and Israel, E. (1987). 'Sibling incest: a study of the dynamics of 25 cases'. *Child Abuse and Neglect*, 11: 101–08.

Smith, P.K. and Sharp, S. (eds.) (1994). *School Bullying: Insights and Perspectives*. London: Routledge.

Soler, H., Vinayak, P. and Quadagno, D. (2000). 'Biosocial aspects of domestic violence'. *Psychoneuroendocrinology*, 25: 721–39.

Sternberg, R.J. (2002). 'Everything you need to know to understand the controversies you learned from psychological research: a comment on the Rind and Lillenfeld controversies'. *American Psychologist*, 57: 193–97.

Stith, S.M., Liu, T., Davies, L.C., Boykin, E.L., Alder, M.C., Harris, J.M. et al. (2009). 'Risk factors in child maltreatment: a meta-analytic review of the literature'. *Aggression and Violent Behavior*, 14: 13–29.

Stith, S.M., Smith, D.B., Penn, C.E., Ward, D.B. and Tritt, D. (2004). 'Intimate partner physical abuse perpetration and victimization risk factors: a meta-analytic review'. *Aggression and Violent Behavior*, 10: 65–98.

Thompson, M.P. and Kingree, J.B. (2006). 'The roles of victim and perpetrator alcohol use in intimate partner violence outcomes'. *Journal of Interpersonal Violence*, 21: 163–77.

Toro-Alfonso, J. and Rodríguez-Madera, S. (2004). 'Domestic violence in Puerto gay male couples: perceived prevalence, intergenerational violence, addictive behaviors, and conflict resolution skills'. *Journal of Interpersonal Violence*, 19: 639–54.

UNICEF (2000). Domestic Violence *against Women and Girls*. Innocenti Digest No. 6. Sienna, UNICEF Innocenti Research Centre.

Updegraff, K.A., McHale, S. and Crouter, A.C. (2002). 'Adolescents' sibling relationship and friendship experiences: developmental patterns and relationship linkages'. *Social Development*, 11: 182–204.

Vasquez, D. and Falcone, R. (1997). 'Cross-gender violence'. *Annals of Emergency Medicine*, 29: 427–29.

Vostanis, P. (2004). 'The impact, psychological sequelae and management of trauma affecting children'. *Current Opinion in Psychiatry*, 17: 269–73.

Vung, N.D., Ostergren, P.O. and Krantz, G. (2009). 'Intimate partner violence against women, health effects and health care seeking in rural Vietnam'. *European Journal of Public Health*, 19: 178–82.

Walker, L. (1979). *The Battered Woman*. New York: Harper and Row.

Walker, L.A. (2006). 'Battered woman syndrome: empirical findings'. *Annals of New York Academy of Science*, 1087: 142–57.

Wells, S.J. (2008). 'Child abuse and neglect'. In T. Mizrahi and L. E. Davis (eds.), *The Encyclopedia of Social Work*, www.oxfordreference.com.libproxy.uregina.ca:2048/views/ENTRY.html?subview=Mainandentry=t203.e47 (accessed 30 March 2009).

Wiehe, V.R. (1997). *Sibling Abuse: Hidden Physical, Emotional and Sexual Trauma*, 2nd edn. Thousand Oaks, CA: Sage.

Wilson, L.M., Reid, A.J., Midmer, D.K., Biringer, A., Carroll, J.C. and Stewart, D.E. (1996). 'Antenatal psychosocial risk factors associated with adverse postpartum family outcomes'. *Canadian Medical Association Journal*, 154: 785–99.

Winokur, M., Holtan, A., and Valentine, D. (2009). 'Kinship care for the safety, permanency, and well-being of children removed from the home for maltreatment'. *Cochrane Database of Systematic Reviews*, 1, Art. No.: CD006546.

Wonderlich, S.A., Brewerton, T.D., Jocic, Z., Dansky, B.S. and Abbott, D.W. (1997). 'Relationship of childhood sexual abuse and eating disorders'. *Journal of the American Academy of Child and Adolescent Psychiatry*, 36: 1107–15.

World Health Organization (WHO) (1997). *Violence against Women: A Health Priority Issue*. Geneva: WHO.

WHO (2002). *World Report on Violence and Health: Summary*. Geneva: WHO.

(2005). *Multi-country Study on Women's Health and Domestic Violence against Women: Initial Results on Prevalence, Health Outcomes and Women's Responses*. Geneva: WHO.

Worling, J. (1995). 'Adolescent sibling-incest offenders: differences in family and individual functioning when compared to adolescent nonsibling sex offenders'. *Child Abuse and Neglect*, 19: 633–43.

Young, S.N. and Leyton, M. (2002). 'The role of serotonin in human mood and social interaction: insight from altered tryptophan levels'. *Pharmacology, Biochemistry, and Behavior*, 71: 857–65.

Zwi, K.J., Woolfenden, S.R., Wheeler, D.M., O'Brien, T.A., Tait, P. and Williams, K.W. (2007). 'School-based education programmes for the prevention of child sexual abuse'. *Cochrane Database of Systematic Reviews*, 3. DOI: 10.1002/14651858.CD004380.pub2.

6   Juvenile dating and violence

Rosario Ortega and Virginia Sánchez

Within the complex social world that young people inhabit, in addition to traditional forms of bullying, we find other negative forms of relations which share some characteristics with bullying in terms of dominance and submission. This is true for 'dating violence', which we discuss in this chapter. We explore individual factors in relation to involvement in dating violence (both aggressors and victims) and the way that the peer network can 'cover up' the problem. We address the roles of affective-emotional links and the appearance of interpersonal violence within the network, as well as the inclusion of negative models of couples. We propose that the appearance of dominance–submission–control–violence within the first romantic relationships during adolescence may originate in the behaviours and attitudes of the peer-group. Early data on this topic (Ortega *et al.*, 2008b) suggest that forms of indirect relational violence may appear within dating relationships and are aimed at controlling the behaviour, attitudes and feelings of the partner, and are difficult to detect and difficult to stop. Sexual violence, on the other hand, is worryingly more present during these first dating relationships than we thought.

The importance of the first romantic relationships in adolescence

The biological changes that accompany adolescence play an important role in the changes which occur in the interpersonal relationships of adolescents. With sexual maturity, changes in the levels of hormones and the development of secondary sexual characteristics, adolescents begin to feel sexual attraction for others.

The majority of adolescent couples develop within the larger peer network. Adolescent groups gradually move from being sex-segregated to becoming mixed sex (Maccoby, 1998) and social groups become less centred on play and start to become places where adolescents can express or experiment with these new dimensions of their lives and identity

113

in leisure activities. In this sense, adolescents need to develop ways of managing and expressing their erotic-sexual emotions in accordance with the norms and social conventions of their culture. Dating involves a continuous process of adjustments of desires, attitudes and sexual and emotional behaviours.

Research describes the importance that these early romantic relationships have for adolescents. Approximately 25 per cent of adolescents between 11 and 13 years state that they have had a girlfriend/boyfriend, whilst in later adolescence we find that only one in four have had no experience of dating (Collins, 2003; Furman, 1999; Menesini and Nocentini, 2008; Muñoz-Rivas *et al.*, 2007a). In our recent research (Sánchez *et al.*, 2008) we have found lower levels: only 8 per cent of adolescents between 17 and 20 years had no experience of dating. To have a girlfriend/boyfriend during adolescence appears to impact positively on identity and satisfies the desire and need for intimacy and an emotional and sexual bond with another person (Furman and Shaffer, 2003).

Considering the importance and value of these first romantic relationships, research in this area has not always explored them from a psycho-social or developmental perspective. Many studies on dating have focused on the psycho-social risks for adolescents, particularly on the risk of sexual relationships resulting in teenage pregnancies and early parenthood. It is not surprising therefore that, from this standpoint, it is concluded that the motivations that guide adolescents in search of a partner are sexual, particularly for boys (Hofstede, 1998). However, research conducted in the USA has found that the most important reasons that guide boys to become involved in romantic relationships are emotional and relational (Smiler, 2008), rather than sexual. Furthermore, many studies have confirmed that erotic-sexual relationships tend to strengthen in the long term into the construction of romantic relationships (Carver *et al.*, 2003; Rice, 1990).

In conclusion, research indicates that the romantic relationships formed by adolescents are both an important developmental landmark and an important social context for adolescents. This does not indicate that both dimensions – the individual socio-emotional factors and the dyadic context – are free of difficulties. Adolescents report that one of the main disadvantages of having a boyfriend/girlfriend is the large number of conflicts and discussions that result from the relationship (Overbeek *et al.*, 2007). In addition, research over the past 20 years has found that the adolescent dating relationship can present a particularly violent social context; more so than among adult couples (Jackson *et al.*, 2000). In the following sections we focus on examining this worrying aspect of adolescent relationships further.

Violence in adolescent couples: studies on dating violence

The first consideration to keep in mind when examining violence among adolescent couples is that, historically, research in this area has been strongly influenced by research on domestic violence at both the theoretical and empirical levels (González and Santana, 2001; Magdol *et al.*, 1997; Makepeace, 1981). In particular, this legacy is seen in the instruments used by researchers which come from traditional explorations of gender violence.

The high prevalence rates of aggression and other violent behaviours that are found among adult couples are also found among adolescent couples. However, it may be that researchers have included behaviours in the same category of offensiveness or criminality among adolescents, which may not be similar, because the adolescent couples' relationships are more short-lived. It is also important to consider the ways in which these behaviours are interpreted and accepted (or not) by those involved. Behaviours which are considered as offensive or harassing by someone who is not attracted to the other may be interpreted by someone who is interested as the initiation of dating or vice versa. The analysis of violence within the adolescent couple may be more complex, as it is important to note the developmental dimension and immaturity of young people in relation to dating. This means that many of the patterns of interaction among young couples are still not clearly defined.

In this chapter we examine violence, more or less persistent, which takes place among adolescent couples (dating violence). Forms of dating violence vary from verbal violence (insults) to psychological violence (threats of different types, including emotional blackmail), to physical violence (pushes, slaps, punches, beatings) and sexual violence (from pressure to have sexual contact to rape). Less severe forms of violence are surprisingly frequent, whilst the most serious forms are less frequent, although both form part of the lives of some adolescent couples.

To date, most research has been conducted in the USA and Canada, and only more recently in European countries. Since 1957, when Kanin conducted the first study with university students (noting that 62 per cent of first-year students said that they had suffered aggression at the hands of their partner in the last year), there have been only a moderate number of studies on this topic. However, there has been an increase in this in recent years.

The prevalence rates in studies conducted in Europe and North America have not been less alarming and controversial, with indices which have varied between 20 and 60 per cent (Archer, 2000; Chase *et al.*, 1998; Fernández-Fuertes and Fuertes Martín, 2005; Hird, 2000; Lewis and Fremouw, 2000; Menesini and Nocentini, 2008; Moffit *et al.*, 2002; Muñoz-Rivas *et al.*, 2007a; Sánchez *et al.*, 2008). More recently, Muñoz-Rivas *et al.* (2007a) found that around 90 per cent of students aged 16–20 years had, at some point, verbally abused their partner, whilst 40 per cent had been physically violent towards them. The most severe forms of physical violence (trying to choke, beat up, threaten with a knife or other weapon) were perpetrated by 4.6 per cent of males and 2 per cent of females.

Many researchers have analysed the different prevalence rates found by studies in methodological terms. Researchers have suggested that the different definitions of dating violence used, the type of instrument employed and the age and sex of the participants may have an effect on the results obtained. Additionally, the criteria used to estimate the global level of violence (only one or several indices of violence; only considering frequent and persistent violence or all of those who reported the behaviour regardless of persistence), the temporal criteria used as a reference (during the last year or the last few months) and the consideration of the experience of dating violence ever or the presence of dating violence in the current dating relationship (Archer, 2000; Lewis and Fremouw, 2000; Menesini and Nocentini, 2008; O'Keefe, 2005; Shorey *et al.*, 2008) may influence the prevalence rates recorded.

Without doubt, sex differences have been the most studied and the most controversial aspect of research on dating violence. Some studies have found no difference between males and females in relation to aggression (Brendgen *et al.*, 2002; Moffit *et al.*, 2002); others have found higher prevalence rates among females (Archer, 2000; Sánchez *et al.*, 2008); whilst in Italy, the rates of aggression have been higher among males (Menesini and Nocentini, 2008). These contradictory results are maintained when the different types of violence are examined separately. Research in Spain has concluded that males use more serious physical aggression than females, whilst females use more verbal, relational or psychological forms (Muñoz-Rivas *et al.*, 2007a; Sánchez *et al.*, 2008). In terms of less serious physical forms, the results are less conclusive, with some studies reporting that females are more likely than males to use these forms of violence, whereas others report similar levels across genders. Archer's (2000) meta-analysis clarified this data by illustrating that girls/young women were more likely than boys/young men to physically assault their partners between the ages of 14 and 22 years, whilst between the ages of 23 and 29 years, men were more likely than women to use physical aggression against their partner.

The results are more conclusive in relation to sexual violence. Several studies have shown that adolescent males are more likely to sexually assault their partners (Fernández-Fuertes and Fuertes-Martín, 2005; Menesini and Nocentini, 2008) or their peers (Ortega *et al.*, 2008b). In addition, females report that they suffer more sexual aggression and harassment than males (Bennett and Fineran, 1998; Foshee, 1996; O'Keefe, 2005).

Age is another variable which has been of interest in research on dating violence. However, as has been noted earlier, very few studies have analysed violence from a developmental perspective across adolescence and during the first years of adult life. An important consideration is that most studies which have looked at the effect of age on violence in couples have used samples of young adults, approximately 20 years old or more, and have concentrated on the analysis of violence against the female partner (Capaldi and Kim, 2002; O'Leary, 1999). In this respect, Archer (2000) found that the development of aggression was different among younger and older samples in relation to sex: before the age of 22, females presented higher levels of aggression, whereas after this age, males were more aggressive. Capaldi and Kim (2002) clarified the conclusions of Archer by considering the stability of the couple's relationship as a mediating variable in the development of violence by young men towards their female partners. They found that there was a drop in violence of males towards their female partners between the ages of 20 and 27 years. When examining those couples whose relationship was relatively stable, the pattern was slightly different. There was still a decline between 20 and 25 years, but violence then increased after the age of 25. However, when there was lower stability in the couple's relationship, there was an increase in male violence between the ages of 20 and 25 years which then began to decrease after this age. The authors explain this peak in violence at 25 years in part by the higher level of involvement in romantic relationships at this age in comparison to earlier ages (Capaldi *et al.*, 2005).

Most research in this area has been cross-sectional, and only recently have longitudinal studies been carried out. This means that currently little is known about the development of dating violence during early and mid-adolescence. Nocentini (2008) conducted one of the first longitudinal studies of the development of physical violence in adolescent couples between the ages of 16 and 18 years. Nocentini concluded that, controlling for couple stability, there was a decrease in violence between 16 and 18 years, and that girls began to decrease their levels of physical aggression towards partners earlier than boys.

One area of recent interest among researchers is the prevalence of dating violence among gay, lesbian and bisexual adolescents (GLBA). Results are mixed, with some studies showing that dating victimisation among GLBA couples is as frequent as among heterosexual couples (e.g. Freedner *et al.*, 2002); some showing lower (e.g. Halpern *et al.*, 2004) and others higher (e.g. Trish *et al.*, 2003) rates. Regarding specific sexual minorities, studies seem to conclude that bisexual adolescents and young adults are more likely to suffer any type of dating violence in comparison to lesbian and gay adolescents (Freedner *et al.*, 2002; Moore and Waterman, 1999), and that girls in same-sex relationships suffer more psychological violence and physical violence than boys.

One of the main conclusions of these studies is the methodological considerations to bear in mind in order to understand this disparity in the results. For example, one important issue is the sample size and the difficulty in recruiting representative samples of GLBA (Freedner *et al.*, 2002). Another methodological issue is the consideration of sexual behaviour or sexual identity in the definition of GLBA (Savin-Williams, 1995). For example, Trish *et al.* (2003) found that 40 per cent of adolescents in their study were still questioning their sexual orientation, whilst just 9 per cent self-identified as gay or lesbian. In this respect, Freedner *et al.* (2002) underline the important effect of the sex of the partner when examining dating violence among GLBA, because many of them may be in relationships with someone of the opposite sex (i.e. have not 'come out'). In conclusion, GLBA dating violence rates are very worrying, or at least as worrying as those among heterosexual adolescent couples.

Dating violence and the quality of romantic relationships

One of the most conclusive findings on this topic has been that there is a higher level of violence in more stable relationships, although that is not to say that they are couples who are more satisfied with their relationship (Furman and Buhrmester, 1992; Menesini and Nocentini, 2008; Shulman and Scharf, 2000). It is necessary to highlight the importance of relationship satisfaction and the functioning of the couple in trying to understand dating violence. Studies demonstrate that couples characterised by higher levels of violence also present higher levels of conflict, a greater imbalance of power within the couple, more discussions and less satisfaction in general with the relationship (Bookwala *et al.*, 1994; Sánchez *et al.*, 2008).

We have recently examined this relationship between quality and violence. Ortega *et al.* (2008b) conducted a study with 524 adolescents between the ages of 15 and 20 years, and found that adolescents with a current or previous partner (within the last six months) whose relationship involved aggressive behaviours with their partner felt that there was a lot of conflict and inequality of power within their relationship. However, paradoxically, they also stated that they felt very satisfied and had positive expectations for the future of their relationship, even more so than those who were not involved in dating violence. The fact that these adolescents had relationships with partners which were stable over time (one year or more) appears to suggest that, for some adolescents, the benefits of the emotional-relational dynamic of the relationship appear to be contaminated by violence and conflict, although this does not make them think about breaking up or changing the nature of the relationship. We have called this perception of intimate relationships 'dirty dating' (Ortega *et al.*, 2008b). Although we are still examining this phenomenon, we hypothesise that a passive acceptance that being part of a couple includes a certain inequality of power, toleration of aggressive conflicts and direct violence may be at the heart of young people's understanding of these relationships.

One of the most relevant findings from research is the large number of adolescents who assault their partners and are assaulted by them at the same time. Gray and Foshee (1997) found that 66 per cent of students in their study were involved in mutual violence, results that have been confirmed by later studies in other countries (Capaldi *et al.*, 2004; Hird, 2000; Menesini and Nocentini, 2008; Whitaker *et al.*, 2007). These studies confirm that, in more adolescent couples than previously expected, there exists a violent and reciprocal dynamic which includes large inequalities of power and dominance of one over the other.

Theories and hypotheses for dating violence in adolescence

As Shorey *et al.* (2008) have underlined, little attention has been paid to the development of theories that could help to understand these behaviours among adolescents. To date, there is no clear theoretical model which can successfully explain the large variety of types of aggression which are found within this context and this age group.

Traditionally, four theoretical models have been proposed regarding dating violence (Shorey *et al.*, 2008; Werkele and Wolfe, 1999): social learning theory, attachment theory, feminist theory and coercion/conflict theory. Recently new research has used integrative approaches to the four models, presenting very interesting results which contribute to the research on this topic.

Attachment theory

Attachment theory explains the unique and powerful nature of the different forms of emotional attachment in terms of the ways in which they impact on the individual's life. From secure and stable attachments, which are flexible and well developed, to those which are insecure, unstable, rigid or scarcely operating, one can describe a continuum of attachment which relates to general psychological adjustment and the presence/absence of personal and social psychological problems. According to the theory developed by Bowlby (1969), in the first years of life and through the formation of emotional relationships with parents or caregivers, children develop general styles of relating with others (attachment styles). Through these relationships they develop internal mental representations, which are then used as a basis for later relationships. Applied to problems of dating violence, attachment theory suggests that victims and aggressors are those individuals whose attachments with their primary caregivers are based on a lack of trust, on the continuum of dominance–submission and emotional control. Research conducted in this area has confirmed that boys and girls who have insecure attachments come from families in which they have been mistreated; they present a higher risk of becoming involved in dating violence (Werkele and Wolfe, 1998). Nevertheless, other studies have questioned whether there is a direct link between attachment and dating violence, as it has been found that a significant number of adolescents who have secure attachments assault their partners (Schwartz *et al.*, 2006).

Social learning theory

Bandura (1977) postulated that human beings learn by exposure to and imitation of the behaviour of others. Applying this to violence, repeated exposure to violent contexts within life, as a witness or direct recipient, could provide the basis for a later expression of violence in different contexts and situations. Learning violent behaviour within the family setting could explain the expression of violence in other contexts, such as the dating relationship (O'Leary, 1988). A number of studies have supported this model, some reporting that being exposed to family violence during infancy increases the risk of behaving aggressively with a partner (González and Santana, 2001; Linder and Collins, 2005). Others have emphasised the moderating role of other variables, such as the quality of the couple's relationship or individual personality. So, the regulation and expression of anger may be influenced by the inter-generational transmission of violence. Wolfe and Foshee (2003) dem-onstrated that the way in which an individual learns to express anger as a result of his or her family context is related to the way in which anger is expressed in adolescence. The authors classified adolescents in rela-tion to the different styles they used to express anger, finding that the destructive style, characterised by aggression towards the person who is the object of the anger, was directly related to aggression within the adolescent dating relationship.

One of the most important contributions of social learning theory is that it can explain the transmission of aggression and violence across contexts. Connolly *et al.* (2000) and Pepler *et al.* (2006) analysed the predictive effect of bullying among peers on dating violence from a developmental perspective, taking into account the predictive or mod-erating effect of the physical and biological changes that accompany adolescence. The authors considered that bullying is a behaviour that is aimed at obtaining power and domination over others, a tendency which aggressive individuals then take to the new forms of relationships which appear during adolescence, i.e. early dating relationships. The authors interviewed 479 students between the ages of 13 and 19 years, using measures of direct involvement in bullying, being the recipient or perpetrator of sexual harassment, involvement in dating violence and changes related to puberty. The authors concluded that, whilst the prevalence of bullying decreased across adolescence, the presence of sexual harassment and dating violence increased. The appearance of these new types of violence also coincided with changes related to puberty, with those who passed puberty early becoming involved in these new types of aggression earlier on as well. In spite of the differ-ent trajectories of bullying, sexual harassment and dating violence, the results showed positive correlations between the three forms of aggres-sion among peers, demonstrating, therefore, the important risk fac-tor that involvement in bullying during primary and secondary school poses for the personal and social adjustment of adolescents.

Work by Ortega and colleagues (Ortega and Mora-Merchán, 2008; Ortega *et al.*, 2008a) has also analysed the transmission of violence across contexts, within the peer-group, from the peer-group, to the couple. The authors examined the key role that dominance–submission within the relationship plays in the dynamic of violence and how this is maintained and repeated in different relational contexts. To date, the authors have found important correlations between sexual harass-ment among peers, and within the couple, and weak correlations for victimisation in these two contexts. The correlation between sexually harassing others and being sexually harassed in different contexts was weak. Nevertheless, highly significant correlations appeared between aggression and victimisation in the couple scenario, which suggests the important effect of the couple as an individual and specific context in the appearance and maintenance of violence.

Feminist theory

Feminist theory (Walker, 1989) suggests that violence within couples is the expression of an inequality of social power which exists between men and women as a consequence of the patriarchal society in the majority of Western and non-Western societies. This imbalance of power places men in a dominant position and women in a more submissive position, placing the latter at higher risk of suffering violence at the hands of their partners. Various factors support the feminist explanation of violence within young couples: the desire for control and the maintenance of power by men over women (Barnett *et al.*, 1997; González and Santana, 2001), as well as rigid sexist attitudes about male and female roles based on misogyny and blaming women for violence. Recent research has found these beliefs to still be present among young people, including university students (Ferrer *et al.*, 2006), and to be particularly representative and defining of the personalities of those who are violent towards their partners (Lichter and McClosey, 2004).

From this perspective, aggression by girls and women towards their male partners is analysed in terms of self-defence rather than being motivated by a desire for control or power. Nevertheless, a vision of women solely being reactive is not fully supported, as girls are equally (Moffit *et al.*, 2002), if not more (Muñoz-Rivas *et al.*, 2007b), likely to start the aggression. Similarly, other studies have found that among the motivations used by girls/women to assault their partner are those which are personal and based on the established dynamics in the intimate relationship more than self-defence (Stuart *et al.*, 2006) or intense emotional states such as momentary anger or rage (Muñoz-Rivas *et al.*, 2007b).

Conflict or coercion theory

Conflict or coercion theory locates the origin of dating and domestic violence in much more proximal factors, in particular the conflict dynamics which are found among some adolescent and adult couples. From this point of view, relationships where coercion and control are used as a way of resolving conflicts would be where we would be more likely to find aggression between the couple (Feld and Straus, 1989). It is therefore a perspective that considers reciprocal conflict and violence as an interactional style used by the couple, which begins in adolescence and becomes more established and perpetuates itself over time. This approach does not focus exclusively on the individual characteristics of each member of the couple, but on the styles of interaction that occur between them.

Gray and Foshee (1997) have confirmed this perspective, noting that these couples are also at higher risk for conflicts, discussions and dissatisfaction with their partner. Werkele and Wolfe (1999) confirmed that these couples have serious difficulties in the use of prosocial strategies and finding solutions. They also have significant problems in emotion regulation (Cummings and Davies, 1996), which in some way reinforces the use of coercive and aggressive strategies in the day-to-day life of the couple. This also increases the likelihood that they will continue to use aggression within their relationship and that it will become a habitual form of interaction (Feld and Strauss, 1989; Werkele and Wolfe, 1999). One of the aspects that has been most studied in this area has been the regulation of anger, which in many studies has been found to be directly related to aggression in adolescent and adult couples (Muñoz-Rivas et al., 2007b; Nocentini, 2008; Riggs and O'Leary, 1989).

Nevertheless, Katz et al. (2000) concluded that, although conflict resolution strategies which involve coercion and control are found within couples where violence is a problem, they are also found within couples where violence does not occur.

The dynamic developmental systems approach

Capaldi et al. (2003) and O'Leary and Slep (2003) have noted the importance of the development of models which prioritise the study of the dyad rather than models which have been centred on the study of the individual. From this, Capaldi et al. (2004) and Capaldi and Kim (2007) have developed a theoretical model which attempts to explain the behaviour of the couple as a dynamic developmental system. In this sense, the behavioural dynamic which is established by the couple is understood as an intrinsically interactive system but, at times, defined by the individual developmental characteristics of both members of the couple and by contextual factors which affect each member of the couple.

The contribution of this model rests in the possibility of considering the different aspects which are involved in the explanation of violence in couples' relationships. These are aspects which relate to the biology of those involved, their individual characteristics, contextual factors and their social experiences in the different micro-contexts in which they participate, principally family and peers (Capaldi *et al.*, 2005). The way in which these aspects develop over time will also form part of the process under investigation; the characteristics of each member of the couple are a product of their development and include biological aspects as well as socialisation, and therefore evolve and change over time.

According to this model, three main factors are important in understanding the origin and development of violence among adolescent couples:

- The individual characteristics of the couple which may affect their relationship, such as aspects of personality, psychopathological characteristics and those characteristics which were learnt and reinforced within the family and peer contexts.
- The contextual risk factors which could be influential in increasing the likelihood of aggressive episodes towards the partner, such as the use of alcohol or drugs.
- The nature of the relationship of the couple, the patterns of interaction which are established in the couple and the way in which these evolve and develop over time.

From this point of view, they consider the interaction styles and the aggressive dynamics which are established within the relationship as being predictive factors and factors which may reinforce violence within these early dating relationships (Capaldi and Kim, 2007; Capaldi *et al.*, 2004).

Capaldi's approach, which is developmental, multi-factorial, multi-probabilistic and integrates diverse perspectives, allows for a much richer and comprehensive view, not only of violence during adolescence and adulthood, but also of its development and stability over time. Research by Capaldi *et al.* (2003) found that some young people who were involved in risky relationships in which physical violence occurred were more likely to continue to be violent (male partners only) if two years later the couple were still together, whilst this probability decreased if the couple had separated and they had started dating other people. Nocentini (2008) found a decrease in physical aggression in adolescent couples from mid- to late adolescence. This decrease was affected by factors related to certain family characteristics and individual experiences, as well as individual factors and factors from within the dyadic relationship such as antisocial behaviour and the perception of victimisation by the partner. In sum, the study concluded that low educational level of mother and the number of previous partners the adolescent had had placed them at higher risk of being aggressive at age 16 compared with the rest of those studied. On the other hand, the use of physical aggression towards a partner in addition to exhibiting other forms of antisocial behaviour and with the perception of being victimised by a partner delayed the tendency for the decrease in physical aggression between mid- and late adolescence. These were the adolescents, according to the study, who were most vulnerable and at the greatest risk.

Risk factors in the appearance and maintenance of dating violence

In order to evaluate the risk factors and to provide intervention or prevention programmes for dating violence, it is important that attention is paid to a large body of research. In this sense, multi-dimensional and probabilistic perspectives seem to be the most appropriate to understand the appearance of dating violence as well as the conditions in which these problems tend to repeat themselves (Cáceres and Cáceres, 2006; Lewis and Fremouw, 2000).

Many of the risk factors identified for dating violence come directly from research carried out from the different perspectives and theoretical models mentioned earlier. Some researchers have focused on family experiences, social contexts (particularly peer contexts), sociodemographic factors, individual difference factors (such as certain personality factors) and the co-occurrence of other risk factors (such as smoking, drinking alcohol or drug taking).

Research into the influence of sociodemographic factors in the prediction of dating violence has not yet produced many conclusive results. Traditionally, the variables studied have been family composition, socioeconomic status (SES), place of residence, ethnicity and gender. Some studies have indicated that boys who are from a low SES background are more at risk of involvement in violence (Makepeace, 1987; O'Keefe, 1998), although for many authors these results are not entirely conclusive (O'Keefe, 2005). In relation to the area of residence, research appears to conclude that violence among adolescent couples occurs independently of the zone of residence. Some studies have found that there is more violence in urban areas (Makepeace, 1987) whilst others have found that there are higher levels of dating violence in rural areas (Reuterman and Burcky, 1989). Several different studies have shown that adolescents from single-parent families are more at risk of being involved in dating violence (Foshee et al., 2008) and that low levels of parental education increase the risk of being involved in dating violence, especially when mediated by sexist attitudes or family violence (Foshee *et al.*, 2008).

With respect to family factors, parents who show neglectful educational styles and whose relationships with their children are characterised by an abuse of power place their children at an increased risk of becoming involved in violent behaviour during adolescence. A study conducted by Straus and Savage (2005), with university students from 17 countries, found that neglect and a lack of material care (e.g. lack of hygiene, lack of help or support with school tasks) by parents during childhood were related to dating violence during adolescence. Boys who had received poor levels of care from their parents during infancy and childhood were more at risk of physically assaulting their partner during adolescence, a probability which increased exponentially if the social context in which they lived was violent.

In the same vein, O'Keefe (1998) found that experiencing physical abuse during infancy significantly predicted victimisation of girls in dating relationships in adolescence. However, this did not predict victimisation or aggression for boys. Kinsfogel and Grych (2004) found that young people who had witnessed high levels of violence in the family home were more at risk of becoming a victim and aggressor of their partner later on. However, the adolescent's beliefs and attitudes about violence emerged as a mediating factor. The authors suggest that some young people who have witnessed violence may have learnt that this is justifiable within dating relationships. However, this result was only significant for boys and not girls.

The peer context and experiences with peers have also been an important focus of research on dating violence. Various studies have concluded that being violent with peers predicts violent behaviour with a partner (Capaldi *et al.*, 2001), particularly for boys (Chase *et al.*, 1998). Additionally, having violent friends who have positive attitudes towards violence predicts aggressive behaviour towards a partner in adolescence (Arriaga and Foshee, 2004; Connolly *et al.*, 2000). Arriaga and Foshee (2004) found that witnessing dating violence among peers and interparental violence significantly predicted violence within their own relationship, either as an aggressor or victim. When looking at the relative strengths of the predictive relationships, they found that dating violence by peers was a stronger predictor than interparental violence. In general, many studies have confirmed that proximal factors, such as peers, the consumption of substances and the context of the dating relationship, are more important than distal factors, but that these distal factors influence dating violence in an indirect way, often mediated by proximal factors (Foshee *et al.*, 2008; Magdol *et al.*, 1997; O'Keefe, 2005).

Different personality variables and interpersonal abilities have been found to be fundamental in the explanation of dating violence. Low self-esteem is a strong indicator of dating aggression for boys (O'Keefe, 1998), whereas for girls it is more strongly related to victimisation. In this respect, some authors reflected on the important influence of self-esteem in the normalisation of violence in the context of the couple and in the explanation of the complex process of victimisation (Lewis and Fremouw, 2000).

Another important psychological factor is conflict resolution style. As mentioned earlier, from the perspective of coercion and conflict theories, several studies have described how some young people present serious difficulties regulating anger and frustration when faced with conflict (Muñoz-Rivas *et al.*, 2007a; Werkele and Wolfe, 1999) and are aggressive, impulsive and tend to attribute guilt to their partner, which reinforces this aversive relational context and results in an increase in conflicts and discussions. As we have noted, adolescents who are involved in dating violence find themselves in relationships which are violent and aggressive, with high levels of conflict and reciprocal and mutual violence. In this respect, research has demonstrated that one important predictor of aggression in the adolescent couple is aggression and violence by the partner, at least for physical violence (Capaldi *et al.*, 2003; O'Leary and Slep, 2003). Therefore, it is probable that those adolescents who lack skills in conflict resolution and the regulation of stress are more likely to form relationships with other violent individuals who have similar patterns of conflict resolution. This leads to a relational dynamic in which conflicts escalate and may lead to violence.

Other influential factors are the beliefs held by the individual regarding their own ability to resolve conflicts and their feelings of self-efficacy in regulating their own emotions. Nocentini (2008) carried out one of the first studies on the impact of the perception of self-control of aggression towards a partner on actual physical and psychological dating violence. The research concluded that the perception of self-efficacy in the self-regulation of emotions in intimate relationships was related to physical and psychological aggression via rumination and conflict. Adolescents who thought that they could not exercise any control over their anger and rage in the face of conflicts with their partner were more likely to use rumination, increasing the desire to extract revenge or hurt their partner. In consequence, it was more likely that conflicts would not be resolved and would in fact worsen, involving the use of negative strategies for conflict resolution such as physical and psychological aggression.

Finally, it is important to restate the significance of other proximal factors, such as the presence or co-ocurrence of other behaviour problems during adolescence. The use of alcohol and other substances has repeatedly been found to be one of the most important predictive factors for delinquent behaviour, as well as dating violence (O'Keefe, 1998; Silverman *et al.*, 2001). However, some studies have not found this relationship (Loh and Gidycz, 2006) and others report that it is an important predictor of sexual aggression by males (Casey *et al.*, 2009) and sexual aggression by males towards their partner (Koss and Dinero, 1989). It is suggested that this may occur because alcohol and other drugs may diminish control over behaviour and distort the perception of the situation and the other person's intentions. Risky sexual behaviour, such as having numerous partners at an early age, has also been found to be a predictive factor of dating violence (Makepeace, 1987; Nocentini, 2008; O'Keefe, 2005; Werkele and Wolfe, 1999).

We do not want to finish this section without considering that these variables are not cause–effect variables, but are dimensions which increase or decrease the probability of an individual becoming involved in dating violence. It is important to underline the summative and/or multiplicative interactions of the co-occurrence of these factors in the explanation and prediction of dating violence. In synthesis, we can say that it is a multi-determined phenomenon, affected by diverse proximal and distal factors and it is the analysis of these factors which may help in the design of prevention and intervention programmes.

Implications for intervention and prevention

The development and implementation of intervention and prevention programmes is only relatively recent and is derived directly from the studies of risk factors for dating violence. Interventions have focused on communication strategies and conflict resolution orientated towards the constructive resolution of problems and increasing awareness of dating violence and its consequences.

Most prevention and intervention programmes have been developed from and within the educational context (Avery-Leaf *et al.*, 1997; Lavoie *et al.*, 1995) and have been primary intervention programmes. Knowledge of their effectiveness is still controversial, as a result of methodological problems which have limited the generalisability of the results. On many occasions these programmes have been implemented with a small number of adolescents; in others the intervention period has been very short or the pre–post evaluation has been carried within a limited timeframe and without the analysis of a comparison control group (Werkele and Wolfe, 1999; Whitaker *et al.*, 2006). However, we describe here two programmes which have been implemented and evaluated satisfactorily, whose design has tried to overcome those methodological problems highlighted and which have presented promising results in changing the attitudes and beliefs of young people, as well as in reducing violent behaviour.

The Safe Date Project (Foshee *et al.*, 1998, 2004) is a community intervention programme which involved 14 schools from North Carolina and was conducted with adolescents aged between 14 and 15 years. The programme focused on challenging sexist attitudes, increasing knowledge about dating violence, developing conflict resolution strategies and the establishment of networks of support and help for those involved in dating violence. The students involved in the study were randomly assigned to a control group or the experimental group, and the evaluation of the effectiveness of the intervention was conducted one month post-intervention, one year later and two to three years later. The focus of the evaluation was on the change in sexist attitudes and attitudes towards violence, as well as the reduction of physical, relational or sexual violence in the dating relationships. The results were mixed. On one hand, the one-month post-test assessment revealed a significant decrease in aggression towards partners, as well as higher levels of knowledge and sensitivity and less tolerance towards this type of violence. However, results relating to a decrease in violent behaviour were not found in the follow-up one year later. Further, a follow-up several years later concluded that the decrease in dating violence was maintained up to four years after the end of the programme (Foshee *et al.*, 2004).

The Youth Relationships Project (Wolfe *et al.*, 2003) is a community project whose results have also been promising. This programme focused on those young adolescents who were at particular risk, specifically those who had a history of family abuse. The young people who took part in the programme received group sessions aimed at improving their conflict resolution skills and emotional well-being and communication skills, as well as their knowledge about abusive relationships, and aimed at decreasing their tolerance towards these. In spite of the fact that more than 160 young people took part in the programme, the experimental design continuously assessed the efficacy of the intervention sessions. The results, although not entirely conclusive, reported reductions in the rates of physical aggression among the participants in this programme.

In spite of the fact that the results of the programmes mentioned above are positive and promising, it remains to be seen whether these interventions will be able to reach those who need them most. As we have mentioned, the dating violence programmes developed have been focused on primary prevention, and few have carried out systematic interventions with at-risk populations. It is important to state that, until now, researchers and theorists have paid little attention to the at-risk populations who are in most need of these interventions.

Conclusions

In this chapter we have analysed the pervasive phenomenon of dating violence. Research suggests that this problem is more frequent than expected and involved boys and girls in similar proportions. Multidimensional and multi-probabilistic theoretical models contribute to the explanation of dating violence, concluding that, other than family and sociodemographic factors, proximal factors related to beliefs about violence, love, sexist attitudes, behavioural problems and coping styles increase the probability of involvement in dating violence. The identification of these risk factors has recently facilitated the design of prevention and intervention programmes. In this respect, results seem to be mixed but promising in relation to reducing dating violence and indicate that, when sensitisation campaigns are directly focused on the positive benefits of the intervention, adolescents' intentions to participate increase considerably.

Acknowledgements

This chapter was developed within the Juvenile Dating Violence project (SEJ-2007–60673), financed by the Plan Nacional I+D. We are also grateful for a grant (2008-Pr.Ex- 0106) received by the first author enabling her to spend an eight-month sabbatical in the Department of Psychology and Counselling at the University of Greenwich, which enabled the preparation of this chapter.

REFERENCES

Archer, J. (2000). 'Sex differences in aggression between heterosexual partners: a meta-analytic review'. *Psychological Bulletin*, 126: 651–80.

Arriaga, X.B. and Foshee, V.A. (2004). 'Adolescent dating violence: do adolescents follow in their friends', or their parents', footsteps?' *Journal of Interpersonal Violence*, 19: 162–84.

Avery-Leaf, S., Cascardi, M., O'Leary, K.D. and Cano, A. (1997). 'Efficacy of a dating violence prevention program on attitudes justifying aggression'. *Journal of Adolescent Health*, 21: 11–17.

Bandura, A. (1977). *Social Learning Theory*. Englewood Cliffs, NJ: Prentice Hall.

Barnett, O.W., Millen-Perin, C. and Perrin, R.D. (1997). *Family Violence across the Life-span: An Introduction*. Thousand Oaks, CA: Sage.

Bennett, L. and Fineran, S. (1998). 'Sexual and severe physical violence of high school students: power beliefs, gender, and relationship'. *American Journal of Orthopsychiatry*, 68: 645–52.

Bowlby, J. (1969). *Attachment and Loss*, vol. 1, *Attachment*, 2nd edn. New York: Basic Books.

Bookwala, J., Frieze, I. and Grote, N. (1994). 'Love, aggression, and satisfaction in dating relationships'. *Journal of Social and Personal Relationships*, 11: 625–32.

Brendgen, M., Vitato, F., Tremblay, R.E. and Wanner, B. (2002). 'Parent and peer effects on delinquency-related violence and dating violence: a test of two mediational models'. *Social Development*, 11: 225–44.

Cáceres, A. and Cáceres, J. (2006). 'Violencia en relaciones íntimas en dos etapas evolutivas [Violence in intimate relationships in two developmental stages]'. *International Journal of Clinical and Health Psychology*, 6: 271–84.

Capaldi, D.M. and Kim, H.K. (2002). 'Aggression toward a partner in young adulthood: longitudinal patterns and predictors'. Paper presented at the Annual Meeting of the Association for Advancement of Behavior Therapy. Reno, Nevada, November.

(2007). 'Typological approaches to violence in couples: a critique and alternative conceptual approach'. *Clinical Psychology Review*, 27: 253–65.

Capaldi, D.M., Dishion, T.J., Stoolmiller, M. and Yoerger, K. (2001). 'Aggression toward female partners by at-risk young men: the contribution of male adolescent friendships'. *Developmental Psychology*, 37: 61–73.

Capaldi, D.M., Kim, H.K. and Shortt, J.W. (2004). 'Women's involvement in aggression in young adult romantic relationships: a developmental systems model'. In M. Putallez and K.L. Bierman (eds.), *Aggression, Antisocial Behavior, and Violence among Girls: A Developmental Perspective* (pp. 223–41). New York: Guilford Press.

Capaldi, D.M., Shortt, J.W. and Crosby, L. (2003). 'Physical and psychological aggression in at-risk young couples: stability and change in young adulthood'. *Merrill-Palmer Quarterly*, 49: 1–27.

Capaldi, D.M., Shortt, J.W. and Kim, H.K. (2005). 'A life span developmental systems perspective on aggression toward a partner'. In W. Pinsof and J. Lebow (eds.), *Family Psychology: The Art of the Science* (pp. 141–67). Oxford and New York: Oxford University Press.

Carver, K., Joyner, K. and Udry, J.R. (2003). 'National estimates of adolescent romantic relationships'. In P. Florsheim (ed.), *Adolescent Romantic Relations and Sexual Behavior: Theory, Research, and Practical Implications* (pp. 23–56). Mahwah, NJ: Lawrence Erlbaum.

Casey, E.A., Beadnell, B. and Lindhorst, T.P. (2009). 'Predictors of sexually coercive behavior in a nationally representative sample of adolescent males'. *Journal of Interpersonal Violence*, 24: 1129–47.

Chase, K.A., Treboux, D., O'Leary, K.D. and Strassberg, Z. (1998). 'Specificity of dating aggression and its justification among high-risk adolescents'. *Journal of Abnormal Child Psychology*, 26: 467–73.

Collins A.W. (2003). 'More than myth: the developmental significance of romantic relationships during adolescence'. *Journal of Research on Adolescence*, 13: 1–24.

Connolly, J.A., Pepler, D., Craig, W. and Taradash, A. (2000). 'Dating experiences of bullies in early adolescence'. *Child Maltreatment: Journal of the American Professional Society on the Abuse of Children*, 5: 299–311.

Cummings, E.M. and Davies, P. (1996). 'Emotional security as a regularity process in normal development and the development of psychopathology'. *Development and Psychopathology*, 8: 123–39.

Feld, S.L. and Straus, M.A. (1989). 'Escalation and desistance of wife assault in marriage'. *Criminology*, 27: 141–61.

Fernández-Fuertes, A.A. and Fuertes Martín, A. (2005). 'Violencia sexual en las relaciones de pareja de los jóvenes [Sexual violence in the relationships of young couples]'. *Sexología Integral*, 2: 126–32.

Ferrer, V., Bosh, E., Ramis, M.C., Torres, G. and Navarro, C. (2006). 'La violencia contra las mujeres en la pareja: creencias y actitudes en estudiantes universitarios/as [Couples violence against women: beliefs and attitudes of university students]'. *Psicothema*, 18: 359–66.

Foshee, V.A. (1996). 'Gender differences in adolescent dating: abuse prevalence, types and injuries'. *Health Education Research*, 11: 275–86.

Foshee, V.A., Bauman, K.E., Arriaga, X.B., Helms, R.W., Koch, G.G. and Linder, G.F. (1998). 'An evaluation of safe dates, and adolescents dating violence prevention program'. *American Journal of Public Health*, 88: 45–50.

Foshee, V.A., Bauman, K.E., Ennet, S.T., Linder, G.F., Benefield, T. and Suchindran, C. (2004). 'Assessing the long-term effects of the Safe Dates Program and a booster in preventing and reducing adolescent dating violence, victimization and perpetration'. *American Journal of Public Health*, 94: 619–25.

Foshee, V.A., Karriker-Jaffe, K.J., Reyes, H.L.M., Ennett, S.T., Suchindran, C., Bauman, K.E. and Benefield, T.S. (2008). 'What accounts for demographic differences in trajectories of adolescent dating violence? An examination of intrapersonal and contextual mediators'. *Journal of Adolescent Health*, 42: 596–604.

Freedner, N., Freed, L.H., Yang, Y.W. and Austin, S.B. (2002). 'Dating violence among gay, lesbian, and bisexual adolescents: results from a community survey'. *Journal of Adolescent Health*, 31: 469–74.

Furman, W. (1999). 'Friends and lovers: the role of peer relationships in adolescent heterosexual romantic relationships'. In W.A. Collins and B. Laursen (eds.), *Relationships As Developmental Contexts: The 29th Minnesota Symposium on Child Development*. Hillsdale, NJ: Lawrence Erlbaum.

Furman, W. and Buhrmester, D. (1992). 'Age and sex differences in perceptions of networks of personal relationships'. *Child Development*, 63: 103–15.

Furman, W. and Shaffer, L. (2003). 'The role of romantic relationships in adolescent development'. In P. Florsheim (ed.), *Adolescent Romantic Relations and Sexual Behavior: Theory, Research, and Practical Implications* (pp. 3–22). Mahwah, NJ: Lawrence Erlbaum.

González, R. and Santana, J.D. (2001). 'La violencia en parejas jóvenes [Violence in young couples]'. *Psicothema*, 13: 127–31.

Gray, H.M. and Foshee, V. (1997). 'Adolescent dating violence'. *Journal of Interpersonal Violence*, 12: 126–42.

Halpern, C.T., Young, M.L., Waller, M.W., Martin, S.L. and Kupper, L.L. (2004). 'Prevalence of partner violence in same-sex romantic and sexual relationships in a national sample of adolescents'. *Journal of Adolescent Health*, 35: 124–31.

Hird, M.J. (2000). 'An empirical study of adolescent dating aggression in the UK'. *Journal of Adolescence*, 23: 69–78.

Hofstede, G. (1998). 'Comparative studies of sexual behaviour: sex as achievement or as a relationship?' In G. Hofstede (ed.), *Masculinity and Femininity: Taboo Dimensions of National Culture* (pp. 153–78). Thousand Oaks, CA: Sage.

Jackson, S.M., Cram, F. and Seymour, F.W. (2000). 'Violence and sexual coercion in high school students' dating relationships'. *Journal of Family Violence*, 15: 23–36.

Kanin, E.J. (1957). 'Male aggression in dating-courting relations'. *American Journal of Sociology*, 63: 197–204.

Katz, J., Jones, D.J. and Beach, S.R.H. (2000). 'Distress and aggression during dating conflict: a test of the coercion hypothesis'. *Personal Relationships*, 7: 391–402.

Kinsfogel, K. and Grych, J. (2004). 'Interparental conflict and adolescent dating relationships: integrating cognitive, emotional and peer influences'. *Journal of Family Psychology*, 18: 505–15.

Koss, M.P. and Dinero, T. (1989). 'Discriminant analysis of risk factors for sexual victimization among a national sample of college women'. *Journal of Consulting and Clinical Psychology*, 57: 242–54.

Lavoie, F., Vezina, L., Piche, C. and Boivin, M. (1995). 'Evaluation of a prevention program for violence in teen dating relationships'. *Journal of Interpersonal Violence*, 10: 516–24.

Lewis, S. and Fremouw, W.J. (2000). 'Dating violence: a critical review of the literature'. *Clinical Psychology Review*, 21: 105–27.

Lichter, E.L. and McClosey, L.A. (2004). 'The effects of childhood exposure to marital violence on adolescent gender-role beliefs and dating violence'. *Psychology of Women Quarterly*, 28: 344–57.

Linder, J.R. and Collins, W.A. (2005). 'Parent and peer predictors of physical aggression and conflict management in romantic relationships in early adulthood'. *Journal of Family Psychology*, 19: 252–62.

Loh, C. and Gidycz, C.A. (2006). 'A prospective analysis of the relationship between childhood sexual victimization and perpetration of dating violence and sexual assault in adulthood'. *Journal of Interpersonal Violence*, 21: 732–49.

Maccoby, E. (1998). *The Two Sexes: Growing Up Apart, Coming Together.* Cambridge, MA: Harvard University Press.

Magdol, L., Moffit, T., Caspi, A., Newman, D., Fagan, J. and Silva, P. (1997). 'Gender differences in partner violence in a birth cohort of 21-year-olds: bridging the gap between clinical and epidemiological approaches'. *Journal of Consulting and Clinical Psychology*, 65: 68–78.

Makepeace, J. M. (1981). 'Courtship violence among collegue students'. *Family Relations*, 30: 97–102.

(1987). 'Social factors and victims offender differences in courtship violence'. *Family Relations*, 36: 87–91.

Menesini, E. and Nocentini, A. (2008). 'Aggressività nelle prime esperienze sentimentali in adolescenza [Aggression in the first sentimental experiences in adolescence]'. *Giornale Italiano di Psicologia*, 2: 407–34.

Moffitt, T.E., Caspi, A., Rutter, M. and Silva, P.A. (2002). *Sex Differences in Antisocial Behaviour: Conduct Disorder, Delinquency and Violence in the Dunedin Longitudinal Study*. Cambridge: Cambridge University Press.

Moore, C.D. and Waterman, C.K. (1999). 'Predicting self-protection against sexual assault in dating relationships among heterosexual men and women, gay men, lesbians, and bisexuals'. *Journal of College Student Development*, 4: 132–40.

Muñoz-Rivas, M.J., Graña, J.L., O'Leary, K.D. and González, M. P. (2007a). 'Aggression in adolescent dating relationships: prevalence, justification and health consequences'. *Journal of Adolescent Health*, 40: 298–304.

(2007b). 'Physical and psychological aggression in dating relationships in Spanish university students'. *Psicothema*, 19: 102–07.

Nocentini, A. (2008). 'Dating aggression across adolescence: a developmental-contextual analysis'. Unpublished doctoral dissertation, Inter-university Center for Research on the Development and Genesis of Prosocial and Antisocial Motivations, Universitá della Sapienza di Roma.

O'Keefe, M. (1998). 'Factors meditating the link between witnessing inter-parental violence and dating violence'. *Journal of Family Violence*, 13: 39–57.

(2005). *Teen Dating Violence: A Review of Risk Factors and Prevention Efforts*. Harrisburg, PA: National Resource Center on Domestic Violence.

O'Leary, K.D. (1988). 'Physical aggression between spouses: a social learning theory perspective'. In V.B. Van Hasselt, R.L. Morrison, A.S. Bellack and M. Hersen (eds.) *Handbook of Family Violence* (pp. 31–55). New York: Plenum Press.

(1999). 'Developmental and affective issues in assessing and treating partner aggression'. *Clinical Psychology: Science and Practice*, 6: 400–14.

O'Leary, K.D. and Slep, A. (2003). 'A dyadic longitudinal model of adolescent dating aggression'. *Journal of Clinical Child and Adolescent Psychology*, 32: 314–27.

Ortega, R. and Mora-Merchán, J.A. (2008). 'Las redes de iguales y el fenómeno de la violencia escolar: explorando el esquema del dominio sumisión [Peer networks and the phenomenon of school violence: exploring the dominance–submission schema]'. *Infancia y Aprendizaje*, 31: 515–28.

Ortega, R., Ortega-Rivera, J. and Sánchez, V. (2008a). 'La violencia sexual entre compañeros/as y en la pareja: un estudio exploratorio [Sexual violence between companions and in couples: an exploratory study]'. *Internacional Journal of Psychology*, 8: 63–72.

Ortega, R., Sánchez, V. and Ortega-Rivera, J. (2008b). 'Quality of dating relationships in Spanish adolescents: a study of dating violence'. Paper presented at the IV World Conference of Violence in School and Public Policies, Lisbon. Portugal, June.

Overbeek, G., Ha, T., Scholte, R., Kemp, R. de and Engels, R.C.M.E. (2007). 'Brief report: intimacy, passion, and commitment in romantic relationships – validation of a triangular love scale for adolescents'. *Journal of Adolescence*, 30: 523–28.

Pepler, D.J., Craig, W.M., Connolly, J.A., Yuile, A. and McMaster, L. (2006). 'A developmental perspective of bullying'. *Aggressive Behavior*, 32: 376–84.

Reuterman, N. and Burcky, W. (1989). 'Dating violence in high school: a profile of the victims'. *Psychology: A Journal of Human Behavior*, 26: 1–9.

Rice, F.P. (1990). *The Adolescent: Development, Relationships, and Culture*. Needham Heights, MA: Allyn and Bacon.

Riggs, D. and O'Leary, K. (1989). 'A theoretical model of courtship aggression'. In M. Pirog-Good and J. Stets (eds.), *Violence in Dating Relationships: Emerging Issues* (pp. 53–70). New York: Praeger.

Sánchez, V., Ortega-Rivera, J., Ortega, R. and Viejo, C. (2008). 'Las relaciones sentimentales en la adolescencia: satisfacción, conflictos y violencia [Sentimental relationships in adolescence: satisfaction, conflicts and violence]'. *Escritos de Psicología*, 2: 97–109.

Savin-Williams, R.C. (1995). 'Lesbian, gay male, and bisexual adolescents'. In A. D'Augelli and C. Patterson (eds.), *Lesbian, Gay, and Bisexual Identities over the Lifespan: Psychological Perspectives* (pp. 165–89). New York: Oxford University Press.

Schwartz, J.P. Hage, S.M, Bush, I. and Burns, L.K. (2006). 'Unhealthy parenting and potential mediators as contributing factors to future intimate violence'. *Trauma, Violence and Abuse*, 7: 206–21.

Shorey, R.C., Cornelius, T.C. and Bell, K.M. (2008). 'A critical review of theoretical frameworks for dating violence: comparing dating and marital fields'. *Aggression and Violent Behavior*, 13: 185–94.

Shulman, S. and Scharf, M. (2000). 'Adolescent romantic behaviors and perceptions: age- and gender-related differences, and links with family and peer relationships'. *Journal of Research on Adolescence*, 10: 99–118.

Silverman, C.G., Raj, A., Mucci, L.A. and Hathaway, J.E. (2001). 'Dating violence against adolescent girls and associated substance use, unhealthy weight control, sexual risk behavior, pregnancy, and suicidality'. *Journal of the American Medical Association*, 286: 572–79.

Smiler, A.P. (2008). 'I wanted to get to know her better: adolescent boys' dating motives, masculinity ideology, and sexual behaviour'. *Journal of Adolescence*, 31: 17–32.

Straus, M. and Savage, S. (2005). 'Neglectful behaviour by parents in the life history of university students in 17 countries and its relation to violence against dating partners'. *Child Maltreatment*, 10: 124–35.

Stuart, G.L., Moore, T.M., Gordon, K.C., Hellmuth, H.C., Ramsey, S.E. and Kahler, C.W. (2006). 'Reasons for intimate partner violence perpetration among arrested women'. *Violence against Women*, 12: 609–21.

Trish, W., Connolly, J., Pepler, D. and Craig, W. (2003). 'Questioning and sexual minority adolescents: high school experiences of bullying, sexual harassment and physical abuse'. *Canadian Journal of Community Mental Health*, 22: 47–58.

Walker, L.E. (1989). 'Psychology and violence against women'. *American Psychologist*, 44: 695–702.

Werkele, C. and Wolfe, D.A. (1998). 'The contribution of a history of child maltreatment and adolescent insecure attachment style to adolescent dating violence'. *Development and Psychopathology*, 10: 571–86.

—— (1999). 'Dating violence in mid-adolescence: theory, significance, and emerging prevention initiatives'. *Clinical Psychology Review*, 19: 435–56.

Whitaker, D.J., Haileyesus, T., Swahn, M. and Saltzman, L.S. (2007). 'Differences in frequency of violence and reported injury between relationships with reciprocal and non-reciprocal intimate partner violence'. *American Journal of Public Health*, 97: 941–47.

Whitaker, D.J., Morrison, S., Lindquist, C., Hawkins, S.R., O'Neil, J.A., Nersuis, A.M. *et al.* (2006). 'A critical review of interventions for the primary prevention of perpetration of partner violence'. *Aggression and Violent Behavior*, 11: 151–66.

Wolfe, D.A. and Foshee, V.A. (2003). 'Family violence, anger expression, and adolescent dating violence'. *Journal of Family Violence*, 18: 309–16.

Wolfe, D.A., Werkele, C., Scott, K., Straatman, A.L., Grasley, C. and Reitzel-Jaffe, D. (2003). 'Dating violence prevention with at-risk youth: a controlled outcome evaluation'. *Journal of Consulting and Clinical Psychology*, 7: 279–91.

7 Bullying in prisons: bringing research up to date

Jane L. Ireland

As a topic of academic study, bullying between prisoners has not seen the same volume of research as that dedicated to other populations, such as bullying among children or within the workplace. Indeed, the first studies into prison bullying were published only in 1996 (Connell and Farrington, 1996; Ireland and Archer, 1996), and even now there is a tendency for research into prison aggression to be published which makes no reference to the concept of bullying (Blitz *et al.*, 2008) nor to any UK prison-based research. This is despite the fact that the UK has led this area, coupled with a marked increase in prison bullying research across the last decade (e.g. Ireland and Ireland, 2008), which has included in excess of 50 publications. Bullying among prisoners is a topic of particular interest on a number of grounds: *academically,* you have the opportunity to explore aggression between sex-segregated groups representing extreme samples of the general population, samples who are residing in unique environments that arguably serve to promote bullying behaviour (Ireland, 2005); and on *practice-grounds,* there is a need to refine and evaluate prison-based anti-bullying strategies and approaches, accounting for the elevated levels of bullying reported in comparison to other populations, and the absence of theory evident in current strategies (Ireland, 2005).

The current chapter aims to provide readers with an outline of some core findings and developments in this important field of study, developments that have occurred over the last decade. The ultimate aim is to provide a timely and current understanding of prison bullying which can serve to promote empirical research and drive the development of theoretically and empirically justified intervention programmes. Developments across the last decade have been most significant in the areas of defining prison bullying; the nature and extent of bullying and the influence of methods of measurement; in predicting and defining group membership; and in recognising the role of the environment and the underpinning value of theory. Each of these areas will be considered in turn, with the chapter concluding by identifying, based on the research and theoretical developments, how bullying within prisons can be effectively managed.

Defining prison bullying

Early research focused on bullying as a subsection of aggressive behaviour, viewing it as somehow distinct from other forms of aggression (e.g. Olweus, 1978). Although developed primarily with an application to schoolchildren, such views permeated early prison bullying research, leading to researchers essentially measuring the extent to which school-based definitions of bullying applied to prison samples (e.g. Connell and Farrington, 1996). This in itself was problematic and led to concerns being raised in relation to the extent to which such definitions really applied to environments which were significantly different from schools, housing entirely different populations. As the prison-based literature has developed, researchers have argued strongly against the application of school-based criteria of bullying to prisons; for example, arguing against the use of the criteria that it must be repeated, based on an imbalance of power and intentional (see Ireland, 2005; Ireland and Ireland, 2003, 2008). These arguments are made on the following grounds:

- Aggression in prisons does not have to be repeated in order to be classed as bullying, with the *fear* of being aggressed, rather than the actual incidence, considered of more importance in determining bullying.
- Some behaviour common to prison settings may not be based on an overt imbalance of power. One such behaviour would be 'baroning', where goods are provided to prisoners at a high rate of interest by another prisoner acting as a 'baron'. This is essentially extortion, but the behaviours are not immediately based on a power imbalance since the victim enters this relationship voluntarily. Such behaviours are commonly identified as bullying by prisoners and staff and yet would not be considered as such if standard definitions of bullying were applied.
- Not all bullying may be intentional; indeed the concept of 'accidental' bullying does exist, whereby a prisoner may perpetrate bullying without fully considering the consequences of their actions. Impulsive, ill-considered actions are not uncommon among prisoner groups and may apply in particular to prisoners using more indirect (e.g. Björkqvist, 1994) and subtle forms of aggression (i.e. gossiping, spreading rumours, etc.) without really considering them to represent

aggression. Such aggression is particularly favoured in prisons, where bullies can ensure that they impact negatively on victims and yet reduce their chances of being caught by the authorities.

Since approximately 1999 prison researchers have begun to opt for much broader definitions of bullying, with Ireland (2002) arguing that such definitions need to account for:

- the perception of the victim;
- the fact that it can include a single incidence of aggression, particularly if severe;
- the fear of repeated aggression;
- the potential absence of an obvious or explicit imbalance of power;
- both direct and indirect types of aggression;
- bullies not intending the consequences of their actions;
- unintentional provocation on the part of the victim.

In the same text (p. 26), I also offered a broad definition of bullying which attempted to encapsulate these elements:

An individual is being bullied when they are the victim of direct and/or indirect aggression happening on a weekly basis, by the same perpetrator or different perpetrators. Single incidences of aggression can be viewed as bullying, particularly where they are severe and when the individual either believes or fears that they are at risk of future victimisation by the same perpetrator or others. An incident can be considered bullying if the victim believes that they have been aggressed towards, regardless of the actual intention of the bully. It can also be bullying when the imbalance of power between the bully and his/her victim is implied and not immediately evident.

What attempts at definition do not resolve, however, are the problems associated with trying to find a fixed definition of bullying and accounting also for the use of the term 'bullying', which in itself is very problematic. What has become increasingly apparent is the futility in achieving a fixed measurable definition of a concept which varies from culture to culture, with this most significantly highlighted in the especial environment of a prison. For example, the term 'bullying' is an emotive one with childish connotations, which prisoners report being reluctant to admit to (Ireland and Ireland, 2003), nor does it translate well as a term in some languages, notably those with no term equivalent to 'bullying' (e.g. Spanish). A good example of this is perhaps evident in the aboriginal prisoners housed within the Canadian correctional service, where, in one aboriginal language, the term 'bullying' does not exist; the closest to it being 'key-kit-tah-may' (Ojibwah Indians), meaning to 'place fear in someone' (Esquash, 2008). The term does not translate beyond this. It seems, therefore, that what researchers have tried to do is develop a definition around a term which in itself is culturally sensitive and does not translate across cultures or even age groups.

Despite the problems of definition, however, the term 'bullying' is useful as a concept to focus intervention strategies and research initiatives. Indeed, more recently I have reached the conclusion that 'bullying' is nothing more than an 'umbrella term' (i.e. essentially a hypernym – a term used to cover a broad category of behaviours and concepts rather than one specific concept) to describe 'intra-group' aggression among prisoners, specifically (Ireland and Ireland, 2008). We should be researching aggressive behaviours that occur within a group context rather than focusing on a single term that can lead to a narrow understanding of such behaviour and, more importantly, an underestimation of the nature and extent of bullying which occurs within prisons.

Nature and extent of bullying, and the influence of method of measurement

Estimates of the extent of bullying vary widely in accordance with the method used, with interviews tending to produce much lower estimates of bullying than anonymous questionnaire methods and group-administered methods producing the smallest estimates of bullying – arguably because of prisoners not feeling assured of anonymity. Despite differences in estimates there is a consensus that bullying in prisons occurs more frequently than that reported among schoolchildren (Ireland, 2005). If prisoners are asked directly 'have you bullied?' or 'have you been bullied?', estimates average at 21 and 23 per cent (Ireland, 2002). There are, however, significant variations in this, with some estimates for perpetration in early studies as high as 57 per cent (e.g. Livingston *et al.*, 1994) and 67 per cent (e.g. Falshaw, 1993).

If, however, you adopt a more behavioural method of measurement where the term 'bullying' is avoided and instead present prisoners with a range of discrete behaviours to consider, average weekly estimates fall at *c.* 50 per cent for both victimisation and perpetration (Ireland, 2005). To date, there is just one behavioural checklist that is routinely used to assess behaviours indicative of bullying among prisoners – the Direct and Indirect Prisoner Behaviour Checklist (DIPC), either in a dichotomous form or in a scaled version (DIPC-SCALED), where the frequency of behaviour can also be accounted for (Ireland and Ireland, 2008).

Although it can be reliably assumed that asking prisoners directly 'have you bullied/been bullied?' is likely to automatically produce lower estimates owing to the emotive and 'childish' connotations of bullying mentioned earlier, there also remains the importance of accounting for prisoner perceptions of what constitutes bullying behaviour. When you ask a prisoner 'have you bullied?' or 'have you been bullied?', you are essentially stating, 'I want you to think about how you would define bullying and then tell me if you have experienced it or engaged in it'. Invariably, prisoners will focus on the more direct forms of aggression in answering such a question, such as physical, verbal, theft-related and sexual forms of bullying (Ireland and Ireland, 2003). Early research was certainly guilty of focusing solely on these forms (e.g. Connell and Farrington, 1996), but since around 1999 attention to indirect forms of bullying has been increased (e.g. Ireland, 1999; Ireland and Monaghan, 2006). Indirect forms of aggression are subtle and represent those in which either the aggressive intent is unclear to those external to the perpetrator–victim relationship or the perpetrator is unknown. It includes behaviours such as engaging in malicious gossip, spreading rumours and ostracising (Björkqvist, 1994).

Such behaviours are particularly valuable within a prison setting, where the risk of being punished for engaging in bullying if caught is high, coupled with the added distress that can be caused to victims who by virtue of their detention are largely unable to escape from such abuse. Any abusive activity which impacts on a prisoner's integration and acceptance in a peer-group from which the potential for physical escape is limited (such as being ostracised by a prisoner peer-group) can be considered to have a more pronounced effect on them than if residing in a non-incarcerated community (Ireland, 2005; Ireland and Qualter, 2008). It should not be a surprise, therefore, that indirect forms of bullying are reported as frequently, if not more so, than direct forms of bullying within prison settings, both by perpetrators and by their victims. For example, in Ireland and Ireland (2008), 43 per cent of prisoners reported direct perpetration, compared to 63 per cent reporting indirect perpetration. For victimisation, estimates were 68 and 72 per cent, respectively. Researchers therefore wishing to provide comprehensive coverage of the nature of prison bullying do so by ensuring an equal focus on both indirect and direct aggression (Ireland and Ireland, 2008).

It is perhaps the case, however, that research exploring the nature and extent of bullying is no longer required, since this largely descriptive branch of the research field has probably reported all that it can (Ireland, 2005), with coverage now extending to all prisoner groups, i.e. men, women, adults and adolescents. Instead, more recently attention has sought to move towards understanding in more depth the groups involved in bullying and how these are classified, coupled with focusing on the importance of the environment in understanding bullying. The starting point for this, however, is a more detailed understanding of individual models of bullying and how these have been refined.

Predicting and defining group membership

Early prison-based bullying research tended to focus on two groups of individuals involved: perpetrators and victims (e.g. Ireland and Archer, 1996; Power *et al.*, 1997). This tendency was influenced by school-based research. However, whereas school-based research then progressed to the use of peer-nomination techniques (e.g. Thunfors and Cornell, 2008) to include 'leader bullies', 'reinforcer bullies', 'assistant bullies', 'victims', 'defenders' and 'outsiders', prison-based researchers were unable to do this since such classification systems were based on a peer-nomination approach. Such methods are not viable in prisons on two counts: first, because prisoners would be unlikely to name their peers as doing so would be considered 'grassing' (informing); and second, peer-groups in prisons are larger and more fluid than those in schools, with prison wings holding over 100 prisoners in many instances. Thus prison research has focused on systems whereby prisoners report what behaviours they have engaged in and this is then used by the research to classify them into one of four groups – 'pure bullies', 'pure victims', 'bully/victims' and 'not-involved' (Ireland, 1999).

Although these groupings are arguably crude, they have proven to be reliable with regards to the proportions of prisoners being classified into each group, regardless of the time period of interest (i.e. exploring behaviours occurring over the past week or the past month). 'Bully/victims' (prisoners reporting both perpetration and victim behaviours simultaneously) have been found to represent the most commonly occurring group, with proportions around 40–45 per cent depending on the specific study. On the other hand, 'pure bullies' (sole perpetrators) represent the least reported, with proportions around 15 per cent. The proportion of prisoners being classified into these groups has remained remarkably consistent within populations, holding for men, women, adults, young offenders and juveniles. The classification system has also been of value in identifying the characteristics likely to be associated with each group, with behavioural characteristics identified to be the most reliable and significant predictors of group membership (e.g. Ireland, 1999). Behavioural characteristics are identified as fluid individual differences which are specific to an individual's presentation within a prison.

Three groups of behaviours have been explored – negative behaviours (e.g. disciplinary infractions; engagement in aggression towards staff, etc.), drug-related behaviours (e.g. buying, selling and using illicit substances) and positive/proactive behaviours towards others (e.g. making new friends on the unit; helping others) (Ireland and Monaghan, 2006). Of these behaviours, the most reliable and consistent finding has been reported in relation to the bully/victim group, with this group most likely to be predicted by increased demonstrations of negative behaviours towards others. This finding has held across populations, and their increased use of negative behaviour in comparison to the other groups has been described as a functional behaviour in that it may serve to:

- *Function 1* – ensure that they are monitored more closely by staff.
- *Function 2* – increase the chances that they may be removed from the unit and segregated, moved to another unit or transferred out of the prison.
- *Function 3* – ensure that their reputation among peers remains intact and that they are not viewed as submissive or weak prisoners.

Displaying negative behaviour, therefore, is a functional response to being bullied by peers in that it is a face-saving way of ensuring that future opportunities for them to be bullied are reduced, either as a result of staff observing them more closely as they are labelled as 'unpredictable' or 'disruptive' (Function 1); by ensuring their removal from the environment in which they are placed, affording respite (Function 2); or by increasing or maintaining a reputation for non-submission (Function 3). This leads into the notion that disruptive and aggressive behaviour may be adaptive in certain situations, accounting for the environment in which it occurs. Such a notion is consistent with information-processing models and specifically those which have attempted to apply to secure settings (Ireland, 2008; Ireland and Murray, 2005) and those which have extended this to how fear can motivate prisoners to behave in specific ways (e.g. the applied fear response model; Ireland, 2005).

Both models outline how aspects of the social and physical environment affect the behaviour of prisoners when presented with a difficult/conflict-provoking situation such as bullying. They also each argue for the importance of recognising that aggression can be adaptive in prisons, and should not be considered automatically as an example of an unskilled behaviour. Indeed, these models argue for the instrumental function of negative behaviour in this instance, considering the functions that they serve as either positively or negatively reinforcing. The importance of recognising the 'bully/victim' group, however, has been noted on several occasions in the literature, particularly when consideration becomes focused on the appropriate intervention with this group. Treating them as 'either' a victim or a perpetrator group will not address their needs. It is also worth noting at this point that, although there has been some recognition of mutuality between perpetrators and victims in the school bullying literature (e.g. Craig, 1998), it is not an area that has been accounted for routinely in other fields of aggression research, where the focus has been on the *exclusivity* of victimisation and perpetration. Within the workplace bullying field (e.g. Jennifer *et al.*, 2003) and in the general offence-focused literature, attention has been on the development *from* victimisation (in childhood) to the later perpetration of violent offending, sometimes referred to as the 'cycle of offending' or intergenerational transmission of violence (Falshaw *et al.*, 1996). Instead, the issue of mutuality with victims and perpetrators appears to have been a stronger focus within the prison bullying literature (Ireland and Ireland, 2008).

More recent advances in this area, however, have begun to consider the role of frequency of behaviours within these groups to explore whether it will help identify differences within the groups. All of the four groups of interest – pure bullies, pure victims, bully/victims and those not involved – have largely been treated as if they are homogenous groups, when this may not be the case (Ireland and Ireland, 2008). Until the further development of behavioural methods applied to measure bullying behaviour it was not possible to explore this further. However, the development of the DIPC-SCALED allowed researchers to account for both the presence of bullying behaviours and for their frequency.

In a recent application of this method, Ireland and Ireland (2008), using the DIPC-SCALED, classified a sample of 605 adult prisoners (487 men and 118 women) into groups using three methods which allowed for median-split and intense groups to be identified:

• *The traditional method* of separating participants into one of four groups: pure bullies, pure victims, bully/victims and not-involved, with classification into each category determined on the basis of the DIPC-SCALED results. Those reporting at least one perpetration item and no victim items were classified as 'pure bullies'; those with at least one victim item and no perpetrator items as 'pure victims'; those reporting at least one perpetrator and one victim item were classified as 'bully/victims' and those reporting no perpetrator or victim items were classified as 'not-involved'.

• *The median-split analysis method*, where the sample was separated into five groups. Those scoring above the median on perpetration items were coded as 'above median bullies'; those scoring above the median on victimisation items as 'above median victims'; and those above the median on perpetration *and* victimisation as 'above median bully/victims'. Those reporting either no perpetration or victimisation *or* whose frequency of behaviours was either at or below the median were classified as 'low frequency-causal involvement'.

• *The intensity frequency method*, whereby, based on the frequency of involvement in perpetration or victimisation, three further groups were identified: intense victims, intense bullies and intense bully/victims. These groups were calculated using the mean for victimisation and perpetrator items on the DIPC-SCALED. Prisoners scoring 1 SD (standard deviation) above the mean on perpetration were coded intense bullies; those 1 SD above the mean on victimisation as intense victims; and those above 1 SD above the mean on victimisation and perpetration as intense bully/victims.

Table 7.1 presents the classification on the basis of the traditional (dichotomous) method and the median-split method, including the overlap between the two groups using contingency coefficients and Cramer's V. With regard to intense groups, one fifth of the sample could be classified into one of the intense groups. These are illustrated in Table 7.1. Gender differences were not found across any of the methods of group classification.

What Ireland and Ireland (2008) demonstrated was a significant overlap between the traditional and median-split methods for all four groups, with contingency coefficients indicating that the groups look similar regardless of the type of method used to classify them. Thus, although adopting a frequency approach to classifying the groups may be of interest, it does not appear to be superior to a traditional dichotomous approach. It was acknowledged, however, that the overlap could be a result of a high proportion but comparatively *low frequency* of aggressive behaviours reported (Ireland and Ireland, 2008). However, the potential value of adopting a frequency approach to classification, particularly for populations with prevalent aggression, lies in its capacity to allow for more sophisticated statistical procedures designed for metric data. Further, regardless of whether a traditional dichotomous or a median-split classification method was adopted, the mutual perpetrator–victim (bully/victim) group remained the most prevalent, highlighting further the importance of recognising that aggression and victimisation can co-exist *within* an individual's presentation. This simultaneous and non-exclusive nature of prison aggression and victimisation (Ireland and Ireland, 2008) is not a concept routinely recognised in wider aggression research (e.g. Falshaw *et al.*, 1996; Jennifer *et al.*, 2003).

Table 7.1 *Membership of different groups across the sample (*n = 605) *using the dichotomous and frequency methods*

Group			
Traditional (dichotomous) method			
Pure bully % (*n*)	Pure victim % (*n*)	Bully/victim % (*n*)	Not-involved % (*n*)
6.1 (37)[a]	20.2 (122)	60.8 (368)	12.9 (78)
Median-split (frequency) method			
Above median bully % (*n*)	Above median victim % (*n*)	Above median bully/victim % (*n*)	Casual/low frequency [b] % (*n*)
14.7 (89)[a]	12.4 (75)	32.1 (194)	40.8 (247)
Intense groups (frequency) method using median split			
Intense bully % (*n*)	Intense victim % (*n*)	Intense bully/victim % (*n*)	
6 (36)	10 (60)	2 (12)	
Contingency coefficients for each group [Cramer's V]			
0.20**	0.46**	0.48**	0.42**
[0.20]	[0.52]	[0.55]	[0.46]

Note: Table first appeared in Ireland and Ireland (2008).
[a] The 'pure bully' and 'pure victim' groups are smaller than the 'above median bully' and 'above median victim' group because a proportion of 'bully/victims' were reclassified as 'above median bully' following the median-split analysis.
[b] Including those reporting no perpetration/victimisation behaviours.
** $P < 0.001$.

Thus, with regard to the rates and measurement of prison bullying the field to date has pointed to remarkable similarity both across and within samples (i.e. men, women, young offenders, juveniles) and across methods of group classification (Ireland and Ireland, 2008). Also indicated is the importance of accounting for both indirect and direct aggression, with the former reported to the same extent, if not more frequently, than direct aggression (Ireland, 2002; Ireland and Ireland, 2008). The similarities across samples, and the preference for indirect aggression in some instances, points beyond individual differences as an explanation for prison bullying. This, coupled with an absence of reliable demographic differences across the bully and victim groups (with age, gender, sentence length and offence type, to name but a few, failing to distinguish between groups; Ireland, 2002, 2005), arguably points to another, more overarching factor that may be having a significant influence on how bullying presents within prisons, and on how individuals come to be categorised as pure bullies, pure victims, bully/victims or those not involved. For a number of years, this factor has been thought to be the social and physical environment of a prison (Ireland, 2002, 2005), with the environment thought to both promote bullying between prisoners and to dictate to a certain extent how it may present. This will be explored in the next section.

The role of the environment and the underpinning value of theory

This topic has already been touched upon in the previous section, with reference both to the applied information processing model and the applied fear response model. One of the main criticisms of the prison bullying field, and indeed a criticism of early school-based research, was the absence of theory. This was undoubtedly a result of an early focus on describing the nature and extent of bullying behaviour within prisons, a descriptive tendency which is not unusual to new populations under study. A recognition of the existence of 'bully/victims' was a driving force behind developing inclusion of theory where researchers were interested in trying to explain *what* was driving the behaviour of this group and their apparent responses to victimisation. Of the theoretical models that have been developed, there are perhaps six which have been either applied to or developed for the area of prison bullying over the past decade. These are described in the following sections.

Effect–danger ratio theory

The effect–danger ratio theory (Björkqvist, 1994) argues that aggressors will choose an aggressive strategy based on an evaluation of the effect of their aggression and the associated personal danger. Thus the most preferred strategy for a perpetrator is one involving a high cost for a victim, coupled with a low cost for the perpetrator. This theory has been used to explain why indirect bullying has been consistently shown to be at least as prevalent as direct bullying, if not more so, among prisoners (e.g. Ireland, 1999, 2005). The theory essentially argues that indirect bullying carries a high cost for the victim in terms of negative impact, but has a low cost for the bully in terms of detection by staff and/or retribution by other prisoners. This is due to the subtle nature of indirect bullying, which ensures it is either not detected, or is not considered to be aggression by those being made aware of the behaviour, and thus not responded to (Ireland, 2005).

Developmental theories of aggression development

Developmental theories are closely tied to the previous point, and are a further explanation of the trajectory of aggression use across an individual's lifespan. Essentially, such theories consider the use of indirect aggression to be a result of developmental change, whereby adults and older adolescents will use indirect aggression to supplement an existing repertoire of (direct) aggression (e.g. Björkqvist, 1994; Björkqvist *et al.*, 1992). Since prison populations deal primarily with older adolescents and adults (where developmentally you would expect an increased use of indirect aggression anyway), this is used to further explain why indirect forms of aggression should therefore be more expected within prisons (Ireland, 1999).

Interactional model of prison bullying

The interactional model of prison bullying (MIP; Ireland, 2005) was the first theoretical model designed to explain the development and maintenance of prison bullying. It aimed to demonstrate how bullying was not solely a product of individual prisoner characteristics, but rather was also a result of the social and physical environment of a prison serving to interact with individual characteristics (such as low levels of empathy and enhanced experience with prison culture) to promote bullying.

Social environmental elements within this model considered to promote bullying included: the inmate culture; attitudes supportive or dismissive of bullying; and the existence of hierarchy which supported the value of dominance and power over submissive behaviours such as being victimised. Physical environmental aspects included limitations on the availability of material goods, which promote a culture of competitiveness; overt measures of security, which serve to promote hostility; and the predictability of staff supervision, which makes opportunities for bullying more likely. This model de-emphasises individual pathology models, arguing against the notion that prisoners bully solely as a product of the individual characteristics that they possess, favouring instead the role of the environment (Ireland, 2002, 2005).

Applied fear response model

The applied fear response model (AFRM; Ireland, 2003, 2005) focuses on understanding victim responses in the context of classic fear responses, specifically outlining avoidance, aggression and self-injurious behaviour in the context of fight and flight responses. It was developed further in 2005 to incorporate the more classic literature relating to fear of crime (e.g. Ferraro, 1996), and more recent work exploring fear and prison victimisation (e.g. Edgar *et al.*, 2003). It argues both for the value of the concept of fear in explaining victim reactions and for the existence of a 'delayed flight response'. Such a response is considered highly relevant to a setting where, by virtue of their incarceration, victims are afforded little immediate opportunity to escape (flight). Thus some flight responses (which could include aggression towards others and self-injurious behaviour, since both would lead to later removal from a unit and placement into a segregation unit or health-care centre, respectively) are delayed. The model therefore argues against viewing an aggressive response from a victim as a pure fight response.

Applied information processing model

The applied information processing model (AIPM; Ireland and Murray, 2005) builds on classic information-processing models, primarily the integrated model of Huesmann (1998), which considers aggression to be driven by an individual's interpretation of events, coupled with their existing aggressive beliefs, cognitions and ability to manage emotions effectively. The applied model simply illustrates how this may be presented in a prison setting, accounting for bullying representing an adaptive behaviour in prisons and indicative of well-refined social problem-solving skills. The latter is not a widely accepted view and is inconsistent with models built on the notion that bullying is maladaptive and therefore those that display it must present with deficits in specific skills (Ireland, 2005). Within prisons, however, it is argued that displaying what is classically considered 'poor problem solving', namely aggression towards self or others, may actually represent adaptive coping. This is due to such behaviour being likely to produce a desired outcome (e.g. removal from a unit where a prisoner is being bullied). In essence, the applied information processing model accounts for the adaptive, non-deficit, qualities of what have been traditionally considered manifestations of poor problem solving.

Biological, psychological and ecological interactional

The biological, psychological and ecological model (Gilbert, 2005) has some similarities in principle with the aforementioned interactional model of prison bullying (IMP), although it extends both the environmental and individual factors, accounting also for the value of evolutionary theory. One of the core tenets of this model is its attempt to de-psychopathologise bullying behaviour by outlining it as a behaviour with functional elements that have been repeated throughout history. It includes a role for biological factors (e.g. genes, hormones, neurochemistry and immunity), and calls for attention to what inhibits and what promotes prosocial behaviour, with the latter an area often neglected in bullying research. It outlines the clear evolutionary advantage that bullying may allow for, accounting for the biological predispositions that some individuals may have to engage in aggression. Arguably such predispositions are most likely to be found in those with a history of aggression (e.g. prisoners detained for violent offences). The model applies particularly well to prison settings, where the environment fosters a culture of competition, limited material goods and raised threat. Evolutionary advantages are therefore raised, with those biologically predisposed to aggression most likely to use this to meet their needs and essentially to 'survive', i.e. 'survival of the fittest'.

Although the development of theory is essential to the development of research, it is perhaps true to say that prison bullying research remains in its infancy with regard to detailed testing of these theoretical models. Research has focused perhaps most significantly on the first four theoretical models presented here, although this still remains relatively limited with reference to the applied fear response model. The theory has, however, proven of value in assisting with the development of intervention and management strategies focused on the reduction of bullying behaviours within prisons. Such strategies are now able to take advantage of an increasing literature base outside of schools. The final section of this chapter will attempt to summarise a selection of the core recommendations which can be made to assist the development of empirically driven 'anti-bullying' strategies.

Developing empirically driven intervention and management strategies

Significant contributions to recommendations for intervention and management can be collapsed into five broad areas: (1) recognition of the nature and extent of bullying, particularly the need to include indirect aggression as a target for reduction and the recognition of a lack of differences between men and women prisoners (Ireland, 2002, 2005); (2) the importance of not psychopathologising bullying and instead considering it a behaviour largely driven by the environment (and hence where interventions should be focused) and not the individual (Ireland, 2007); (3) the value in exploring what promotes non-aggression and focusing on the value of a 'community' approach to managing bullying behaviour (Ireland, 2007); (4) recognition that the aim of any intervention programme should be to reduce bullying to a minimum and not eradicate it completely since the latter is an unachievable goal (Ireland, 2007); and (5) recognising that bullying may represent an adaptive behaviour within prisons which is not necessarily indicative of a skills deficit (Ireland and Murray, 2005).

Importantly, what the research has indicated over the past decade is the likely problems associated with trying to ascertain individual 'risk factors' associated with bullying. Such an approach is inconsistent with more holistic views which account for the role of the environment and which seek to avoid a focus on creating 'typologies' of perpetrators and victims. Such typologies do little to drive effective intervention programmes, since they promote a use of labelling and fail to account for the dynamic nature of the different groups involved in bullying. Rather, what has been suggested as core valuable principles for the effective management of prison bullying is a focus on environmental changes (see Ireland, 2002, 2007).

Focusing on promoting cultural change

Working towards changing the social ecology that is accepting of bullying is a useful starting point for prison intervention (Gilbert, 2005). This can include raising awareness of the nature and extent of bullying and promoting a sense of 'community' through the development and ownership of community principles and community-focused activities (Ireland, 2007). Bullying is a product of the peer-group and not a behaviour that occurs in isolation. Change therefore needs to account for the entire peer-group, including those not involved in bullying, and to attend to the involvement of both prisoners and staff. Culture change is undoubtedly a significant element to attempt to change and will take a considerable amount of time and input to progress, but this is not to say it should not be focused on. Both research and theory have focused on the importance of the social environment in promoting and maintaining bullying, of which culture forms an important part (Edgar et al., 2003; Ireland, 1999). Ultimately the main change that is aimed for is an increase in the social retribution for those engaging in bullying behaviour. If the social retribution is raised among the wider peer-group, then bullying should be expected to decrease since the cost for those bullying becomes higher, producing an increased cost to the victim and an increased cost to the bully (e.g. a clear application of the 'effect–danger ratio' theory; Björkqvist, 1994).

Managing the importance of currency

As noted earlier, currency is an important aspect of the physical environment, with limits on material goods promoting competition. Competition in turn promotes bullying as a 'solution' to the deprivation perceived in material allowances (Gilbert, 2005; Ireland, 2002, 2005). Although strategies are in place to monitor material goods in prisons, there is a need to continually revise strategies in accordance with the type of goods featuring as significant currency. Again, as before, the focus here is on raising the cost of bullying for the perpetrator so that the cost outweighs the potential gains (e.g. raising the penalties for being caught bullying others; for example, disallowing prisoners anything above standard socialisation periods with their peers, removing goods from them and/or adding days to sentences).

Supervision style

Predictably, staff supervision is identified as an important factor both in promoting bullying and in determining victim responses (Ireland, 2005), with opportunities for bullying increasing as the more predictable supervision becomes. Prisons operate with clear regimes, where supervision patterns are largely predictable. The recommendations from research focus on the value of trying to reduce the predictability of supervision and in driving a focus away from the amount of supervision since this may not prove the key area of importance. Put simply, if prisoners are less able to identify periods of time when they are most able to bully others without fear of detection by staff, then this reduces the risk for bullying by raising the risk for detection and subsequent retribution. The notion of unpredictable supervision fits well with the 'effect–danger ratio' theory, which predicts that raised danger (e.g. the risk of being caught) serves to discourage perpetration by reducing the likely impact on victims and increasing the risk of punishment for perpetrators.

What the research and theory has also been valuable in recommending has been approaches that should be avoided if an intervention programme is to be considered a success.

Avoiding school-based approaches Avoidance of adopting school-based approaches, primarily on the basis that school and prison environments are quantifiably different and focus on populations at different developmental stages with regard to aggression use (i.e. children versus older adolescents/adults). The development of prison-based research over the past decade ensures that there is no longer a need to focus on a different research base to design prison-based intervention programmes.

Avoiding a focus on two 'groups' – bullies and victims Such an approach fails to account for the importance of the wider peer-group and also the mutual group – bully/victims. A focus on 'groups' involved in bullying is also a product of typology-driven approaches to understanding aggression, which, as noted earlier, do not have theoretical advantage over more holistic environmental understandings. Similarly, concerns here extend to any suggestion of developing 'bully' or 'victim' intervention programmes. Such programmes will undoubtedly not succeed owing to their failure to account for the wider environmental influences; the problems in being assured that you can clearly define an individual as a 'bully' or a 'victim' once you account for mutuality across these groups; and a risk that any such individual 'victim' or 'bully' groups will become quickly labelled – usually in a negative fashion (e.g. it is not unusual for 'victim' intervention groups to be given a negative label such as a 'muppet' or 'herbert' group; Ireland, 2002).

Avoiding punishment-orientated approaches Although such approaches are rarely marketed as 'punishment', they undoubtedly fit the principles of this. Examples include the use of 'anti-bullying' units or wings, where reported perpetrators are placed in order to have their behaviour 'corrected' before returning to a standard wing or unit (Ireland, 2007). They also include the use of 'stage systems', where perpetrators have privileges removed from them each time they are known to have bullied. Here, the number of privileges are removed in accordance with the number of times an individual is reported, with each report and its corresponding action leading to another 'stage' being instigated. The final stage in such systems tends to be the removal of perpetrators from the prison to another prison (Ireland, 2002). What is not attended to by these interventions, however, is the function of the bullying behaviour or the environment in which the bullying is taking place.

For example, with 'anti-bullying' units, although there are claims for 'treatment', the perpetrator is essentially returned to the original environment in which the bullying first occurred. How can any behaviour change be expected to be sustained if the environment driving the behaviour has not been amended in any way (Ireland, 2007)? It is also not possible to be assured that the 'perpetrators' based in these units are not in fact mutual victims. 'Treating' victims in this way simply reinforces their use of aggression as an effective method of placing them in another unit, away from their perpetrator(s), where they will be watched more closely by staff (and hence the opportunities to be bullied by others will consequently be reduced).

These approaches, although marketed as rehabilitation, are in fact punishment-orientated approaches. It is perhaps valuable to note here the problem in trying to use punishment as a method of behaviour change, particularly in relation to bullying. First, in order for punishment to be 'effective', it must be inevitable, immediate and severe, and include alternative options to the negative behaviour, with the link between the negative behaviour and the punishment understood by the perpetrator (McGuire and Priestly, 2000). Thus, in order to be effective in managing bullying, the approach needs to respond to each and every occasion of bullying; to occur immediately after the bullying; to match the severity of the bullying; and to provide bullies with an attractive alternative to using aggression. Such conditions, most notably the first three, cannot be met (see Ireland, 2007).

Conclusion

The current chapter has attempted to bring together the core developments that have occurred in the field of prison bullying research in the last decade and show how these have influenced research direction and intervention. The research has grown significantly across the last 10 years, with a clear move away from focusing on the nature and extent of bullying to exploring more detailed areas likely to contribute to the advancement of the research field. Research into prison bullying remains, however, in its infancy; considerable work is still required and there is a significant need for a wider group of researchers to become involved in studying and publishing in this important area. The three core areas which would prove particularly valuable as topics to research include: more focused testing of the theories proposed; studies focusing on the evaluation of prison-based anti-bullying interventions; and longitudinal research exploring the changes in bullying behaviours and group involvement across time. The research field is now in a position where these areas can be addressed, with refinements in measurement and definition at a stage where more informed studies can be conducted with an overall focus on *furthering* this area of study in a way that will assist with meaningful changes being made to intervention and management programmes.

REFERENCES

Björkqvist, K. (1994). 'Sex differences in physical, verbal, and indirect aggression: a review of recent research'. *Sex Roles*, 30: 177–88.
Björkqvist, K., Österman, K. and Kaukiainen, A. (1992). 'The development of direct and indirect aggressive strategies in males and females'. In K. Björkqvist and P. Niemela (eds.), *Of Mice and Women: Aspects of Female Aggression* (pp. 51–64). San Diego, CA: Academic Press.

Blitz, C.L, Wolff, N. and Shi, J. (2008). 'Physical victimisation in prison: the role of mental illness'. *International Journal of Law and Psychiatry*, 3: 385–93.

Connell, A. and Farrington, D. (1996). 'Bullying amongst incarcerated young prisoners: developing an interview schedule and some preliminary results'. *Journal of Adolescence*, 19: 75–93.

Craig, W. (1998). 'The relationship among bullying, victimization, depression, anxiety and aggression in elementary school children'. *Personality and Individual Differences*, 24: 123–30.

Edgar, K., O'Donnell. I. and Martin, C. (2003). *Prison Violence: The Dynamics of Conflict, Fear and Power*. Hove: Willan Publishing.

Esquash, M. (2008). Personal communication. Canadian Correctional Service.

Falshaw, L. (1993). 'Why me? Can incarcerated young offenders be identified as potential victims of bullying by their behaviour within the penal environment?' Unpublished BSc thesis, Aston University.

Falshaw, L., Browne, K.D. and Hollin, C. (1996). 'Victim to offender: a review'. *Aggression and Violent Behavior: A Review Journal*, 4: 389–404.

Ferraro, K.F. (1996). 'Women's fear of victimisation: shadow of sexual assault?' *Social Forces*, 75: 667–90.

Gilbert, P. (2005). 'Bullying in prisons: an evolutionary and biopsychosocial approach'. In J.L. Ireland (ed.), *Bullying among Prisoners: Innovations in Theory and Research* (pp. 188–223). Hove: Willan Publishing.

Huesmann, L.R. (1998). 'The role of social information processing and cognitive schema in the acquisition and maintenance of habitual aggressive behavior'. In R.G. Geen and E. Donnerstein (eds.), *Human Aggression: Theories, Research, and Implications for Social Policy* (pp. 73–109). New York: Academic Press.

Ireland, J.L. (1999). 'Bullying behaviours amongst male and female prisoners: a study of young offenders and adults'. *Aggressive Behavior*, 25: 162–78.

—— (2002). *Bullying among Prisoners: Evidence, Research and Intervention Strategies*. London: Brunner-Routledge.

—— (2003). *Bullying among Prisoners: The Role of Fear in the Psychology of Fear*. New York: Nova Science Publishers.

—— (2005). 'Bullying among prisoners: the need for innovation'. In J.L. Ireland (ed.), *Bullying among Prisoners: Innovations in Theory and Research* (pp. 3–26). Hove: Willan Publishing.

—— (2007). 'The effective management of bullying among prisoners: working towards an evidence-based approach'. In G. Towl (ed.), *Psychological Research in Prisons* (pp. 95–115). Oxford: BPS Blackwell.

—— (2008). 'Therapeutic assessment issues to consider with violent offenders'. In J.L. Ireland, C.A. Ireland and P. Birch (eds.), *Violent and Sexual Offenders: Assessment, Intervention and Management Strategies* (pp. 153–178). Hove: Willan Publishing.

Ireland, J.L. and Archer, J. (1996). 'Descriptive analysis of bullying in male and female adult prisoners'. *Journal of Community and Applied Social Psychology*, 6: 35–47.

Ireland, J.L. and Ireland, C.A. (2003). 'How do offenders define bullying? A study of adult, young and juvenile male offenders'. *Legal and Criminological Psychology*, 8: 159–73.

(2008). 'Intra-group aggression among prisoners: bullying intensity and exploration of victim–perpetrator mutuality'. *Aggressive Behavior*, 34: 76–87.

Ireland, J.L. and Monaghan, R. (2006). 'Behaviours indicative of bullying among young and juvenile male offenders: a study of perpetrator and victim characteristics'. *Aggressive Behavior*, 32: 172–80.

Ireland, J.L. and Murray, E. (2005). 'Social problem-solving and bullying: are prison bullies really impaired problem solvers?' In J.L. Ireland (ed.), *Bullying among Prisoners: Innovations in Theory and Research* (pp. 150–75). Hove: Willan Publishing.

Ireland, J.L. and Qualter, P. (2008). 'Bullying and social and emotional loneliness in a sample of adult male prisoners'. *International Journal of Law and Psychiatry*, 31: 19–29.

Jennifer, D., Cowie, H. and Ananiadou, K. (2003). 'Perceptions and experience of workplace bullying in five different working populations'. *Aggression and Violent Behavior: A Review Journal*, 29: 489–96.

Livingston, M., Jones, V. and Hussain, S. (1994). 'The extent of bullying amongst adult prisoners at HMP/YOI Moorland'. Unpublished Psychology Research Report, 20.

McGuire, J. and Priestly, P. (2000). 'Reviewing what works: past, present and future'. In J. McGuire (ed.), *What Works: Reducing Reoffending – Guidelines from Research and Practice*. London: Wiley.

Olweus, D. (1978). *Aggression in Schools: Bullies and Whipping Boys*. Washington, DC: Hemisphere Press.

Power, K.G., Dyson, G.P. and Wozniak, E. (1997). 'Bullying among Scottish young offenders: prisoners' self-reported attitudes and behaviour'. *Journal of Community and Applied Social Psychology*, 7: 209–18.

Thunfors, P. and Cornell, D. (2008). 'The popularity of middle school bullies'. *Journal of School Violence*, 7: 65–82.

8   Bullying in the workplace

Iain Coyne

For those interested in workplace bullying, it is difficult to conceive that attention and systematic investigation into this topic is relatively recent. However, before the late 1980s, research tended to be anecdotal and awareness was minimal. Since then, interest in the topic has increased rapidly. From an initial focus in Scandinavia (e.g. Björkqvist *et al.*, 1994; Leymann, 1996), workplace bullying is studied globally, in Africa (Marais-Steinman, 2003), Asia (Seo and Leather, 2008), Australia (e.g. Djurkovic *et al.*, 2005), Europe (e.g. Hoel *et al.*, 2001; Nielsen *et al.*, 2009), North America (e.g. Ferris, 2004; Lutgen-Sandvik *et al.*, 2007) and South America (De Souza and De Souza, 2008).

As well as advancing a global perspective on bullying, research techniques and methodologies have also become more varied. Understandably dominated early on by large-scale prevalence surveys, increasing use of different quantitative and qualitative approaches has methodologies showing an ensured more systematic research that has rapidly changed our understanding of this complex phenomenon. Although no one can claim to have solved the problem, researchers, practitioners and other stakeholders are becoming increasingly aware of what workplace bullying is and how it can be managed.

This chapter aims to provide readers with an outline and discussion of the research and practice relating to workplace bullying as it currently stands. The intention is to discuss the advances made in theory and practice, highlight areas for future development and consider the development/evaluation of interventions to reduce workplace bullying.

Conceptualising workplace bullying

A number of different labels have been used to conceptualise bullying at work, with the term 'bullying' itself being widely used within the UK. 'Mobbing' has been the preferred label in some Nordic and German-speaking countries (Zapf and Einarsen, 2001), whilst in the USA, similar constructs include 'workplace harassment' (Brodsky, 1976), 'abusive supervision' (Tepper, 2000), 'victimisation' (Aquino and Bradfield, 2000), 'emotional abuse' (Keashly and Harvey, 2005), 'workplace incivility' (Pearson *et al.*, 2005) and 'social undermining' (Crossley, 2009). Although variations in definitions occur, in practice 'mobbing' and 'bullying' have tended to be used interchangeably, and as our recognition of the nature of bullying advances we may find that constructs become more refined. Pearson *et al.* (2005) distinguish 'incivility' as low intensity, 'bullying' as low to moderate intensity and 'mobbing' as moderate to high intensity deviant behaviour. Lutgen-Sandvik *et al.* (2007) propose a three-level hierarchical model to encapsulate negative workplace behaviours. The superordinate level includes overarching concepts (e.g. aggression, counterproductive behaviour, deviance) and underneath this an intermediate level including more general (bullying, emotional abuse, mobbing) or specific (sexual harassment) forms of abuse. The final, subordinate level denotes forms of intermediate act (e.g. victimisation, verbal abuse, incivility). They argue that higher-level behaviours subsume those below and highlight that bullying (intermediate) includes acts of incivility or victimisation (subordinate) but is itself a form of aggression (superordinate). The usefulness of this approach is that academics and practitioners can consider bullying from a broader perspective of counterproductive behaviour and develop an understanding of why such behaviour emerges in the organisation and ways to control it (which may also control levels of bullying); or they can focus more directly on examining and controlling bullying, which may have a positive influence on other higher-level behaviours.

With the above discussion in mind, the rest of the chapter will use the term 'bullying', although it will include research on mobbing, victimisation, etc. Whilst there is no one agreed definition of workplace bullying, some agreement of a definition is important from an academic (obtaining a clearer notion of the concept being investigated), a practitioner/organisation (knowing what the behaviour is and what support is needed), a worker (knowing if you are being bullied or not) and a legal (when cases go to tribunals) perspective.

Initially, researchers suggested bullying should involve frequency and duration, the victim's perception of being harassed, negative outcomes for the individual and a power imbalance (e.g. Keashly and Harvey, 2005; Zapf and Einarsen, 2001). Yet these criteria have tended to be 'measured' from an individual's perspective and this element of subjectivity in defining bullying will always present challenges to researchers and practitioners, as what may be seen as bullying by one person may not be perceived in the same manner by another. In an attempt to achieve consensus, Einarsen *et al.* (2003, p. 15) offer a definition of bullying:

Bullying at work means harassing, offending, socially excluding someone or negatively affecting someone's work tasks. In order for the label bullying (or mobbing) to be applied to a particular activity, interaction or process it has to occur repeatedly and regularly (e.g. weekly) and over a period of time (e.g. about six months). Bullying is an escalating process in the course of which the person confronted ends up in an inferior position and becomes the target of systematic negative social acts. A conflict cannot be called bullying if the incident is an isolated event or if two parties of approximately equal 'strength' are in conflict.

Rayner and Cooper (2006) question the notion of persistency, arguing that it could provide a perpetrator with a rationale for undertaking a one-off negative act and that it deters investigations into one-off events. Additionally, as organisational harassment policies tend to ask the target to note down cases and examples of behaviour over time, there is an ethical question of allowing negative behaviour to occur until one can deem it to be bullying.

Saunders *et al.* (2007) contend that researcher and legal definitions of bullying are similar to each other, but differ from practitioner definitions. The former involve negative effects, frequency, persistence, self-labelling and power imbalance; whilst the latter are more generally worded and emphasise types of behaviour and negative outcomes. They go so far as to suggest that negative behaviours and perceptions of harm are the only essential defining features of bullying. In a study of individual definitions of workplace bullying from 1,095 adults across Australia, Canada, the USA and the UK, negative acts, harmful effects, power imbalance and persistence were identified within the definitions provided. Two additional components of violation of expected treatment and deliberate and intentional behaviour also emerged.

These findings imply that target/user definitions will differ from standard academic definitions in some of the key features inherent within the behaviour. To some extent, practitioner definitions have already moderated aspects within academic definitions, even removing the imbalance of power component (Rayner and Cooper, 2006). Establishing stakeholder definitions has obvious positives for those attempting to prevent bullying behaviour within organisations, but it causes problems from an academic and legal perspective. Perhaps in the future some of these practitioner/target developed definitions will start to feed into academic research and legal case work.

Taxonomies of behaviour

Initially, Leymann (1996) proposed five categories of mobbing: effects on victim's possibility to communicate adequately; effects on victim's possibility to maintain social contact; effects on victim's possibility to maintain personal reputation; effects on victim's occupational status; and effects on victim's physical health. Zapf *et al.* (1996) proposed seven factors: organisational measures; social isolation; attacking the victim's private life; physical violence; attacking the victim's attitudes; verbal aggression; and rumours. Rayner and Hoel (1997) suggested that bullying is grouped into threat to professional status; threat to personal standing; isolation; overwork; and destabilisation. Re-analysis of the Revised Negative Acts Questionnaire (NAQ-R) produced a three-factor solution of personal bullying (e.g. insults, criticism); work-related bullying (e.g. unreasonable deadlines); and physical intimidation (Einarsen *et al.*, 2009). Overall, workplace bullying has an element of personal abuse (attacking the person directly or indirectly), work-related abuse (overwork and work pressure) and social isolation (ostracism). Physical bullying can also occur in the workplace, but this tends to be not as common as the more psychological forms of bullying.

Reflecting more on how bullying originates than on specific behavioural taxonomies, Einarsen (1999) distinguished broad categories of predatory bullying (where the victim has done nothing provocative to justify the aggression towards him or her) and dispute-related bullying (which develops from grievances and is triggered by work-related conflict). Within these, similar types of behaviour may emerge, although the process of why the bullying occurred in the first place and why that particular individual was targeted is different.

Returning to the notion of target-defined conceptualisations of bullying, Liefooghe and MacKenzie-Davey (2001) identified institutionalised bullying within UK call centre staff. Qualitative analysis of focus groups indicated that employees distinguished between interpersonal and organisational bullying, with the latter being seen as part of organisational systems (e.g. monitoring of call time, performance-related pay), threats from the organisation regarding job security, a fear of speaking up and a lack of negotiation.

The prevalence of workplace bullying

Earlier prevalence studies reported rates of 3.5 per cent in Sweden (Leymann, 1996), 7.8 per cent in Austria (Niedl, 1996), 8.6 per cent in Norway (Einarsen and Skogstad, 1996), 10.1 per cent in Finland (Vartia,

1996) and 53 per cent in the UK (Rayner, 1997). Later examples indicated levels in the UK of 10.6 per cent (Hoel *et al.*, 2001), in the USA of 28 per cent (Lutgen-Sandvik *et al.*, 2007), in Ireland of 6.2 per cent (O'Moore and Lynch, 2007), in Finland of 8.8 per cent (Salin, 2001) and in Denmark of 8 per cent (Mikkelsen and Einarsen, 2002). Some of these rates are high and when one adds in data on the number of people who witness bullying in their workplace (e.g. 29.9 per cent, Ólafsson and Jóhannsdóttir, 2004; 30 per cent, Salin, 2001; 69 per cent, Quine, 2004), it provides a strong cause for concern.

However, methodological problems, including differences in the criteria used to classify individuals as targets or non-targets, have made comparison across countries and studies difficult (Cowie *et al.*, 2002). Further, studies have tended to use either a subjective (self-reported victimisation in relation to a definition) or an operational (exposure to a set of negative workplace behaviours in a set time period) approach to identifying victims of bullying (Mikkelsen and Einarsen, 2001). In the former the individual is judging whether she or he is a victim of bullying or not; whereas the latter tends not to make any reference to bullying. Using these approaches, Nielsen *et al.* (2009) found different rates for subjective (2.0–4.6 per cent) and operational (6.2–14.3 per cent) methods. However, the operational approach does not assess an individual's perception of being bullied and, whilst they may face certain negative acts at work, they may not construe them as bullying – hence this method may overestimate the level. By contrast, self-labelling to a definition could result in under-reporting, as an individual is likely to have an idiosyncratic conceptualisation of what bullying is, which may not match the given definition.

Another criticism is the lack of verification (such as peer-nominations) of bullying incidences (Cowie *et al.*, 2002). The majority of the research has tended to concentrate on the victim's perceptions of bullying without obtaining any information to verify the behaviour or without even obtaining the views of other parties (such as the bully or other employees). Other reports may be difficult to obtain as third parties would need to be guaranteed anonymity (Björkqvist *et al.*, 1994) and, given organisational power and politics, peers are often not in a neutral position. However, Coyne *et al.* (2003), using different criteria based on a definition of self-report, peer-report or a combination of self- and peer-report, found victim rates ranged from 3.9 to 39.6 per cent, whilst perpetrator rates ranged from 2.7 to 19.3 per cent.

Overall, methodological issues have meant that, whilst data is available, there are difficulties in making comparisons over time, across organisations and across countries. Nevertheless, Zapf *et al.* (2003)

suggested that within Europe a rate of 1–4 per cent for serious bullying generally occurs and 20 per cent for occasional exposure to negative acts. Surveys are, and continue to be, an important tool in workplace bullying research. Yet, to counter methodological issues in bullying rates, there is a developing norm to use a combination of self-reporting to a definition and reporting experiences of negative acts. Additionally, some authors have argued that latent class cluster analysis provides a better estimate of victim rates, with victim rates of 6.8 per cent reported (Nielsen *et al.*, 2009).

Risk factors for workplace bullying

Gender

A number of studies have found small (Paice *et al.*, 2004; Tehrani, 2004) and others larger (Quine, 2004; Salin, 2003a; Vaez *et al.*, 2004) effects of gender, with females more likely to be targets than males. By contrast, no differences in victim rates between males and females have been reported (Hogh and Dofradottir, 2001; Vartia and Hytti, 2002), and some research has even found that males are more likely to be exposed to more negative acts than females (Ólafsson and Jóhannsdóttir, 2004; Seo and Leather, 2008).

Males are more often reported as the bullies (Ólafsson and Jóhannsdóttir, 2004), with Zapf *et al.* (2003) suggesting this may be a function of males more often operating in a supervisory role which provides a level of legitimate power. By contrast, Djurkovic *et al.* (2004) found no difference in perpetrator status between males and females. More consistent findings have shown that same-gender bullying is more common than mixed-gender bullying (Einarsen and Skogstad, 1996; Hoel *et al.*, 2001) – although a higher rate for males bullying females (20–30 per cent) than for females bullying males (3–10 per cent) emerges.

In general, there is a mixed picture regarding gender as a risk factor and, whilst there are some consistent patterns in terms of same-gender bullying, research suggests gender is not a simple direct risk factor for exposure to or engagement in workplace bullying. Any gender effects may be an artefact of the samples used, the level of the person in the organisation or even cultural differences in terms of reporting bullying.

Status

As with gender, whilst some research indicates that bullying differs across job levels/grades (Salin, 2001), with those at lower levels facing more bullying, in general job status does not appear to have a substantial effect on victim levels (Aquino and Bradfield, 2000; Quine, 2004). On the other hand, bullies are more often rated as senior to the target of the bullying (Hoel *et al.*, 2001; Quine, 1999), with supervisors, managers and line managers often judged the main perpetrators. This is not universal, with some studies showing peer bullying to be more common than hierarchical bullying (Hogh and Dofradottir, 2001; Ortega *et al.*, 2008b) and no differences across bullying levels (Paice *et al.*, 2004). Akin to the gender issue, there is more support for the notion of status/job level as a risk factor for perpetrator than victim status, although, even here, Zapf *et al.* (2003) suggest this may be a function of cultural values of low power distance and high femininity rather than status *per se*.

Organisational sector

Workplace bullying is not necessarily limited to one sector or one type of organisation. Even though organisational differences have not emerged (e.g. Hoel *et al.*, 2001; Mikkelsen and Einarsen, 2001), other evidence has identified higher rates in industry (Einarsen and Skogstad, 1996), education (Hubert and van Veldhoven, 2001) and the health sectors (Ortega *et al.*, 2008b), with workplace bullying tending to be more prevalent in public sector than private sector organisations (Leymann and Gustaffson, 1996; Salin, 2001). In a large-scale study in France, Niedhammer *et al.* (2008) found an interaction effect with gender, where high-risk sectors for males were services and associated professionals and for females the highest risk was with government-associated professionals.

Given some evidence that the public sector is more at risk, Calvert (2008) proposes three hypotheses as to why this may be the case:

- Greater organisational changes have emerged within the public sector as compared to the private sector, leading to the creation of competitive climates, tighter controls on workers, closer scrutiny as a result of governmental regulation and more pressure on managers to deliver. As Lewis (2004, p. 281) suggests, in relation to UK further and higher education, this market-orientated approach has resulted in such institutions being run according to a more business-focused model and has created 'an environment where bullying has become a synonym for tough managerial styles'.
- Public sector organisations are more likely to have well-developed policies and procedures on workplace bullying, promoting a culture of intolerance of such behaviour and creating processes to deal with and report such acts. Rather than true rates being higher in public sector

organisations, individuals are more likely to report bullying in public sector organisations. Coupled with a stronger union presence, this may create an environment where individuals feel safe in reporting bullying.

- Traditional characteristics of public sector employment (job security, long-term jobs, reduction in job mobility) mean that such workers are less likely to seek employment elsewhere than private sector workers. Rates of bullying may be higher as individuals stay longer in one position and hence continue to be a target. However, this notion seems to contradict that presented in the first point above and it is likely that, with such rapid change in the public sector, this hypothesis can be rejected.

Other risk factors which have been less researched include age (Ortega *et al.*, 2008a) and being bullied at school (Smith *et al.*, 2003), with the suggestion that older workers are more likely to be bullied than younger workers and that a previous history of bullying correlates with workplace bullying. However, demographic risk factors *per se* tend to only show only small effects on levels of workplace bullying and relationships are more likely attributable to a third related factor (e.g. increasing organisational change).

Individual and organisational effects of workplace bullying

Individual psychological and physical effects

Table 8.1 illustrates that victims experience a wide variety of psychological, psychosomatic and physiological effects as a consequence of being bullied at work. Indeed, victims have shown higher levels of post-traumatic stress disorder (PTSD) symptoms and psychiatric distress when compared to war-zone personnel, individuals facing downsizing, recently divorced people and parents of children involved in a bus accident (Matthiesen and Einarsen, 2004). However, victims are not the only group affected, as witnesses of bullying also experience some negative health effects (Hoel *et al.*, 2004; Lutgen-Sandvik *et al.*, 2007), suggesting a ripple effect throughout the organisation.

Nevertheless, a stressor–strain model is too simplistic, as negative affectivity (Djurkovic *et al.*, 2004) and mental toughness (Coyne *et al.*, 2006) may act as mediators, with self-efficacy (Mikkelsen and Einarsen, 2002) and coping style (Keashly and Harvey, 2005) as moderators of the relationship between bullying and health outcomes.

Table 8.1 *Consequences of bullying on targets*

General effects	Specific effects	Example reference
Psychological	Low self-esteem	Zapf *et al.* (1996)
	Stress and strain	Lutgen-Sandvik *et al.* (2007)
	Anxiety	Quine (1999)
	Depression	Agervold and Mikkelsen (2004)
	Fear and health concern	Matthiesen and Einarsen (2001)
	Burnout/fatigue/vitality	Bowling and Beehr (2006)
	Negative emotion	Mikkelsen and Einarsen (2002)
	Irritation	Niedl (1996)
	General mental health	Hoel *et al.* (2004)
Psychosomatic	Physical symptoms	Djurkovic *et al.* (2004); Hoel *et al.* (2004); Bowling and Beehr (2006)
	Psychosomatic	Mikkelsen and Einarsen (2002); Agervold and Mikkelsen (2004)
	Pain	Vaez *et al.* (2004)
Physiological	Chronic disease	Kivimäki *et al.* (2000)
	Cardiovascular problems	Kivimäki *et al.* (2003)
PTSD	PTSD or severe psychiatric distress	Leymann and Gustafsson (1996); Matthiesen and Einarsen (2004); Tehrani (2004)

In trying to account for why bullying relates to severe negative outcomes in victims, Einarsen and Mikkelsen (2003) propose two theoretical models:

- *Cognitive model* – this model suggests that bullying destroys our basic schemas of the world as meaningful and ourselves as decent and deserving individuals. Such schemas relate to our core beliefs, and bullying attacks these positive schemas, starts to dissolve our core self-beliefs (which becomes threatening and stressful) and requires us to develop new schemas. It is this destruction of our view of the world and the ability or not to produce new schemas which results in the severe negative effects of bullying.

- *Social-biological model* – an evolutionary perspective would suggest that individuals have a basic fear of being excluded and ostracised from a group as this may threaten our survival. As bullying is often characterised by exclusion from a work group, this creates anxiety, fear and a feeling of life being threatened, and hence may explain the severe negative effects reported by victims.

Individual coping styles

Victims are more likely to adopt avoidance or resignation coping styles than problem-solving styles when compared to non-victims (Hogh and Dofradottir, 2001; Ólafsson and Jóhannsdóttir, 2004). Such an approach may enhance the negative impact on the victim as the bullying is never resolved and the victim either ignores it or leaves the organisation in order to escape it. Supporting the notion of unresolved conflict, Smith *et al.* (2003) found a higher rate of workplace bullying for those individuals who reported they did not cope with bullying at school (the effect being stronger for females). However, both Niedl (1996) and Zapf and Gross (2001) revealed that victims tended to begin with more constructive coping styles and reverted to more destructive styles as the bullying escalated. Further, Richman *et al.* (2001) found unsuccessful direct/active coping led to a greater risk of alcohol use and abuse in a sample of US university employees. Therefore, whilst ultimately victims tend not to cope well with bullying and in the main end up avoiding the perpetrator, quitting the organisation or suffering long-term negative effects, it appears that initially they do try to focus more on constructive problem solving, which for some reason does not work. It is not simply that victims are poor copers; rather, they have exhausted all other avenues and have nothing left to do except accept the situation or leave the organisation.

Organisational outcomes

Bullying has been shown to relate to negative perceptions of individual or team performance (Coyne *et al.*, 2004), reduced job satisfaction and commitment (Bowling and Beehr, 2006; Lutgen-Sandvik *et al.*, 2007), absenteeism (Agervold and Mikkelsen, 2004; Kivimaki *et al.*, 2000), intention to leave (Djurkovic *et al.*, 2004) and actual turnover (Rayner, 1997). Coupled with other potential costs such as litigation, industrial action, replacement and training costs, as well as the ripple effect which causes reduced morale and motivation in other employees, the impact on organisations can be considerable. As an example, Hoel *et al.* (2003) detail the cost of a bullying case involving a UK local authority. In total, the actual cost to the organisation (e.g. absence, replacement costs and costs of the disciplinary process) was £28,109.

Given this, Rayner and McIvor (2008) suggest that organisations need to present a business case centred on costs to illustrate why interventions aimed at dealing with bullying are required and ultimately are cost-effective. As part of the UK's Dignity at Work project (www.dignityatwork.org), interviews with a range of individuals involved in dealing with bullying identified three costs which can become part of a business case:

- *Direct costs* – sickness absence, disruption costs of someone leaving and replacement costs.
- *Indirect costs* – lowered morale and disruption to productivity affecting an organisation's competitive edge.
- *Reputation damage* – media coverage and standing in the eyes of the profession or the local/national community affecting the ability of an organisation to recruit and retain high quality staff.

Antecedents of workplace bullying

Organisational antecedents

Most of the focus on the antecedents of workplace bullying has tended to consider the impact of organisational factors on promoting or reducing bullying behaviour. Bullying has been shown to be promoted within an organisational climate with little encouragement for personal development, uninteresting and unchallenging work, and little variation (Einarsen et al., 1994); when the working environment is strained and competitive (Vartia, 1996); when organisational changes occur under authoritarian leadership (O'Moore et al., 2003); and when the working conditions and social climate are perceived to be poor (Vartia and Hyyti, 2002).

Hoel and Salin (2003) propose four types of organisational antecedent:

- *Changing nature of work* – conomic globalisation, increased competition, organisational restructuring and downsizing have changed the nature of work and this leads to decreased morale and motivation, a goal-driven focus and a sense by managers that they are justified in using whatever means needed to manage individuals (Sheehan, 1999). For example, Skogstad et al. (2007) found positive relationships between bullying and organisational changes during the previous 12 months. Further, Harvey et al. (2006) suggest that a rapid rate of change, increased diversity of people and values, a lack of correctly trained managers, and cultural differences in acceptance of bullying are conditions within global organisations that may promote bullying.

- *Work organisation* – strained and stressful work environments can create an avenue for interpersonal conflict or frustrations which may result in bullying. In particular, role ambiguity, role conflict, work constraints and low job autonomy have been shown to relate to higher levels of bullying (Hauge *et al.*, 2007). Einarsen (2000) proposes two theoretical models to account for the role of workplace stressors in promoting bullying. First, the revised frustration–aggression hypothesis (Berkowitz, 1989) purports that stress may lead to aggression via a mediating effect of negative emotion. Baillien *et al.* (2009) found bullying often resulted from frustrations in the work environment and the resulting ineffective coping mechanism adopted by the individual experiencing the frustration. In particular, they suggest that an ineffective active coping style resulted in an individual projecting their aggression towards others. The second theory, the Social Interaction Model (Felson and Tedeschi, 1993), proposes that stressful events change the way an individual behaves, which in turn may result in the person violating work norms or expectations and causes them to become the focus of others' annoyance and aggression; a 'passive ineffective coping style' (Baillien *et al.*, 2009).

- *Organisational culture and climate* – an organisational environment conducive to bullying, which is tolerant of such behaviour and in which individuals are socialised into this way of thinking, is likely to see high levels of bullying behaviour. Archer's (1999) research within the fire service shows how bullying behaviours were normalised, seen as tradition and came to be viewed as strong management. O'Moore and Lynch (2007) found Irish bullying victims tended to view the organisational climate as less supportive, more competitive and more hostile than non-victims.

- *Leadership* – poor leadership (especially autocratic leadership and poor management) is one of the most cited reasons by employees for workplace bullying (O'Moore and Lynch, 2007; Woodman and Cook, 2005). Petty tyrannical leadership promotes obedience, de-individualisation of employees, non-contingent punishment and a forcing style of conflict resolution (Ashforth, 1994). As Hoel and Salin (2003) suggest, this may create a climate of fear where individuals are bullied but feel unable to complain or criticise. Conversely, Hauge *et al.* (2007) found a relationship between laissez-faire leadership and bullying, which suggests a leader's inability or unwillingness to deal with bullying in the workplace rather than a predatory, tyrannical approach. Either way, too autocratic a leadership style, the inability/lack of skills to deal with conflict and the lack of willingness to address bullying all appear to promote workplace bullying.

Bringing all these aspects together, Salin (2003b) conceptualised a three-process interactive model of organisational antecedents of workplace bullying. Enabling processes (power imbalances, poor social climate and poor management style/skills) provide the conditions that facilitate bullying. Motivating processes (competitive and politicised work environments and organisational norms that justify bullying) present the individual with a rationale or reward for engaging in bullying; and precipitating processes (organisational change, change in management) provide the trigger mechanism for bullying processes to evolve in the organisation.

Individual disposition of the victim

Individual differences may predispose an individual to be a target of bullying, with research indicating that victims score higher than non-victims in neuroticism (Vartia, 1996), apprehension and sensitivity (O'Moore et al., 1998), depression (Zapf, 1999) and negative affectivity (Aquino and Bradfield, 2000), as well as lower in dominance (O'Moore et al., 1998) and social skills (Zapf, 1999). Victims have also been shown to be lower in extraversion, assertiveness and emotional stability, and higher in conscientiousness than non-victims (Coyne et al., 2000). Glaso et al. (2007) supported the effect of extraversion and stability, but reported their victims scored lower for conscientiousness and agreeableness than non-victims. Further, in relation to incivility, Milam et al. (2009) found higher levels of incivility for individuals low in agreeableness and high in neuroticism. However, both Glaso et al. and Matthiesen and Einarsen (2001) argue that victims are not a homogenous group, as in some cases no differences emerged between victims and non-victims.

The notion of victim characteristics is controversial, as it has been argued that it focuses on blaming the victim for their problems. Further, Leymann (1996) strongly opposed this notion, suggesting changes in personality occur *as a result* of mobbing. However, individual differences may predispose an individual to be a target of bullying. Taking Olweus' (1993) notion of submissive and provocative school victims, researchers (e.g. Aquino et al., 1999; Coyne et al., 2000; Matthiesen and Einarsen, 2001) have suggested:

• Submissive victims may be seen as easy targets because of vulnerabilities in disposition that mean they are either unable to defend themselves, unable to cope or lack a peer support network, which places them in a socially exposed position.

- Provocative victims may provoke aggressive behaviour within another person as a result of envy, being too anxious, being too conscientious and clashing with expected group norms. An individual's disposition will direct the way they respond to conflict, which may in turn result in conflict escalation and ultimately bullying.

Individual disposition provides some evidence for who may be targeted within an organisation where the work environment is conducive to bullying. There is no suggestion that victims are to blame; rather, when bullying is ongoing, personality may provide some explanation as to why certain individuals are targeted and others not. Bullying cannot be solely down to organisational factors, because this does not explain why employees perceive the same environment differently or why some are targeted and others not. Granted, to date, there has not been the long sought-after longitudinal study which helps to answer the directional criticism, although this criticism can also be levelled at research focused on organisational antecedents.

Individual disposition of the perpetrator

Partly because of the difficulty in obtaining perpetrator samples, but also partly because of the focus of attention on victims, relatively little research has focused on whether disposition may predispose an individual to engage in bullying behaviour at work. In terms of perpetrator characteristics, bullies have been shown to be violent (Leather *et al.*, 1990), tyrannical (Ashforth, 1994) and aggressive (Seigne *et al.*, 2007). Zapf and Einarsen (2003) present three mechanisms to explain why characteristics of the perpetrator may result in bullying:

- Individuals with an inflated or unrealistic view of their self-esteem (high narcissism) are likely to perceive a threat to their self-esteem when faced with conflict. In order to preserve their view of themselves and to reduce the negative appraisal of others, they engage in aggressive behaviour towards the source of the threat.
- A lack of social competencies could mean that individuals low in emotional control are likely to vent their anger in an inappropriate manner when faced with stressful and frustrating situations. Additionally, a lack of self-awareness and empathy could result in perpetrators not being aware that their behaviour constitutes bullying and of the effect it has on others.
- Employees may engage in micro-political behaviours within an organisation to enhance their position and to gain power, which could manifest itself in competitive, dominant and assertive behaviours.

Table 8.2 *Victimisation types based on a dyadic interaction*

	Submissive victim	Provocative victim
Dominating perpetrator	Predatory bullying where the perpetrator has a desire to control the victim and the victim is an 'easy target' (e.g. tyrannical leader)	Dispute-related victimisation where dominance is met by resistance, which leads to victimisation (e.g. clash with group norms)
Reactive perpetrator	No or little bullying emerges as there is no trigger and the perpetrator has no motive to dominate	Dispute-related bullying where the perpetrator reacts to perceived provocation from the victim (e.g. via threatened self-esteem)

Source: Table adapted from Aquino and Lamertz (2004).

Based on a dispositional hypothesis, Aquino and Lamertz (2004) propose a dyadic model of victim and perpetrator interaction in predicting victimisation. Table 8.2 illustrates the types of bullying which are hypothesised to emerge from an interaction between submissive and provocative victims and domineering and reactive perpetrators. Under this classification, bullying emerges from a dynamic interplay between two individuals which differs in motive and type of behaviour. The shaded cells involve behaviour which is institutionalised, frequent and with a repeated pattern and hence is synonymous with traditional definitions of bullying. The provocative victim–dominating perpetrator cell involves discrete, episodic behaviour and therefore does not fit into a strict definition of bullying, but certainly involves negative acts. Although only at the dyadic level and focused on individual roles (the authors do discuss organisational moderators such as social power, social capital and formal/informal norms), this model provides some insight into how personality may function within workplace bullying.

Group/social antecedents

Einarsen *et al.* (2003) suggest that, at a group level, bullying can be seen as a scapegoating process whereby groups direct their aggression to a less powerful individual who is not accepted by peers. This results in peer-rejection whereby the individual becomes an outsider in the group and ultimately a victim. Archer (1999) found bullying among fire fighters was seen as indoctrination into a team, whereby new recruits were socialised into the group norm and those who did not conform were isolated. LaVan and Martin (2008) argue that high group cohesiveness may create in-groups and out-groups, whereby some employees find themselves as outsiders and victims of bullying. Further, Neuman and Baron (2003) suggest perceptions of unfair treatment, an increasingly diverse workforce, norms of reciprocity and norm violations are social determinants of aggression which can create in-out-groups and isolation.

Within the framework of Social Identity Theory (Tajfel and Turner, 1986), one can comprehend how, in order to enhance or maintain self-esteem and not be perceived as an outsider by others, an employee will show favouritism towards their in-group at the expense of those deemed outside the group. Therefore, at a group level, there may be a strong cohesive in-group mentality or a collection of individuals fearful of being singled out who are 'led' by a dominating individual. This may also explain why witnesses may not intervene when they see bullying going on.

In arguably a first for workplace bullying research, Coyne *et al.* (2004) used sociometrics to try to examine outsider positions of victims in fire-fighter samples. Contrary to expectations, victims tended not to occupy outsider positions and were generally rated as preferred people to work with. Perpetrators were least preferred people to work with, but bully-victims were more likely to be isolated in the teams. Clearly, more research is needed to examine the group factors involved in workplace bullying and who occupies outsider roles and why.

Integrative theoretical models

Single causal explanations are too simplistic to model the complex phenomenon of bullying at work. As we become more aware of the processes behind bullying, the development of models to explain workplace bullying has advanced rapidly. Theoretical models have emerged for mobbing (Zapf, 1999), workplace bullying (Einarsen *et al.*, 2003), aggression (Neuman and Baron, 2003), emotional abuse (Keashly and Harvey, 2005), workplace harassment (Bowling and Beehr, 2006) and struggling for power as a preliminary stage of bullying (Strandmark and Hallberg, 2007). Table 8.3 briefly illustrates the main elements of these models. While most take a stress perspective and focus on the target, there is agreement that organisational and individual antecedents interact to provide a context conducive to workplace bullying. Individual

Table 8.3. *Models of workplace bullying and related concepts*

Authors(s)	Antecedents	Moderators / mediators	Outcomes	Process/explanatory mechanism
Zapf (1999)	Organisational Social group Person (victim and bully)	Type of behaviour as mediator	Individual well-being	Antecedents lead to behaviour which leads to negative outcomes
Einarsen et al. (2003)	Organisational factors inhibiting aggression Individual, social and contextual factors promoting aggression	Organisational action and victim characteristics as moderators	Effects on the organisation Effects on the individual	Interaction of organisational and individual antecedents which is mediated by perceptual, attributional and emotional processes of the victim
Neuman and Baron (2003)	Social situational Individual differences	Internal states (arousal, negative affect and hostile cognitions) as mediators	Aggressive or non-aggressive response	Individual's appraisal of critical states resulting from antecedents may lead to aggression
Keashly and Harvey (2005)	Situational forces Actor characteristics Target-orientated factors	Features of behaviour and target's experience as mediators Coping and social support as moderators	Psychological Behavioural Physical	Stressor–stress–strain model
Bowling and Beehr (2006)	Organisational culture Human resource systems Perpetrator characteristics Victim characteristics Role stressors	Attributions to self, perpetrator or organisation and justice as mediators	Victim's well-being Attitudes/ behaviour to perpetrator Individual performance outcomes	Primarily a stress model based on a reciprocity and attribution process by a victim towards self, perpetrator or organisation

Table 8.3 (*cont.*)

Authors(s)	Antecedents	Moderators / mediators	Outcomes	Process/explanatory mechanism
Strandmark and Hallberg (2007)	Potential arena for conflict Personal strength or vulnerability	Professional and personal value conflicts	Struggle for power	A conflict model where organisational triggers and individual factors interact; power struggles emerge if value conflicts are not resolved

attributions and appraisal of events influence the types of behaviour experienced, emotional and behavioural reactions to the behaviour and the individual and organisational outcomes of behaviour. Although models differ regarding the role of the appraisal process, this may hold the key to understanding both victim and perpetrator perspectives within workplace bullying.

Creating effective interventions

With increasing knowledge comes an increasing awareness of how to tackle bullying – its causes and its consequences. However, surveys have shown that only just over a half of UK organisations (Woodman and Cook, 2005) and Finnish public sector municipalities (Salin, 2008) have introduced anti-bullying policies. Further, both Ferris (2004) and Rayner and McIvor (2008) suggest organisational differences in tackling bullying, ranging from those that take a proactive stance, acknowledging bullying is harmful and develop a policy coupled with training and counselling, to those where bullying is endemic, normalised and not taken seriously.

Combining ideas from Resch and Schubinski (1996), Hubert (2003) and Rayner and McIvor (2008), Table 8.4 illustrates a three-level intervention framework mapping organisational, group and individual antecedents of workplace bullying. There is also a higher society level proposed that captures the need to consider the impact of society values, laws (e.g. specific laws against bullying or current employment laws such as health and safety), the actions of unions and professional bodies, as well as government guidance/political action on reducing workplace bullying at a national level. This section should also include

Table 8.4. *A framework for workplace bullying intervention*

Society level

Cultural values, legal framework, union/professional body support, guidance from government, anti-bullying associations

	Prevention	Support/ intervention	Remedial
Organisation	Risk assessment Change work design Leadership training Culture change Dignity at work	Staff surveys Monitor absences Support from the top Creation of informal and formal networks	Ensure sanctions are implemented Monitor culture change Monitor and evaluate training
Group	Awareness training for groups Diversity training Foster appropriate group norms	Examine in-group and out-group (team network) Facilitate group meetings and group discussions	External meetings to change norms Change the make-up of the team
Individual	Training (emotion regulation, social skills, anger management, etc.)	Contact person/ buddy system Confidential support and advice Informal and formal procedures	Counselling for victims and perpetrators Support to enact a grievance case

national anti-bullying associations or centres (e.g. Beyond Bullying Association in Australia; Andrea Adams Trust in the UK; Workplace Bullying Institute in the USA), which have dedicated websites and support networks providing advice, guidance and help for individuals and organisations.

At the organisational level, the development of a clear policy setting out the organisation's stance on bullying and aiming to change attitudes of managers and employees to workplace bullying is a minimal requirement (Richards and Daley, 2003). Ultimately, if used correctly, this creates a culture of respect and dignity at work (Rayner and McIvor, 2008). Further, some authors have suggested a risk management approach (Resch and Schubinski, 1996; Spurgeon, 2003) which treats bullying as a psycho-social hazard and considers possible changes to work design (linked to reducing stressors and frustrations) and leadership (through training) as methods of managing the risk of bullying. At the support level, organisations could examine employee morale and absences (as they may be indicators of bullying) and create informal 'buddy' networks, as well as having a clear grievance policy to deal with cases. Finally, if cases develop into a grievance, an organisation needs to ensure that the process is operated effectively and that any sanctions are implemented, as well as monitoring and evaluating the approach used to gauge its success in reducing bullying.

At the group level, the focus is on changing group norms and values, which at the start may be achieved by a programme of awareness training and the development of group norms against bullying. Vartia *et al.* (2003) suggest a role here for occupational health services, which can help with this initial prevention, but can also help mediate group conflict via group meetings to try to obtain a sense of how the group deals with conflict. Finally, if group norms are too entrenched, group interventions with an outside expert are required and as a last resort changing group membership may be needed.

At the individual level, training in emotional regulation, assertiveness and so on could help reduce the vulnerability and submissiveness of the victim as well as the dominance and reactivity of the perpetrator. Also, the individual should be able to access both informal and formal support and help (e.g. dignity at work advisers) and victims should be able to access counselling. Rehabilitation should be provided which supports victim return to work and, if appropriate, perpetrator rehabilitation back into the organisation may be considered (Tehrani, 2003).

Interestingly, whilst there are numerous initiatives in and practical guidance for dealing with bullying, little evidence has emerged to show the effectiveness of such approaches. In the few studies which have attempted to evaluate bullying interventions (e.g. Hoel and Giga, 2006; Mikkelsen *et al.*, 2008), evidence of success is inconclusive.

Conclusions

Workplace bullying research has come a long way in a short space of time and today we have a much clearer sense of the salient issues. The area is being examined from a multidisciplinary perspective (e.g. human resources, counselling, psychology, law), using different methodologies and with strong links between research and practice. However, there are still a number of issues to consider. First, there remains a need to consider the perspectives of others (e.g. perpetrators, bully-victims, witnesses, bystanders) in order to obtain a more rounded view of bullying. Unlike school bullying, there has been a lack of focus on bully-victims and those adopting other participant roles. Second, we need fuller testing of explanatory models within both the academic and applied domains, which is limited at present. Third, interventions need to better map current thinking on workplace bullying as well as undergo increased evaluation. Fourth, we need to examine evidence from other bullying contexts and consider how it may develop our understanding of workplace bullying. Finally, we cannot stand still and view bullying as a static concept. Changes to the nature of bullying (e.g. the emergence of cyberbullying), changes in the legal framework, and significant global changes (e.g. global recessions) are likely change the nature, frequency, antecedents and impact of workplace bullying and revise our ideas about this complex, yet destructive phenomenon.

REFERENCES

Agervold, M. and Mikkelsen, E.G. (2004). 'Relationships between bullying, psychological work environment and individual stress reactions'. *Work and Stress*, 18: 336–51.

Aquino, K. and Bradfield, M. (2000). 'Perceived victimization in the workplace: the role of situational factors and victim characteristics'. *Organization Science*, 11: 525–37.

Aquino, K. and Lamertz, K. (2004). 'A relational model of workplace victimization: social roles and patterns of victimization in dyadic relationships'. *Journal of Applied Psychology*, 89: 1023–34.

Aquino, K., Grover, S.L., Bradfield, M. and Allen, D.G. (1999). 'The effects of negative affectivity, hierarchical status, and self-determination on workplace victimisation'. *Academy of Management Journal*, 42: 260–72.

Archer, D. (1999). 'Exploring "bullying" culture in the para-military organisation'. *International Journal of Manpower*, 20: 94–105.

Ashforth, B. (1994). 'Petty tyranny in organizations'. *Human Relations*, 47: 755–70.

Baillien, E., Neyens, I., De Witte, H. and De Cuyper, N. (2009). 'A qualitative study on the development of workplace bullying: towards a three-way model'. *Journal of Community and Applied Social Psychology*, 19: 1–16.

Berkowitz, L. (1989). 'The frustration–aggression hypothesis: an examination and reformulation'. *Psychological Bulletin*, 106: 59–73.

Björkqvist, K., Österman, K. and Hjelt-Bäck, M. (1994). 'Aggression among university employees'. *Aggressive Behavior*, 20: 173–84.

Brodsky, C.M. (1976). *The Harassed Worker*. Toronto: Lexington Books.

Bowling, N.A. and Beehr, T.A. (2006). 'Workplace harassment from the victim's perspective: a theoretical model and meta-analysis'. *Journal of Applied Psychology*, 91: 998–1012.

Calvert, E. (2008). 'A public or private issue? Sectoral patterns in workplace bullying'. Proceedings of the 6th International Conference on Workplace Bullying, Montreal, Canada (pp. 179–80).

Cowie, H., Naylor, P., Rivers, I., Smith, P.K. and Pereira, B. (2002). 'Measuring workplace bullying'. *Aggression and Violent Behavior*, 7: 33–51.

Coyne, I., Clough, P., Alexander, T. and Clemment, G. (2006). 'Workplace bullying: the role of mental toughness'. In Proceedings of The British Psychological Society Division of Occupational Psychology Annual Conference, Leicester, (pp. 107–10).

Coyne, I., Craig, J. and Smith-Lee Chong, P. (2004). 'Workplace bullying in a group context'. *British Journal of Guidance and Counselling*, 32: 301–17.

Coyne, I., Seigne, E. and Randall, P. (2000). 'Predicting workplace victim status from personality'. *European Journal of Work and Organizational Psychology*, 9: 335–49.

Coyne, I., Smith-Lee Chong, P., Seigne, E. and Randall, P. (2003). 'Self and peer nominations of bullying: an analysis of incident rates, individual differences and perceptions of the working environment'. *European Journal of Work and Organizational Psychology*, 12: 209–28.

Crossley, C.D. (2009). 'Emotional and behavioral reactions to social undermining: a closer look at perceived offender motives'. *Organizational Behavior and Human Decision Processes*, 108: 14–24.

De Souza V.L. and De Souza, M.Z.A. (2008). 'Contemporary practices for performance evaluation and wages: conditioning factors for violence against workers' dignity and reputation'. Proceedings of the 6th International Conference on Workplace Bullying, Montreal, Canada (pp. 212–13).

Djurkovic, N., McCormack, D. and Casimir, G. (2004). 'The physical and psychological effects of workplace bullying and their relationship to intention to leave: a test of the psychosomatic and disability hypotheses'. *International Journal of Organizational Theory and Behavior*, 7: 469–97.

(2005). 'The behavioral reactions of victims to different types of workplace bullying'. *International Journal of Organizational Theory and Behavior*, 8: 439–61.

Einarsen, S. (1999). 'The nature and causes of bullying at work'. *International Journal of Manpower*, 20: 16–27.

(2000). 'Harassment and bullying at work: a review of the Scandinavian approach'. *Aggression and Violent Behavior*, 5: 379–401.

Einarsen, S. and Mikkelsen, E.G. (2003). 'Individual effects of exposure to bullying at work'. In S. Einarsen, H. Hoel, D. Zapf and C.L. Cooper (eds.), *Bullying and Emotional Abuse in the Workplace: International Perspectives in Research and Practice* (pp. 127–44). London: Taylor and Francis.

Einarsen, S. and Skogstad, A. (1996). 'Bullying at work: epidemiological findings in public and private organisations'. *European Journal of Work and Organizational Psychology*, 5: 185–201.

Einarsen, S., Hoel, H. and Notelaers, G. (2009). 'Measuring exposure to bullying and harassment at work: validity, factor structure and psychometric properties of the Negative Acts Questionnaire–Revised'. *Work and Stress*, 23: 24–44.

Einarsen, S., Hoel, H., Zapf, D. and Cooper, C.L. (2003). 'The concept of bullying at work: the European tradition'. In S. Einarsen, H. Hoel, D. Zapf and C.L. Cooper (eds.), *Bullying and Emotional Abuse in the Workplace: International Perspectives in Research and Practice* (pp. 3–30). London: Taylor and Francis.

Einarsen, S., Raknes, B.I. and Matthiesen, S.B. (1994). 'Bullying and harassment at work and its relationship with work environment quality: an exploratory study'. *European Work and Organizational Psychologist*, 4: 381–401.

Felson, R.B. and Tedeschi, J.T. (1993). *Aggression and Violence: Social Interactionist Perspectives.* Washington, DC: American Psychological Association.

Ferris, P. (2004). 'A preliminary typology of organisational response to allegations of workplace bullying: see no evil, hear no evil, speak no evil'. *British Journal of Guidance and Counselling*, 32: 389–95.

Glaso, L., Matthiesen, S.B., Nielsen, M.B. and Einarsen, S. (2007). 'Do targets of workplace bullying portray a general victim personality profile?' *Scandinavian Journal of Psychology*, 48: 313–19.

Harvey, M.G., Treadway, D. and Heames, J.T. (2006). 'Bullying in global organizations: a reference point perspective'. *Journal of World Business*, 41: 190–202.

Hauge, L.J., Skogstad, A. and Einarsen, S. (2007). 'Relationships between stressful work environments and bullying: results of a large representative study'. *Work and Stress*, 21: 220–42.

Hoel, H. and Giga, S.I. (2006). 'Destructive interpersonal conflict in the workplace: the effectiveness of management interventions'. Unpublished report by Manchester Business School, University of Manchester.

Hoel, H. and Salin, D. (2003). 'Organisational antecedents of workplace bullying'. In S. Einarsen, H. Hoel, D. Zapf and C.L. Cooper (eds.), *Bullying and Emotional Abuse in the Workplace: International Perspectives in Research and Practice* (pp. 203–18). London: Taylor and Francis.

Hoel, H., Cooper, C.L. and Faragher, B. (2001). 'The experience of bullying in Great Britain: the impact of organizational status'. *European Journal of Work and Organizational Psychology*, 10: 443–65.

Hoel, H., Einarsen, S. and Cooper, C.L. (2003). 'Organisational effects of bullying'. In S. Einarsen, H. Hoel, D. Zapf and C.L. Cooper (eds.), *Bullying and Emotional Abuse in the Workplace: International Perspectives in Research and Practice* (pp. 145–61). London: Taylor and Francis.

Hoel, H., Faragher, B. and Cooper, C.L. (2004). 'Bullying is detrimental to health, but all bullying behaviours are not necessarily equally damaging'. *British Journal of Guidance and Counselling*, 32: 367–87.

Hogh, A. and Dofradottir, A. (2001). 'Coping with bullying in the workplace'. *European Journal of Work and Organizational Psychology*, 4: 485–96.

Hubert, A.B. (2003). 'To prevent and overcome undesirable interaction: a systematic approach model'. In S. Einarsen, H. Hoel, D. Zapf and C.L. Cooper (eds.), *Bullying and Emotional Abuse in the Workplace: International Perspectives in Research and Practice* (pp. 299–311). London: Taylor and Francis.

Hubert, A.B. and van Veldhoven, M. (2001). 'Risk sectors for undesirable behaviours and mobbing'. *European Journal of Work and Organizational Psychology*, 4: 415–24.

Keashly, L. and Harvey, S. (2005). 'Emotional abuse in the workplace'. In S. Fox and P.E. Spector (eds.), *Counterproductive Work Behavior: Investigations of Actors and Targets* (pp. 201–35). Washington, DC: American Psychological Association.

Kivimäki, K., Elovainio, M. and Vathera, J. (2000). 'Workplace bullying and sickness absence in hospital staff'. *Occupational and Environmental Medicine*, 57: 656–60.

Kivimäki, K., Virtanen, M., Vartia, M., Elovainio, M., Vathera, J. and Keltikangas-Järvinen, L. (2003). 'Workplace bullying and the risk of cardiovascular disease and depression. *Occupational and Environmental Medicine*, 60: 779–83.

LaVan, H. and Martin, W.M. (2008). 'Bullying in the U.S. workplace: normative and process-oriented ethical approaches'. *Journal of Business Ethics*, 83: 147–65.

Leather, P.J., Cox, T. and Farnsworth, W.J.F. (1990). 'Violence at work: an issue for the 1990s'. *Work and Stress*, 4: 3–5.

Lewis, D. (2004). 'Bullying at work: the impact of shame among university and college lecturers'. *British Journal of Guidance and Counselling*, 32: 281–99.

Leymann, H. (1996). 'The content and development of mobbing at work'. *European Journal of Work and Organizational Psychology*, 5: 165–84.

Leymann, H. and Gustafsson, A. (1996). 'Mobbing at work and the development of post-traumatic stress disorders'. *European Journal of Work and Organizational Psychology*, 5: 251–75.

Liefooghe, A.P.D. and MacKenzie Davey, K. (2001). 'Accounts of workplace bullying: the role of the organization'. *European Journal of Work and Organizational Psychology*, 10: 375–92.

Lutgen-Sandvik, P., Tracy, S.J. and Alberts, J.K. (2007). 'Burned by bullying in the American workplace: prevalence, perception, degree and impact'. *Journal of Management Studies*, 44: 837–62.

Marais-Steinman, S. (2003). 'Challenging workplace bullying in a developing country: the example of South Africa'. In S. Einarsen, H. Hoel, D. Zapf and C.L. Cooper (eds.), *Bullying and Emotional Abuse in the Workplace: International Perspectives in Research and Practice* (pp. 312–23). London: Taylor and Francis.

Matthiesen, S.B. and Einarsen, S. (2001). 'MMPI-2 configurations among victims of bullying at work'. *European Journal of Work and Organizational Psychology*, 10: 467–84.

(2004). 'Psychiatric distress and symptoms of PTSD among victims of bullying at work'. *British Journal of Guidance and Counselling*, 32: 335–56.

Mikkelsen, E.G. and Einarsen, S. (2001). 'Bullying in Danish working life: prevalence and health correlates'. *European Journal of Work and Organizational Psychology*, 4: 393–413.

(2002). 'Relationships between exposure to bullying at work and psychological and psychosomatic health complaints: the role of state negative affectivity and generalized self-efficacy'. *Scandinavian Journal of Psychology*, 43: 397–405.

Mikkelsen, E.G., Hogh, A. and Olsen, L.B. (2008). 'Prevention of bullying and conflicts at work: an intervention study'. Proceedings of the 6th International Conference on Workplace Bullying, Montreal, Canada (pp. 40–42).

Milam, A.C., Spitzmueller, C. and Penney, L.M. (2009). 'Investigating individual differences among targets of workplace incivility'. *Journal of Occupational Health Psychology*, 14: 58–69.

Neuman, J.H. and Baron, R.A. (2003). 'Social antecedents of bullying: a social interactionist perspective'. In S. Einarsen, H. Hoel, D. Zapf and C.L. Cooper (eds.), *Bullying and Emotional Abuse in the Workplace: International Perspectives in Research and Practice* (pp. 185–202). London: Taylor and Francis.

Niedhammer, I., David, S. and Degioanni, S. (2008). 'Economic activities and occupations at high risk for workplace bullying: results from a large-scale cross sectional survey in the general working population in France'. *International Archives of Occupational and Environmental Health*, 80: 346–53.

Niedl, K. (1996). 'Mobbing and well-being: economic and personnel development implications'. *European Journal of Work and Organizational Psychology*, 5: 239–49.

Nielsen, M.B., Skogstad, A., Matthiesen, S.B., Glasø, L., Aasland, M.S., Notelaers, G. and Einarsen, S. (2009). 'Prevalence of workplace bullying in Norway: comparisons across time and estimation methods'. *European Journal of Work and Organizational Psychology*, 18: 81–101.

Ólafsson, R.F. and Jóhannsdóttir, H.L. (2004). 'Coping with bullying in the workplace: the effect of gender, age and type of bullying'. *British Journal of Guidance and Counselling*, 32: 319–33.

Olweus, D. (1993). *Bullying at School: What We Know and What We Can Do*. Oxford: Blackwell.

O'Moore, M. and Lynch, J. (2007). 'Leadership, working environment and workplace bullying'. *International Journal of Organizational Theory and Behavior*, 10: 95–117.

O'Moore, M., Lynch, J. and Daéid, N.N. (2003). 'The rates and relative risks of workplace bullying in Ireland, a country of high economic growth'. *International Journal of Management and Decision Making*, 4: 82–95.

O'Moore, M., Seigne, E., McGuire, L. and Smith, M. (1998). 'Victims of workplace bullying in Ireland'. *Irish Journal of Psychology*, 19: 345–57.

Ortega, A., Hogh, A. and Borg, V. (2008a). 'Bullying, absence and presenteeism in the Danish elderly care sector: a one-year follow-up study'. Proceedings of the 6th International Conference on Workplace Bullying, Montreal, Canada (pp. 90–92).

Ortega, A., Hogh, A., Pejtersen, J.H. and Olsen, O. (2008b). 'Prevalence of workplace bullying and risk groups: a representative population study'. *International Archives of Occupational and Environmental Health*, 82: 417–26.

Paice, E., Aitken, M., Houghton, A. and Firth-Cozens, J. (2004). 'Bullying among doctors in training: cross-sectional questionnaire survey'. *British Medical Journal*, 329: 658–59.

Pearson, C.M., Andersson, L.M. and Porath, C.L. (2005). 'Workplace incivility'. In S. Fox and P.E. Spector (eds.), *Counterproductive Work Behavior: Investigations of Actors and Targets* (pp. 177–200). Washington, DC: American Psychological Association.

Quine, L. (1999). 'Workplace bullying in NHS community trusts: staff questionnaire survey'. *British Medical Journal*, 318: 228–32.

(2004). 'Workplace bullying in junior doctors: questionnaire survey'. *British Medical Journal*, 324: 878–79.

Rayner, C. (1997). 'The incidence of workplace bullying'. *Journal of Community and Applied Social Psychology*, 7: 199–208.

Rayner, C. and Cooper, C.L. (2006). 'Workplace bullying'. In E.K. Kelloway, J. Barling and J.J. Hurrell (eds.), *Handbook of Workplace Violence* (pp. 121–45). Thousand Oaks, CA: Sage.

Rayner, C. and Hoel, H. (1997). 'A summary review of literature relating to workplace bullying'. *Journal of Community and Applied Social Psychology*, 7: 181–91.

Rayner, C. and McIvor, K. (2008). Unpublished research report on the Dignity at Work project'. Business School, University of Portsmouth.

Resch, M. and Schubinski, M. (1996). 'Mobbing: prevention and management in organizations'. *European Journal of Work and Organizational Psychology*, 5: 295–307.

Richards, J. and Daley, H. (2003). 'Bullying policy: development, implementation and monitoring'. In S. Einarsen, H. Hoel, D. Zapf and C.L. Cooper (eds.), *Bullying and Emotional Abuse in the Workplace: International Perspectives in Research and Practice* (pp. 248–58). London: Taylor and Francis.

Richman, J.A., Rospenda, K.M., Flaherty, J.A. and Freels, S. (2001). 'Workplace harassment, active coping, and alcohol-related outcomes'. *Journal of Substance Abuse*, 13: 347–66.

Salin, D. (2001). 'Prevalence and forms of workplace bullying among business professionals: a comparison of two different strategies for measuring bullying'. *European Journal of Work and Organizational Psychology*, 10: 425–41.

(2003a). 'The significance of gender in the prevalence, forms and perceptions of bullying'. In D. Salin, 'Workplace bullying among business professionals: prevalence, organisational antecedents and gender differences' (pp. 113–39). Published doctoral thesis, Swedish School of Economics and Business Administration, Helsinki.

(2003b). 'Ways of explaining workplace bullying: a review of enabling, motivating and precipitating structures and processes in the work environment'. *Human Relations*, 56: 1213–32.

(2008). 'The prevention of workplace bullying as a question of human resource management: measures adopted and underlying organizational factors'. *Scandinavian Journal of Management*, 24: 221–31.

Saunders, P., Huynh, A. and Goodman-Delahunty, J. (2007). 'Defining workplace bullying behaviour: professional lay definitions of workplace bullying'. *International Journal of Law and Psychiatry*, 30: 340–54.

Seigne, E., Coyne, I., Randall, P. and Parker, J. (2007). 'Personality traits of bullies as a contributory factor in workplace bullying: an exploratory study'. *International Journal of Organizational Theory and Behavior*, 10: 118–32.

Seo, Y.N. and Leather, P. (2008). 'Workplace bullying in South Korea: an exploratory study'. Proceedings of the 6th International Conference on Workplace Bullying, Montreal, Canada (pp. 64–65).

Sheehan, M. (1999). 'Workplace bullying: responding with some emotional intelligence'. *International Journal of Manpower*, 20: 57–69.

Skogstad, A., Matthiesen, S.B. and Einarsen, S. (2007). 'Organizational changes: a precursor of bullying at work?' *International Journal of Organizational Theory and Behavior*, 10: 58–94.

Smith, P.K., Singer, M., Hoel, H. and Cooper, C.L. (2003). 'Victimization in the school and the workplace: are there any links?' *British Journal of Psychology*, 94: 175–88.

Spurgeon, A. (2003). 'Bullying from a risk management perspective'. In S. Einarsen, H. Hoel, D. Zapf and C.L. Cooper (eds.), *Bullying and Emotional Abuse in the Workplace: International Perspectives in Research and Practice* (pp. 327–38). London: Taylor and Francis.

Strandmark, M.K. and Hallberg, L.R.-M. (2007). 'The origin of workplace bullying: experiences from the perspective of bully victims in the public service sector'. *Journal of Nursing Management*, 15: 332–41.

Tajfel, H. and Turner, J. (1986). 'The social identity theory of intergroup behavior'. In S. Worchel and W.G. Austin (eds.), *Psychology of Intergroup Relations* (pp. 7–24). Chicago: Nelson.

Tehrani, N. (2003). 'Counselling and rehabilitating employees involved with bullying'. In S. Einarsen, H. Hoel, D. Zapf and C.L. Cooper (eds.), *Bullying and Emotional Abuse in the Workplace: International Perspectives in Research and Practice* (pp. 270–84). London: Taylor and Francis.

(2004). 'Bullying: a source of chronic post traumatic stress?' *British Journal of Guidance and Counselling*, 32: 357–66.

Tepper, B.J. (2000). 'Consequences of abusive supervision'. *Academy of Management Journal*, 43: 178–90.

Vaez, M., Ekberg, K. and Laflamme, L. (2004). 'Abusive events at work among young working adults: magnitude of the problem and its effect on self-rated health'. *Industrial Relations*, 59: 569–84.

Vartia, M. (1996). 'The sources of bullying: psychological work environment and organizational climate'. *European Journal of Work and Organizational Psychology*, 5: 203–14.

Vartia, M. and Hyyti, J. (2002). 'Gender differences in workplace bullying among prison officers'. *European Journal of Work and Organizational Psychology*, 11: 113–26.

Vartia, M., Korppoo, L., Fallenius, S. and Mattila, M. (2003). 'Workplace bullying: the role of occupational health services'. In S. Einarsen, H. Hoel, D. Zapf and C.L. Cooper (eds.), *Bullying and Emotional Abuse in the Workplace: International Perspectives in Research and Practice* (pp. 285–98). London: Taylor and Francis.

Woodman, P. and Cook, P. (2005). *Bullying at Work: The Experience of Managers*. London: Chartered Management Institute.

Zapf, D. (1999). 'Organisational, work group related and personal causes of mobbing/bullying at work'. *International Journal of Manpower*, 20: 70–85.

Zapf, D. and Einarsen, S. (2001). 'Bullying in the workplace: recent trends in research and practice – an introduction'. *European Journal of Work and Organizational Psychology*, 10: 369–73.

    (2003). 'Individual antecedents of bullying'. In S. Einarsen, H. Hoel, D. Zapf and C.L. Cooper (eds.), *Bullying and Emotional Abuse in the Workplace: International Perspectives in Research and Practice* (pp.165–84). London: Taylor and Francis.

Zapf, D. and Gross, C. (2001) 'Conflict escalation and coping with workplace bullying: a replication and extension'. *European Journal of Work and Organizational Psychology*, 10: 497–522.

Zapf, D., Einarsen, S., Hoel, H. and Vartia, M. (2003). 'Empirical findings on bullying in the workplace'. In S. Einarsen, H. Hoel, D. Zapf and C.L. Cooper (eds.), *Bullying and Emotional Abuse in the Workplace: International Perspectives in Research and Practice* (pp. 103–26). London: Taylor and Francis.

Zapf, D., Knorz, C. and Kulla, M. (1996). 'On the relationship between mobbing factors and job content, the social work environment and health outcomes'. *European Journal of Work and Organizational Psychology*, 5: 215–37.

9   Elder abuse and bullying: exploring
     theoretical and empirical connections

*Christine A. Walsh, Gabrielle D'Aoust
and Kate Beamer*

Adults aged 65 years and older represent one of the fastest-growing seg-
ments of the population in Western countries. It has been suggested that,
with the increasing population of older adults, enhanced dependency
and care-giving responsibilities there will likely occur a concomitant
rise in all forms of violence against older adults (Fulmer *et al.*, 2000;
Glendenning, 1997). Over the course of the past three decades, the
maltreatment of older adults has been increasingly examined, although
there is a paucity of research on bullying in this population. This chapter offers theoretical explanations and reviews current information
regarding the nature and scope of elder abuse and how bullying might
be conceptualised within this framework. The chapter concludes with
directions for further research.

Definitions of bullying and elder abuse

In reviewing the literature, information on bullying of older adults is
absent. A small body of research focuses on bullying of adults within
the workplace (i.e. Gabrielle *et al.*, 2008), offering little insight into the
nature of bullying among older adults in other contexts. In this chapter,
elder bullying will be conceptualised within the typology of interpersonal violence developed in 2004 by the World Health Organization
(2004) as 'violence between family members and intimate partners and
violence between acquaintances and strangers that is not intended to
further the aims of any formally defined group or cause' (p. x).

Bullying, defined as chronic aggression with 'deliberate intent to
cause physical or psychological distress to others' (Randall, 1997, p. 4),
comprises three key elements: power differential, repetition and motivation. Power imbalances are contextually based and fluid in nature
and can be derived through physical advantage (size or strength),
social advantage (dominant social role), social status or systemic power
(racial, cultural or economic status, sexual orientation, etc.) (Craig
and Pepler, 2007; Rigby, 2002) or using knowledge of another person's

vulnerability to cause distress. Bullying is typically repeated over time and, with each incident, power differentials between bully and target are reinforced (ibid.).

Following from these conceptualisations of bullying behaviours, elder bullying which shares the common features of intent, differences in power and repetition may be considered within the broader phenomenon of elder abuse, made up of both abuse and neglect. There are some important differences, however, which will be examined.

Bullying behaviour can be understood as one form of violence against older adults coming under the term elder abuse. There is no universally accepted definition for elder abuse; it was first described in 1975 as 'granny battering' (Baker, 1975; Burston, 1975) and subsequently labelled as 'battered elder syndrome', 'elder mistreatment', 'parent battering' and 'old age abuse' (Daly and Jogerst, 2001). More recently, the concept has evolved to encompass a variety of forms of maltreatment.

In 1995, Action on Elder Abuse (AEA), based in the UK, advanced a definition of elder abuse as 'a single or repeated act, or lack of appropriate action, occurring within a relationship where there is an expectation of trust, which causes harm or distress to an older dependent person'. It has been widely used and was subsequently adopted in 2002 by the International Network for the Prevention of Elder Abuse (INPEA), the World Health Organization (WHO) and the Toronto Declaration on the Global Prevention of Elder Abuse.

Elder abuse and bullying differ on the basis of intentionality and an expectation of trust in the relationship. The maltreatment of older adults includes intentional or unintentional harm. Unintentional maltreatment refers to a situation in which inadvertent action results in harm to an older adult, typically as a result of inexperience, lack of ability or ignorance on the part of a caregiver, whereas intentional maltreatment refers to a conscious, deliberate attempt to inflict injury or harm on an older adult (Aravanis *et al.*, 1993).

Elder abuse occurs within a relationship where there is an expectation of trust, such as familial or care-giving relationships (Dauvergne, 2003; Lithwick *et al.*, 1999). In community settings, elder abuse is perpetrated most often by adult children and spouses (Brozowski and Hall, 2004).

Prevalence of elder abuse and bullying

In contrast to some other forms of bullying (e.g. school and workplace bullying), elder bullying is only beginning to draw public, professional and political attention. Although reports of elder bullying and abuse emerged in medical journals over 30 years ago, it has remained isolated from public consciousness until relatively recently (Abbey, 2009; Dong, 2005). According to Anetzberger (2005a, p. 2), 'the 1980s are widely acknowledged as the decade for public awakening and broadening professional action regarding elder abuse'. However, it was not until the early 1990s that national studies on elder abuse began to emerge in Canada and elsewhere (Brozowski and Hall, 2004). Reasons for the topical isolation of elder abuse include low report rates, social isolation on the part of older adults (either in their homes or in care) and a perceived lack of older adults' credibility as a result of dementia, Alzheimer's, and so on (Abbey, 2009).

International prevalence rates, or the number of cases of elder abuse, range between 4 and 10 per cent in studies from Amsterdam (Comijs et al., 1999), Australia (Kurrle and Naughtin, 2008), Denmark and Sweden (Tornstam, 1989), Canada (Podnieks, 1992), Germany (Hirsch and Brendebach, 1999), Finland (Kivela et al., 1992), the UK (Biggs et al., 2009) and the USA (Laumann et al., 2008). However, accurate estimates of elder abuse are difficult to determine as most cases are hidden, undetected or unreported (Bomba, 2006). Reported cases represent only the tip of the iceberg (McDonald and Collins, 2000). Only 1 to 2 per cent of cases are reported (Beaulieu and Leclerc, 2006) and are typically severe cases of physical abuse and active neglect (Gordon and Brill, 2001).

Forms of elder abuse and bullying

Although there is some overlap in the forms of violence between elder abuse and bullying, according to the 'Missing Voices' report (INPEA and WHO, 2002), elder abuse is more broadly conceptualised according to three major themes: neglect, including isolation, abandonment and social exclusion; the violation of human, legal and medical rights; and the deprivation of choices, decisions, status, finances and respect. Under these themes five primary categories of elder abuse are recognised: physical abuse, psychological or emotional abuse, sexual abuse, financial or material abuse and neglect (Lachs and Pillemer, 2004).

Physical abuse refers to the use of physical force or violence towards an older adult, resulting in physical pain or discomfort, bodily injury or impairment. Physical abuse might include hitting, striking, beating, shaking, pushing, biting, choking, kicking and burning, or activities such as force-feeding, physical coercion, involuntary seclusion and the use of chemical or physical restraints.

Sexual abuse comprises sexual contact of any kind with an older adult that occurs without full knowledge or consent on the part of that older adult. It may include sexual harassment, unwanted kissing, fondling or touching, all forms of sexual assault or violence, as well as sexually explicit photographing.

Emotional or psychological abuse refers to verbal or non-verbal acts which result in the infliction of distress, fear or pain on the part of an older adult. Emotional or psychological abuse might include harassment, insults, humiliation, intimidation, 'ignoring' or deception, and might arise from a failure to provide companionship, separation from family and friends, a failure to impart important information, unannounced changes in routine or intentional social isolation.

Financial or material abuse includes the improper or illegal use, exploitation or concealment of an older adult's resources, funds, property or assets. Abusive acts include theft or misuse of funds or personal property, loss of or damage to assets or property, unauthorised withdrawal of funds, forging of financial transactions, misuse of guardianship or power of attorney, use (or attempted use) of persuasion, trickery or coercion to obtain money or property, pressuring of an older adult to alter legal documents that he or she does not fully understand or pressuring of an older adult to give money or property to caregivers or relatives.

Neglect refers to a refusal or failure to fulfil caretaking/caregiving duties or obligations, or to provide an older adult with necessary goods and services. Neglect might include the failure to ensure adequate personal hygiene; provide adequate food or meal preparation; provide adequate clothing; ensure hygienic, safe and comfortable housing/living conditions (including required utilities); provide necessary and proper medication or health devices; treat or attend to health concerns; provide sufficient personal privacy; or provide adequate social support and companionship (Anetzberger, 2005b; Bomba, 2006; CNPEA, 2006).

Emerging forms of elder abuse include medical abuse (i.e. overmedication, lack of health-care services) and systemic institutional abuse (i.e. abuse on the part of the government, including inadequate pensions, restrictive immigration policies) (Walsh *et al.*, 2007). Individuals often experience multiple forms of elder abuse simultaneously or different forms throughout their life course (Dauvergne, 2003; Walsh *et al.*, 2007).

Theoretical frameworks

A number of theoretical frameworks have been proposed in an effort to explain the phenomenon of elder abuse which may also contribute to our understanding of bullying among older adults. These theories offer intra-individual explanations of maltreatment, caregiver burden, dependency, transgenerational violence and the structural or systemic marginalisation of older adults (Gainey and Payne, 2006; McDonald et al., 1991). These theoretical frameworks have been borrowed and modified from other fields of family violence (McDonald and Collins, 2000; McDonald et al., 1991). Few have been empirically tested and most offer incomplete explanations and are insufficient to account for the complex, multi-level, multi-dimensional nature of elder abuse (Glendenning, 1997).

Situational model

Rooted in a framework initially applied to child abuse and family violence, the situational model was one of the first explanations of elder abuse advanced (Glendenning, 1997; McDonald et al., 1991). This model postulates that caregiver burden, or the pressure or strain experienced by a care provider resulting from caring for an older adult (Van Den Wijngaart et al., 2007), causes caregivers to engage in abusive behaviours toward the older adult care recipients (Dauvergne, 2003; Perel-Levin, 2008). Abuse is viewed as an irrational response by a caregiver to the stress caused by an older adult's physical or mental impairment (McDonald and Collins, 2000). According to Phillips (1989, p. 198), 'as the stress associated with certain situational and/or structural factors increases for the abuser, the likelihood increases of abusive acts directed at a vulnerable individual who is seen as being associated with stress'.

Contextual variables associated with the situational model include characteristics of the caregiver, the older adult and the socioeconomic/structural factors (McDonald and Collins, 2000; Phillips, 1989; Van Den Wigngaart et al., 2007). Specific stressors related to caregiver burden include the social and behavioural difficulties of the older adult, the perception of the caregiving role as a threat and perceived or actual lack of instrumental caregiving support or assistance (Anetzberger, 2000; Gainey and Payne, 2006; Van Den Wijngaart et al., 2007). Thus a caregiver becomes burdened when there is an imbalance between the stressors (the care-load) and daily life functional capacity (Van Den Wigngaart et al., 2007).

The situational model has been criticised on the basis of its potential for blaming the victim (McDonald and Collins, 2000), and not all caregivers engage in abusive behaviours (Gainey and Payne, 2006). According to Anetzberger (2000, p. 47), 'although caregiving can be an important context for victim–perpetrator interaction and the dynamics of caregiving can certainly lead to abuse, caregiving is not the sole context in which elder abuse occurs'.

Social exchange theory

The social exchange theory assumes that 'social interaction involves an exchange of rewards and punishments between at least two people, and that all people seek to maximize rewards and minimize punishments' (Phillips, 1989, p. 202). In most social interactions, there are differences in power based on differential access to resources and different service-providing capabilities. In the case of elder abuse, the model suggests that, as older adults become increasingly vulnerable, powerless and physically, emotionally and financially dependent on caregivers, they have less to offer in terms of exchange and are thus at increased risk of abuse (Dauvergne, 2003; McDonald and Collins, 2000; Perel-Levin, 2008). According to this model, older adults may tolerate maltreatment or exploitation on the part of caregivers, for reasons which include the desire for continued relationships, a fear of abandonment or institutionalisation, feelings of responsibility for their experiences of maltreatment or feelings of guilt or shame (Reilly and Spencer, 1995). This theory has been criticised in that not all victims of elder abuse are dependent and powerless and some evidence suggests that dependency on the part of the caregiver exacerbates the risk for elder abuse (McDonald and Collins, 2000).

Social learning theory

The social learning theory focuses on transgenerational or intergenerational learning, conceptualising family violence as a cyclical phenomenon. This theory posits that, as a result of witnessing or experiencing violence, perpetrators of elder abuse are socialised to engage in violent behaviours, while targets of abuse learn to be more accepting of abuse. Violence thus becomes normative and an acceptable mechanism of control or response to stress (Dauvergne, 2003; McDonald and Collins, 2000; Perel-Levin, 2008). The social learning theory is part of the symbolic interaction approach which emphasises all parties' symbolic interpretations of one another's behaviours and of the shared encounter (McDonald and Collins, 2000). According to this theory, abuse is contextually or situationally defined, occurring in social interactions where discrepancies between behaviours and role expectations exist (Anetzberger, 2005a). Elder abuse is then conceptualised as inadequate or inappropriate role enactment (Glendenning, 1997).

The three theoretical frameworks discussed place emphasis on personal or interpersonal dynamics of abuse and thus fail 'to connect either to the wider political or structural processes which reinforce and support abusive situations leaving them to be played out at the micro level amongst carers and "victims"' (Whittaker, 1997, p. 122). Consequently, theoretical explanations ought to account for structural, socio-political factors, such as power imbalances within relationships or the social marginalisation of older adults.

Feminist theories

Feminist theories focus on spousal elder abuse, which constitutes a significant dimension of elder abuse (Crichton *et al.*, 1999; Podnieks, 1992). Some feminist theories suggest that 'wife abuse grown old' (McDonald and Collins, 2000, p. 30) is a consequence of family patriarchy, an ideology which legitimises a social structure in which men have more power than women. These theories highlight the gendered imbalance of power within domestic relationships, which it is argued increase a woman's vulnerability to abuse. Feminist frameworks typically focus on social inequality and marginalisation, examining the ways in which social structures and institutions maintain and reinforce acceptance of certain violent behaviours.

Traditional feminist theories, however, fail to account for the reality that older men are as likely as older women to experience abuse (Podnieks, 1992) for cases of late-onset spousal violence as a result of factors such as illness, disability or family role changes (such as becoming a caregiver) (NCPEA, 2006). Feminist theories need to focus on themes of power imbalances between partners, regardless of gender (McDonald and Collins, 2000).

Ageism

It has been widely recognised that elder abuse reflects negative structural/societal attitudes toward and beliefs about older adults, as well as discriminatory treatment in society (INPEA and WHO, 2002). Public policies and commonly held socio-cultural attitudes serve to foster and institutionalise ageist stereotypes. Ageism often includes the assignation of a devalued social identity to older adults, which often serves to justify societal inequalities (Bugental and Hehman, 2007; Kite *et al.*, 2005). Ageist beliefs refer to negative attitudes towards older adults, which might include assumptions that older adults are 'frail', 'dependent', 'unproductive' and characterised by 'diminished capacities' (Bugental and Hehman, 2007; Podnieks, 2006). Butler (1975) outlines a number of stereotypes associated with older adults, referring to myths of non-productivity, disengagement, inflexibility and senility.

Political economy theory

This approach to elder abuse suggests that violence against older adults arises from the socially created forced dependency and social marginalisation of older adults resulting from exclusion from social life through forced retirement or exclusion from work, experiences of poverty, institutionalisation and restricted domestic and community roles (Biggs *et al.*, 1995; Phillipson, 1997).

A lack of power and status on the part of older adults results in difficulties in accessing information, resources and services, responding to experiences of abuse and neglect and protesting against age-related discrimination (HelpAge International, 2000; Podnieks, 2006). The interplay of these circumstances and processes can result in enhanced vulnerability to abusive situations. Podnieks (2006) concurs, suggesting that age-based prejudices are closely linked to the social isolation and exclusion of older adults, enhancing their vulnerability to abuse. According to McDonald *et al.* (1991: 32), 'these negative attitudes dehumanize elderly persons and thus make it easier for them to be victimized'.

Ecological models

Ecological models of elder abuse examine the phenomenon as an interplay between the interpersonal characteristics of the older adult, their interpersonal relationships with the community in which they live, and broader societal factors such as social policies or collective norms (Krug *et al.*, 2003; Perel-Levin, 2008). Rabiner *et al.* (2004) present an applied ecological perspective of elder abuse which accounts for the 'multiple processes unfolding over time among the victim ... the perpetrator, and other interested parties who are concerned about the older person in the context of his/her physical, psychological, and social environment' (p. 56). At the simplest level, Rabiner *et al.* identify two dimensions of the conceptual framework: micro-level and macro-level factors. *Micro-level* factors include risk-associated characteristics of older adults experiencing abuse and perpetrators of the abuse. Relationships or interactions between the perpetrator and the individual experiencing abuse vary according to the type of social relationship, inequalities in social or economic status and the nature of power and exchange occurring between the two individuals.

Macro-level factors refer to those which exist within the socio-cultural and policy environment, including cultural norms (pertaining to views of older adults), public policies and programmes intended to protect older adults from maltreatment, civil and criminal remedies to cases of maltreatment and preventative efforts (Rabiner *et al.*, 2004).

According to Schiamberg and Gans (1999), the application of an ecological perspective to elder abuse enables a move from a simple, categorical description to a systemic, contextually based focus. Such a focus is necessary because of the complex nature of elder abuse and the fact that risk factors associated with elder abuse extend from the individual characteristics of the individuals experiencing and perpetrating abuse to the socio-cultural environment, as well as the interactions between individuals and their context (Rabiner *et al.*, 2004).

To an increasing extent, elder abuse research indicates a need for theoretical explanations that account for both individual characteristics and the broader context in which maltreatment takes place (Kosberg and Nahmiash, 1996). The need for a more systemic, contextually based conceptual framework is necessary as a basis for an understanding of the phenomenon of elder abuse and the interrelation and interdependence between different risk factors, as well as for the development of relevant, appropriate prevention and intervention programmes (Schiamberg and Gans, 1999).

Determinants of elder abuse and bullying

McDonald and Collins (2000) emphasise the importance of distinguishing between theoretical explanations of elder abuse and the individual risk factors associated with experiences of elder abuse. The WHO (2004) has adopted an ecological model of interpersonal violence, in which risk factors associated with maltreatment are conceptualised according to four interacting contexts:

- *Individual* – demographicic factors, such as age, psychological and personality disorders, education and income, alcohol or substance abuse and a history of violent behaviour or experiences of abuse.
- *Relationship* – family dysfunction, inadequate parenting practices, marital conflict and association with peers engaging in violent or delinquent behaviours.
- *Community* – social isolation, high residential mobility and unemployment and inadequate institutional programmes or policies.
- *Societal* – socio-cultural norms supporting the use of violence, social policies which maintain or increase economic and social inequalities and the availability of means of violence (including arms).

Podnieks (2006) discusses the complex interactive nature of determinants of elder abuse, which include personal, psychological and behavioural, social, economic and environmental factors. Risk factors can be classified according to three general categories: characteristics of the individual experiencing abuse, characteristics of the perpetrator of the abuse and characteristics of the relationship between the abuser and the abused. Anetzberger (2000, p. 48) proposes a model of elder abuse as a 'victim–perpetrator' dyad within which 'each involved party has a role in defining interactions, determining their meaning, and creating their dynamic properties', occurring within a context that brings the dyad together and fosters or triggers the occurrence of the abuse. She suggests that characteristics associated with the perpetrator of elder abuse are more predictive of maltreatment than characteristics associated with the older adult.

Risk factors or risk correlates associated with elder abuse have been examined in a number of studies and have been summarised in recent review articles (Erlingsson *et al.*, 2003; Lachs and Pillemer, 2004). Although variation exists, 'some identifiable patterns among the victim, the abuser, and the type of abuse have emerged' (Brozowski and Hall, 2004, p. 69).

Commonly identified risk factors specific to the older adult experiencing abuse include cognitive impairment (including dementia), physical or functional impairment, low income, low educational attainment, past experiences of abuse, substance abuse and social isolation (including a lack of social support and lack of access to resources) (Anetzberger, 2005a; Cooper *et al.*, 2006; Erlingsson *et al.*, 2003; Fulmer *et al.*, 2005; Lachs *et al.*, 1998; Schofield *et al.*, 2002; Shugarman *et al.*, 2003). Commonly identified risk factors specific to the perpetrator of abuse include mental/psychiatric illness, substance abuse, a history of violence or aggression, dependence (with respect to housing or financial support) of the older adult and inadequate caregiver experience or training (Perel-Levin, 2008; Podnieks, 2008). Other risk factors identified in existing literature include shared living arrangements between the older adult experiencing abuse and the perpetrator of abuse, a history of family violence (spousal or transgenerational violence) and social isolation (Kosberg and Nahmiash, 1996; Podnieks, 2008).

Specific risk factors tend to be associated with particular forms of abuse (Cooney and Mortimer, 1995). A Dutch study of 1,797 independently living older adults by Comijs *et al.* (1999) identified a statistically significant relationships between physical aggression and cases in which the older adult experiencing abuse lived with the perpetrator of abuse and depressive symptoms on the part of the older adult. Chronic verbal aggression was associated with cases in which the older adult experiencing abuse lived with the perpetrator of abuse and poor health on the part of the older adult, while financial mistreatment was associated with living alone, dependence in daily life activities and depressive symptoms on the part of the older adult.

Certain sub-groups of older adults may be particularly vulnerable to maltreatment, with increased vulnerability associated with gender, socioeconomic status, physical and mental health, and culture, ethnicity or race. According to the INPEA and WHO (2002), older women, older adults living in poverty, 'very old' older adults and older adults with limited functional capacity are population sub-groups which may be particularly vulnerable to abuse. Women are considered more likely than men to experience elder abuse (Choi and Mayer, 2000; Fulmer *et al.*, 2004; Straka and Montminy, 2006), particularly physical abuse, sexual abuse, psychological abuse and financial exploitation (Bugental and Hehman, 2007; Lithwick *et al.*, 1999). Other researchers, however, suggest that men are at equal (or even higher) risk of abuse (Kosberg and Nahmiash, 1996). It has been suggested that the older the adult, the higher the risk for maltreatment; adults aged 75 years and older are also considered to be particularly vulnerable (Choi and Mayer, 2000; Cooper *et al.*, 2006). Finally, McDonald and Collins (2000) identify race and ethnicity as two risk factors associated with elder abuse, though they caution that most discussions have been based on speculation.

Despite some level of consensus in existing literature with respect to the identification of these risk factors, methodological limitations preclude the development of hypotheses or the drawing of conclusions with respect to the determinants of elder abuse. These methodological limitations include variability in definitions of elder abuse, the use of non-random research designs, a lack of appropriate control groups, a reliance on retrospective reports and the use of assessment measures with limited reliability and validity (Vida *et al.*, 2002). A nine-year US prospective cohort study of 2,812 community-residing older adults identified non-Caucasian race, low income or poverty, advanced age, functional disability or activities of daily living impairment and cognitive impairment as associated with reported and verified cases of elder abuse and neglect (Lachs *et al.*, 1997). Further research is necessary to identify and distinguish the specificity of risk factors for bullying behaviours and those under the broader conceptualisation of elder abuse and neglect.

Implications of elder abuse

The implications of elder abuse extend to beyond the individual and family, having implications for community and government systems.

While there is a lack of research examining the specific effects of elder abuse on older adults' psychological and physical health and well-being (Choi and Mayer, 2000; Spencer, 2000), experiences of abuse have been said to have a profound impact on the overall health and quality of life of older adults (Bomba, 2006; Fulmer, 2002; Stones, 2007). Elder abuse is associated with various adverse health and life-course outcomes, including anguish, humiliation, damage to self-confidence or self-esteem, pain and injury, a decline in functional abilities, depression and increased withdrawal and social isolation (Abbey, 2009; Choi and Mayer, 2000; Dong, 2005; Perel-Levin, 2008; Stones, 2007).

According to Spencer (2000), the social costs of elder abuse are both tangible (those which can be assigned a monetary value) and intangible (those which cannot easily be assigned a monetary value). The tangible, or material, social implications of elder abuse include increased health and medical costs. Elder abuse might affect an individual's need for counselling or therapy, hospitalisation or placement in long-term care facilities, community-based or in-home health services and medications (Dong, 2005; Heath *et al.*, 2005). Elder abuse has also been associated with a higher risk of mortality (Lachs *et al.*, 1998).

The socioeconomic costs of family violence are substantial (WHO, 2004), although little information specific to elder abuse is available. Worldwide ageing suggests costs related to elder abuse are certain to escalate (Spencer, 2000). This demands attention to the development and implementation of elder abuse intervention and prevention programmes, as well as elder abuse screening and detection processes.

Screening and detection

Approaches to elder abuse intervention can be conceptualised to encompass detection, direct intervention and prevention. With respect to detection, elder abuse, bullying or neglect are known to have occurred if they have been personally observed or if they are reported by the older adult experiencing maltreatment (or by another individual having that knowledge). Elder abuse, bullying or neglect are suspected if certain signs, representing the consequences of maltreatment, are identified. These signs suggest the probability that maltreatment has occurred and are typically identified through the observation and interviewing of older adults in residential or clinical settings (Anetzberger, 2005a). Professionals most often involved in the identification of potential cases of elder abuse include social workers, psychologists, nurses, physicians and law enforcement officers (Teaster, 2003). However, though they are ideally situated to detect and manage cases of elder abuse, elder abuse remains under-recognised on the part of most professionals (Dong, 2005; Yaffe *et al.*, 2008).

According to the Toronto Declaration (WHO, 2002, p. 2) 'primary health care workers have a particularly important role to play as they deal with cases of elder abuse regularly – although they often fail to recognise them as such'. It has been reported that, while physicians are well placed to detect and report cases of elder abuse, they rank tenth among professionals who do so (Dong, 2005; Yaffe *et al.*, 2007).

On the part of health-care professionals, barriers to the detection or reporting of cases of abuse might include a fear of offending the patient or a fear of retaliation on the part of the perpetrator; difficulties in distinguishing between signs of abuse and age-related physical conditions; a lack of appropriate knowledge of elder abuse; uncertainty as to optimal management of, or intervention in, elder abuse cases; and a lack of appropriate or suitable screening instruments or assessment tools for identifying cases of elder abuse (Abbey, 2009; Perel-Levin, 2008; Yaffe *et al.*, 2008). In addition, cases of elder abuse may be difficult to detect unless there are obvious signs of (physical) injury (Dong, 2005). Physicians' perceptions of barriers to detection and management of elder abuse included difficulty in determining which experiences constitute elder abuse, a lack of knowledge of the prevalence of elder abuse, a lack of knowledge as to whom to contact to request assistance and support and a lack of protocols guiding the assessment of (and response to) cases of elder abuse (Krueger and Patterson, 1997).

Adults experiencing maltreatment also face barriers such as under-reporting of abuse which might be rooted in a denial of the maltreatment, shame or embarrassment, fear of stigmatisation, fear of retaliation by the perpetrator, a desire to protect the perpetrator of abuse, a fear of disrupting family solidarity (if the perpetrator is a family member), a fear of disrupting one's living arrangement, a fear of institutionalisation, difficulties in communicating experiences of abuse or lack of trust in clinical professionals. Further, older adults may not be aware of maltreatment as a result of cognitive or other impairments or they may not conceptualise their experiences as abuse on the basis of family background or cultural beliefs (Abbey, 2009; Perel-Levin, 2008; Yaffe *et al.*, 2008).

Screening instruments

A range of elder abuse screening and risk assessment instruments have been developed over the past three decades in an attempt to facilitate the systematic observation, inquiry and detection of elder abuse cases by identifying older adults experiencing abuse, those at risk of abuse or both (Anetzberger, 2005a). Kozma and Stones (1995) identify two general approaches to the measurement of elder abuse: the survey approach and the clinical approach. Survey instruments are concerned with the prevalence, frequency and type of elder abuse within specific population sub-groups, while the clinical approach, based on the use of screening instruments, is concerned primarily with the detection of elder abuse or the confirmation of suspected cases of abuse. Effective measures of abuse they advance ought to be sufficiently sensitive to discriminate among different forms of abuse and neglect, and ought to demonstrate appropriate reliability and validity. Fulmer *et al.* (2004) conclude that there is still much to be done in terms of reaching a consensus as to what constitutes an appropriate instrument for the assessment of elder abuse. The absence of a comprehensive, universal definition of elder abuse has been described as a fundamental obstacle in this regard (Fulmer *et al.*, 2004).

Prevention of and intervention in elder abuse

Across Western countries increasing public, professional and political awareness of elder abuse has stimulated the development and establishment of a variety of programmes and services aimed at preventing the occurrence of elder abuse or intervention strategies directed towards older adults who have been victimised to reduce the recurrence or associated harm.

Primary prevention strategies reduce the need for elder abuse intervention services by alleviating social isolation of older adults through the development of a formal and informal social support network for older adults, which might encompass peers, various care and service providers and participation in community organisations (such as local seniors' centres) (Nerenberg, 2006). Awareness campaigns or the provision of information regarding existing support services might also serve to prevent older adults from being victimised (Choi and Mayer, 2000). As such, education around existing services for older adults ought to be prioritised, in addition to mechanisms of dissemination necessary information in an attempt to prevent the occurrence of elder maltreatment (Nerenberg, 2006). Physical access to existing services, as well as awareness, ought to be ensured through reduction in mobility or financial issue barriers to access (Crichton *et al.*, 1999). Prevention services ought to target caregivers (both professional and non-professional) as well as older adults, and include caregiver stress assessments and caregiving supports (such as caregiver training, respite and home health care, and so on) (Heath *et al.*, 2005; Kurrle and Naughtin, 2008; Podnieks, 2008).

Anetzberger (2000) presents an integrative framework for primary intervention made up of three intersecting components: *primary intervention approaches* (protection, empowerment and advocacy), *primary intervention targets* (the victim–perpetrator dyad or the family system) and *primary intervention functions* (emergency response, support, rehabilitation and prevention). In terms of primary intervention functions, an *emergency response* service includes supports to be accessed during the abuse crisis or just before or after the abuse occurs. These services might include hotlines and temporary shelters. *Support services* are used to manage the elder abuse situation and to improve the situation of the older adult experiencing the abuse, the perpetrator of the abuse and any family members. These services might include personal care supports, meal delivery services and more. *Rehabilitative services* aim to diminish the likelihood of a recurrence of elder abuse by addressing risk factors associated with the older adult experiencing abuse or the perpetrator of abuse. These services might include counselling, substance abuse treatment and more. *Preventative services* aim to change the attitudes and behaviours of individuals, families or communities in order to decrease the likelihood of elder abuse occurrence. These services might include caregiver training, elder abuse education programmes and more.

Anetzberger (2005a) suggests the clinical management of elder abuse consists of detection (previously discussed), assessment, planning, intervention and follow-up. The *assessment* process is intended to evaluate the older adult experiencing abuse, as well as the circumstances of the older adult and the perpetrator of abuse. During this phase, information is collected from a variety of sources, including the older adult experiencing abuse, the caregiver and/or perpetrator, other family members and collateral sources to determine the need for assistance, the immediacy of that need, available resources and priorities for assistance. A number of factors must be considered, including the form of maltreatment, intentionality, the urgency of the situation, the involvement of any other individuals, the cooperation and capabilities of those involved individuals and the older adult's cognitive status and decision-making capabilities (Anetzberger, 2005a). The assessment process improves the accuracy of case identification and provides information to guide the planning of interventions.

In the *planning* phase of elder abuse interventions, two goals are considered: the preservation of the autonomy of the older adult experiencing abuse and the promotion of that older adult's safety. The first goal references the ability and willingness of the older adult to accept assistance and support, and the selection of approaches that are least restrictive with respect to the older adult's independence and decision-making responsibilities. The second goal concerns the adequacy and effectiveness of the assistance, as well as adherence to legislated adult protection mandates or policies (Anetzberger, 2005a).

Broadly, *interventions* refers to the implementation of a safety plan, which might include the application of social, legal and clinical services or procedures, treatment of the consequences of maltreatment, the provision of assistance to alleviate the cause(s) of maltreatment or the application of measures to prevent the occurrence or recurrence of maltreatment. Specific interventions may be directed either towards the older adult experiencing maltreatment or the perpetrator. Specific interventions might include elder abuse education, the provision of emergency or referral information, safe-home or institutional placements, hospitalisation, protective orders, caregiving respite care services, home health or nursing services and the referral of the older adult and/or family members to appropriate support services (social work, counselling, and so on) (Heath *et al.*, 2005; Kurrle and Naughtin, 2008). As they are voluntary interventions, the older adult must be willing to accept these supports. For older adults who are not considered to have the capacity to consent to such supports, adult protective services may be engaged. Protective options might include orders of protection, guardianship, conservatorship, financial management services (cheque-writing services, the designation of a representative payee, and so on) and more (Choi and Mayer, 2000).

Finally, *follow-up* procedures include evaluations of assessment of the effectiveness of the intervention, reassessments of needs and the monitoring of individual situations in order to prevent the recurrence of maltreatment. These processes often include the establishment of an ongoing relationship between the older adult (and, potentially, the perpetrator of maltreatment) and a clinician or service provider (Anetzberger, 2005a). The inclusion of follow-up procedures within an intervention and prevention framework reflects the recognition that victimisation and the associated consequences cannot be solved in a quick or simple manner.

With respect to the development of interventions and preventions, Harbison (1999) distinguish between four separate 'needs discourses'. Through these discourses, older adults who have experienced violence are constructed as 'adults in need of protection', 'victims of domestic violence', 'persons subject to illegal acts' or 'agents for their own lives'. When older adults are considered 'adults in need of protection', programmes and services are specifically directed towards cases of elder abuse and are based on adult protection legislation. When they are considered 'victims of domestic violence', programmes and services aim to alleviate or end experiences of maltreatment. When older adults are considered 'victims of illegal acts', their rights are publicised and they are encouraged to take legal action against the perpetrators of abuse. Finally, when older adults are considered 'agents for their own lives', they may lobby against systemic forces, such as ageism, or participate in public educational programmes. In this context, these constructions are considered to inform three main forms of programme and service that exist in response to the maltreatment of older adults: adult protection programmes, domestic violence programmes and advocacy programmes. Each of these approaches is rooted in a particular set of assumptions about older adults and is characterised by specific intervention strategies and preferred services (Anetzberger, 2005a; McDonald *et al.*, 1991). However, caution is necessary as 'important methodological limitations ... limit our ability to draw conclusions about the effectiveness of these interventions' (Ploeg *et al.*, 2009, p. 187).

Adult protection programmes have traditionally been modelled on child welfare or protection programmes, viewing older adults as vulnerable and in need of protection. These programmes are characterised by legislated or mandated protective actions, such as special powers of investigation and intervention, and mandatory reporting procedures. These may include power of removal and compulsory custody and services (Harbison, 1999; McDonald *et al.*, 1991; McKenzie *et al.*, 1995). Interventions are most often dependent on criminal sanctions or adult protective services in a given community, region or country, illustrating the connection between programmes and services and provincial or federal public policy (Podnieks, 2008).

Adult protection programmes have been criticised for their mandatory reporting, investigation and intervention procedures. Critics claim that such programmes restrict the rights, privacy, confidentiality and decision-making autonomy of individuals who have experienced elder abuse. Adult protection programmes have been said to restrict older adults' choice between intervention and non-intervention, as well as choice as to type of intervention: the older adult experiencing abuse may lose the right to determine what action might be taken with respect to their situation. These programmes have also been criticised on the basis that they 'infantilise' older adults, or that they characterise older adults as dependent and requiring protection from maltreatment in the same manner as children (McDonald *et al.*, 1991; McKenzie *et al.*, 1995).

Domestic violence programmes are often considered an alternative to the 'child welfare model' of adult protection programmes. These typically involve crisis intervention services, (court) orders for protection, emergency sheltering and second-stage housing, support groups for the individual experiencing abuse and the perpetrator of abuse, as well as a range of health, social and legal services. Domestic violence programmes might also include some form of public education (regarding the nature and extent of elder abuse and neglect) (ibid.). However, they typically target the symptoms of the abuse instead of the underlying causes (Anetzberger, 2001). As spousal elder abuse (perpetrated towards women) accounts for a large proportion of elder abuse cases, resources for domestic violence ought to be made available for older women who are experiencing or who have experienced spousal abuse.

Domestic violence programmes have also been criticised in that they typically conceptualise family violence of all forms as a problem of individual families rather than examine structural or systemic explanations of violence (Harbison, 1999; Hugman, 1995; Neysmith, 1995).

Advocacy programmes, which concern speaking for or acting on behalf of an individual or group in order to ensure that certain needs are met or that certain rights are respected (McDonald *et al.*, 1991), might be seen to align with the construction of older adults as 'agents for their own lives'. McDonald *et al.* assert the need to differentiate between legal and social advocacy, and between formal (structured) and informal (voluntary advocacy by relatives or acquaintances, or self-advocacy) forms of advocacy. Advocacy programmes have been described as the least intrusive or restrictive form of intervention or prevention for elder abuse (McDonald *et al.*, 1991). Advocacy programmes might also include 'peer participation' models of intervention within which older adults become involved, as individuals or collectives, in addressing issues of elder maltreatment (Harbison, 1999). Peer education (with respect to protecting oneself and others from maltreatment, for example) or peer counselling have also been advocated as participatory approaches to intervention, to 'provide opportunities for older adults themselves to take ownership of responses to elder abuse and neglect, rather than the current reliance on professional expertise' (Walsh *et al.*, 2007, p. 508).

Harbison (1999) suggests that older adults may be reluctant to engage in political or public action, as few older adults are willing to publicly acknowledge issues of family violence and, when the issue is taken up, it is often done in partnership with 'professional' advocates. Advocates inform older adults of their rights and of alternatives in service provision, and can assist those older adults in carrying out plans of action and working toward specific goals, in an attempt to advance protection, treatment and prevention (Anetzberger, 2001). They might also support older adults in lobbying against structural or systemic forms of oppression and marginalisation (such as ageism) or participation in public education programmes, peer counselling and other programmes and services (Harbison, 1999). Advocates are characterised by their relative independence from the service delivery system, though they often work to facilitate the appropriate and effective delivery of services. Authority and decision-making power rests with older adults experiencing abuse (Anetzberger, 2001).

Many older adults who have experienced violence may decline offered supports and services, which might reflect the identification of inappropriate intervention services or services that may not address an older adult's self-identified needs (Spencer, 2005, as cited in Podnieks, 2008). For older adults who may be unwilling to accept traditional intervention services, a *harm-reduction model* may be the best option, in terms of reducing the negative impacts of elder abuse. The harm-reduction model:

- promotes a non-confrontational, non-judgemental, value-neutral approach to intervention, as opposed to an approach which pathologises or criminalises the perpetrator of abuse (Lithwick *et al.*, 1999);
- prioritises short-term, realistic, realisable goals, as opposed to long-term goals;
- prioritises the reduction of the negative effects of abuse, and the most harmful or severe consequences of maltreatment (self-identified by the older adult) are addressed by immediate measures;
- promotes a bottom-up, empowerment- and advocacy-focused approach to intervention;
- recognises (and values) the roles that might be played by the older adult and the perpetrator of maltreatment in the harm-reduction process;
- focuses on maximising older adults' right to self-determination, placing emphasis on client-centred choice and validating older adults' concerns with respect to their independence, privacy and control (Lithwick *et al.*, 1999; Marlatt, 1996).

With perhaps the exception of advocacy programmes, the majority of elder abuse intervention and prevention approaches respond to individualistic conceptualisations of elder abuse and bullying, as opposed to addressing multiple structural or systemic factors associated with the occurrence of violence. Elder abuse intervention and prevention requires multiple services and strategies that are often situation dependent, given the complex nature of elder abuse experiences (Anetzberger, 2005a). For example, crisis intervention modalities may not be appropriate or effective (Ledbetter Hancock, 1990); programmes and services 'must do more than intervene to stop the abuse; they must provide a healing process for seniors who are abused to strengthen their ability to live free from abuse' (McKenzie *et al.*, 1995, p. 24). Choi and Mayer (2000, p. 23) reiterate the importance of ongoing support for both the older adult who has experienced abuse and the caregiver or perpetrator of the maltreatment, stating the need for 'tangible support to rebuild their lives after violence'. Elder abuse interventions ought to move beyond individual-level approaches in an attempt to direct initiatives towards community organisations, social service agencies and public policy and government legislation (Harbison, 1999).

Directions for future research

It is clear that elder abuse is an important social issue with devastating personal, social and economic consequences. Programme and service delivery for older adults who have experienced interpersonal violence has been significantly affected by the increasing population of older adults and by the concomitant increase in cases of elder abuse. The lack of empirical research evidence regarding the nature, prevalence, determinants and implications of elder abuse, bullying and neglect serves as a significant impediment to detection, reporting and intervention in cases of elder abuse (Fulmer *et al.*, 2004; Perel-Levin, 2008; Yaffe *et al.*, 2008). A lack of empirical research with respect to the effectiveness of existing interventions has hindered the progress of services for older adults experiencing various forms of violence. Accurate information about the risk factors and protective factors associated with elder abuse and bullying is required in order to facilitate the development of theoretically based approaches to elder abuse intervention and prevention, which could serve to moderate the associated harm.

REFERENCES

Abbey, L. (2009). 'Elder abuse and neglect: when home is not safe'. *Clinics in Geriatric Medicine*, 25: 47–60.
Action on Elder Abuse (AEA) (1995). *Action on Elder Abuse Bulletin*, No. 11. (Available from Astral House, 1268 London Road, London SW116 4ER.)
Anetzberger, G.J. (2000). 'Caregiving: primary cause of elder abuse?' *Generations*, 24: 46–51.

(2001). 'Elder abuse identification and referral: the importance of screening tools and referral protocols'. *Journal of Elder Abuse and Neglect*, 13: 3–22.

(2005a). 'Clinical management of elder abuse: general considerations'. *Clinical Gerontologist*, 28: 27–41.

(2005b). 'The reality of elder abuse'. *Clinical Gerontologist*, 28: 1–25.

Aravanis, S.C., Adelman, R.D., Breckman, R., Fulmer, T.T., Holder, E., Lachs, M., O'Brien, J.G. and Sanders, A.B. (1993). 'Diagnostic and treatment guidelines on elder abuse and neglect'. *Archives of Family Medicine*, 2: 371–88.

Baker, A.A. (1975). 'Granny battering'. *Modern Geriatrics*, 5: 20–24.

Beaulieu, M. and Leclerc, N. (2006). 'Ethical and psychosocial issues raised by the practice in cases of mistreatment of older adults'. *Journal of Gerontological Social Work*, 46: 161–86.

Biggs, S., Manthorpe, J., Tinker, A., Doyle, M. and Erens, B. (2009). 'Mistreatment of older people in the United Kingdom: findings from the first National Prevalence Study'. *Journal of Elder Abuse and Neglect*, 21: 1–14.

Biggs, S., Phillipson, C. and Kingston, P. (eds.) (1995). *Elder Abuse in Perspective*. Buckingham: Open University Press.

Bomba, P.A. (2006). 'Use of a single page elder abuse assessment and management tool: a practical clinician's approach to identifying elder mistreatment'. *Journal of Gerontological Social Work*, 46: 103–22.

Brozowski, K. and Hall, D.R. (2004). 'Growing old in a risk society: elder abuse in Canada'. *Journal of Elder Abuse and Neglect*, 16: 65–81.

Bugental, D.B. and Hehman, J.A. (2007). 'Ageism: a review of research and policy implications'. *Social Issues and Policy Review*, 1: 173–216.

Burston, G.R. (1975). 'Granny battering'. *British Medical Journal*, 3: 592.

Butler, R.N. (1975). *Why Survive? Being Old in America*. New York: Harper and Row.

Canadian Network for the Prevention of Elder Abuse (CNPEA) (2006). *What Is Senior Abuse?*, www.cnpea.ca/what_is_abuse.htm (accessed 30 October 2008).

Choi, N.G. and Mayer, J. (2000). 'Elder abuse, neglect, and exploitation: risk factors and prevention strategies'. *Journal of Gerontological Social Work*, 33: 5–25.

Comijs, H.C., Smit, J.H., Pot, A.M., Bouter, L.M. and Jonker, C. (1999). 'Risk indicators of elder mistreatment in the community'. *Journal of Elder Abuse and Neglect*, 9: 67–76.

Cooney, C. and Mortimer, A. (1995). 'Elder abuse and dementia: a pilot study'. *International Journal of Social Psychiatry*, 41: 276–83.

Cooper, C., Katona, C., Finne-Soveri, H., Topinkova, E., Carpenter, G.I. and Livingston, G. (2006). 'Indicators of elder abuse: a crossnational comparison of psychiatric morbidity and other determinants in the Ad-HOC study'. *American Journal of Geriatric Psychiatry*, 14: 489–97.

Craig, W.M. and Pepler, D.J. (2007). 'Understanding bullying: from research to practice'. *Canadian Psychology*, 48: 86–94.

Crichton, S.J., Bond, J.B., Harvey, C.D. and Ristock, J. (1999). 'Elder abuse: feminist and ageist perspectives'. *Journal of Elder Abuse and Neglect*, 10: 115–30.

Daly, J.M. and Jogerst, G. (2001). 'Statute definitions of elder abuse'. *Journal of Elder Abuse and Neglect*, 13: 39–57.

Dauvergne, M. (2003). 'Family violence against seniors'. *Canadian Social Trends*, Statistics Canada Catalogue No. 11–008: 10–14.

Dong, X. (2005). 'Medical implications of elder abuse'. *Clinical Geriatric Medicine*, 21: 293–313.

Erlingsson, C.L., Carlson, S.L. and Saveman, B. (2003). 'Elder abuse risk indicators: results from a literature search and a panel of experts from developed and developing countries'. *Journal of Elder Abuse and Neglect*, 15: 185–203.

Fulmer, T. (2002). 'Elder mistreatment'. *Annual Review of Nursing Research*, 20: 369–95.

Fulmer, T., Guadagno, L., Dyer, C.B. and Connolly, M.T. (2004). 'Progress in elder abuse screening and assessment instruments'. *Journal of the American Geriatrics Society*, 52: 297–304.

Fulmer, T., Paveza, G., Abraham, I. and Fairchild, S. (2000). 'Elder neglect assessment in the emergency department'. *Journal of Emergency Nursing*, 26: 436–43.

Fulmer, T., Paveza, G., VandeWeerd, C., Fairchild, S., Guadagno, L., Bolton-Blatt, M. and Norman, R. (2005). 'Dyadic vulnerability and risk profiling for elder neglect'. *Gerontologist*, 45: 525–34.

Gabrielle, S., Jackson, D. and Mannix, J. (2008). 'Adjusting to personal and organisational change: views and experiences of female nurses aged 40–60 years'. *Collegian*, 15: 85–91.

Gainey, R.R. and Payne, B.K. (2006). 'Caregiver burden, elder abuse and Alzheimer's disease: testing the relationship'. *Journal of Health and Human Services Administration*, 29: 245–59.

Glendenning, F. (1997). 'What is elder abuse and neglect?' In P. Decalmer and F. Glendenning (eds.), *The Mistreatment of Elderly People*, 2nd edn (pp. 13–41). London: Sage.

Gordon, R.M. and Brill, D. (2001). 'The abuse and neglect of the elderly'. *International Journal of Law and Psychiatry*, 24: 183–97.

Harbison, J. (1999). 'Models of intervention for elder abuse and neglect: a Canadian perspective on ageism, participation, and empowerment'. *Journal of Elder Abuse and Neglect*, 10: 1–17.

Heath, J.M., Kobylarz, F.A., Brown, M. and Castaño, S. (2005). 'Interventions from home-based geriatric assessments of adult protective service clients suffering elder mistreatment'. *Journal of the American Geriatrics Society*, 53: 1538–42.

HelpAge International (2000). *The Mark of a Noble Society. Human Rights and Older People*. London: HelpAge International.

Hirsch R.D. and Brendebach, C. (1999). 'Violence against the aged within the family: results of studies by the Bonner HsM (treating vs. mistreating) study'. *Zeitschrift für Gerontologie und Geriatrie*, 32: 449–55.

Hugman, R. (1995). 'The implication of the term "elder abuse" for problem definition and response in health and social welfare'. *Journal of Social Policy*, 24: 493–507.

International Network for the Prevention of Elder Abuse (INPEA) and World Health Organization (WHO) (2002). *Missing Voices: Views of Older Persons on Elder Abuse*, http://whqlibdoc.who.int/hq/2002/WHO_NMH_VIP_02.1.pdf (accessed 14 December 2008).

Kite, M.E., Stockdale, G.D., Whitley, B.E. and Johnson, B.T. (2005). 'Attitudes toward younger and older adults: an updated meta-analytic review'. *Journal of Social Issues*, 61: 242–62.

Kivela, S., Saviaro, P.K., Kesti, E., Pahkala, K., and Ijas, M. (1992). 'Abuse in old age: epidemiological data from Finland'. *Journal of Elder Abuse and Neglect*, 4: 1–18.

Kosberg, J.I. and Nahmiash, D. (1996). 'Characteristics of victims and perpetrators and milieus of abuse and neglect'. In L.A. Baumhorer and S.C. Bell (eds.), *Abuse, Neglect and Exploitation of Older Persons: Strategies for Assessment and Intervention* (pp. 31–50). Baltimore, MD: Health Professions Press.

Kozma, A. and Stones, M.J. (1995). 'Issues in the measurement of elder abuse'. In M.J. MacLean (ed.), *Abuse and Neglect of Older Canadians: Strategies for Change* (pp. 117–28). Toronto, ON: Thompson Educational Publishing.

Krug, E.G., Mercy, J.A, Dahlberg, L.L. and Zwi, A.B. (2003). 'The world report on violence and health'. *The Lancet*, 360: 1083–94.

Krueger, P. and Patterson, C. (1997). 'Detecting and managing elder abuse: challenges in primary care. The Research Subcommittee of the Elder Abuse and Self-Neglect Task Force of Hamilton-Wentworth'. *Canadian Medical Association Journal*, 157: 1095–2000.

Kurrle, S. and Naughtin, G. (2008). 'An overview of elder abuse and neglect in Australia'. *Journal of Elder Abuse and Neglect*, 20: 108–25.

Lachs, M.S. and Pillemer, K. (2004). 'Elder abuse'. *The Lancet*, 364: 1263–72.

Lachs, M.S., Williams, C.S. and O'Brien, S. (1998). 'The mortality of elder abuse'. *Journal of the American Medical Association*, 280: 428–32.

Lachs, M.S., Williams, C.S., O'Brien, S., Hurst, L. and Horwitz, R. (1997). 'Risk factors for reported elder abuse and neglect: a nine-year observational cohort study'. *The Gerontologist*, 37: 469–74.

Laumann, E.O., Leitsch, S.A. and Waite, L.J. (2008). 'Elder mistreatment in the United States: prevalence estimates from a nationally representative study'. *Journals of Gerontology Series B: Psychological Sciences and Social Sciences*, 63: S248–54.

Ledbetter Hancock, B. (1990). *Social Work with Older People*, 2nd edn. Englewood Cliffs, NJ: Prentice Hall.

Lithwick, M., Beaulieu, M., Gravel, S. and Straka, S.M. (1999). 'The mistreatment of older adults: perpetrator–victim relationships and interventions'. *Journal of Elder Abuse and Neglect*, 11: 95–112.

Marlatt, G.A. (1996). 'Harm reduction: come as you are'. *Addictive Behaviors*, 21: 779–88.

McDonald, L. and Collins, A. (2000). *Abuse and Neglect of Older Adults: A Discussion Paper*. Family Violence Prevention Unit, Health Canada, www.phac-aspc.gc.ca/ncfv-cnivf/familyviolence/pdfs/age-abuseneglect-discussion_e.pdf (accessed 16 December 2008).

McDonald, P.L., Hornick, J.P., Robertson, G.B. and Wallace, J.E. (1991). *Elder Abuse and Neglect in Canada*. Toronto, ON: Butterworth.

McKenzie, P., Tod, L. and Yellen, P. (1995). 'Community-based intervention strategies for cases of abuse and neglect of seniors: a comparison of models, philosophies and practice issues'. In M.J. MacLean (ed.), *Abuse and Neglect of Older Canadians: Strategies for Change* (pp. 17–26). Toronto, ON: Thompson Educational Publishing.

National Committee for the Prevention of Elder Abuse (NCPEA) (2006). *Domestic Violence*, www.preventelderabuse.org/elderabuse/domestic.html (accessed 5 March 2009).

Nerenberg, L. (2006). 'Communities respond to elder abuse'. *Journal of Gerontological Social Work*, 46: 5–33.

Neysmith, S. 1995. 'Power in relationships of trust: a feminist analysis'. In M.J. MacLean (ed.), *Abuse and Neglect of Older Canadians: Strategies for Change* (pp. 43–54). Toronto, ON: Thompson Educational Publishers.

Perel-Levin, S. (2008). *Discussing Screening for Elder Abuse at Primary Health Care Level*. Ageing and Life Course, World Health Organization, www.who.int/ageing/publications/Discussing_Elder_Abuseweb.pdf (accessed 19 December 2008).

Phillips, L.R. (1989). 'Issues involved in identifying and intervening in elder abuse'. In R. Finlinson and S. Ingman (eds.), *Elder Abuse: Practice and Policy* (pp. 197–217). New York: Human Sciences Press.

Phillipson, C. (1997). 'Abuse of older people: sociological perspectives'. In P. Decalmer and F. Glendenning (eds.), *The Mistreatment of Elderly People* (pp. 102–15). London: Sage.

Ploeg, J., Fear, J., Hutchison, B., MacMillan, H. and Bolan, G. (2009). 'A systematic review of interventions for elder abuse'. *Journal of Elder Abuse and Neglect*, 21 (3): 187–210, www.informaworld.com/10.1080/08946560902997181 (accessed 19 August 2009).

Podnieks, E. (1992). 'National Survey on Abuse of the Elderly in Canada'. *Journal of Elder Abuse and Neglect*, 41: 5–58.

—— (2006). 'Social inclusion: an interplay of the determinants of health – new insights into elder abuse'. *Journal of Gerontological Social Work*, 46: 57–79.

—— (2008). 'Elder abuse: the Canadian experience'. *Journal of Elder Abuse and Neglect*, 20: 126–50.

Rabiner, D.J., O'Keeffe, J. and Brown, D. (2004). 'A conceptual framework of financial exploitation of older person'. *Journal of Elder Abuse and Neglect*, 16: 53–73.

Randall, P.E. (1997). *Adult Bullying: Victims and Perpetrators*. London: Routledge.

Reilly, C. and Spencer, C. (1995). 'Ethical dilemmas in abuse and neglect-cases'. Paper presented at the 24th Annual Conference of the Canadian Association on Gerontology, Vancouver, Canada, October.

Rigby, K. (2002). *New Perspectives on Bullying*. London: Jessica Kingsley.

Schiamberg, L.B., and Gans, D. (1999). 'An ecological framework for contextual risk factors in elder abuse by adult children'. *Journal of Elder Abuse and Neglect*, 11: 79–103.

Schofield, M.J., Reynolds, R., Mishra, G.D., Powers, J.R. and Dobson, A.J. (2002). 'Screening for vulnerability to abuse among older women: Women's Health Australia Study'. *Journal of Applied Gerontology*, 21: 24–39.

Shugarman, L.R., Fries, B.E., Wolf, R.S. and Morris, J.N. (2003). 'Identifying older people at risk of abuse during routine screening practices'. *Journal of the American Geriatrics Society*, 51: 24–31.

Spencer, C. (2000). *Exploring the Social and Economic Costs of Abuse in Later Life*. Health Canada, Family Violence Prevention Unit, http://129.3.20.41/eps/le/papers/0004/0004006.pdf (accessed 16 December 2008).

— (2005). 'Harm reduction and abuse in later life'. Paper presented at the World Conference on Family Violence, Banff, Canada, 26 October.

Stones, M.J. (2007). 'Age differences in ratings of elder abuse'. *Senior Care Canada*, 2: 22–24.

Straka, S.M. and Montminy, L. (2006). 'Responding to the needs of older women experiencing domestic violence'. *Violence Against Women*, 12: 251–67.

Teaster, P. (2003). *A Response to the Abuse of Vulnerable Adults: The 2000 Survey of State Adult Protective Services*, www.elderabusecenter.org/pdf/research/apsreport030703.pdf (accessed 23 August 2010).

Tornstam, L. (1989). 'Abuse of the elderly in Denmark and Sweden: results from a population study'. *Journal of Elder Abuse and Neglect*, 1: 35–44.

Van Den Wijngaart, M.A.G., Vernooij-Dassen, M.J.F.J. and Felling, A.J.A. (2007). 'The influence of stressors, appraisal and personal conditions on the burden of spousal caregivers of persons with dementia'. *Aging and Mental Health*, 11: 626–36.

Vida, S., Monks, R.C. and DesRosiers, P. (2002). 'Prevalence and correlates of elder abuse and neglect in a geriatric psychiatry service'. *Canadian Journal of Psychiatry*, 47: 459–67.

Walsh, C.A., Ploeg, J., Lohfeld, L., Horne, J., MacMillan, H. and Lai, D. (2007). 'Violence across the lifespan: interconnections among forms of abuse as described by marginalized Canadian elders and their care-givers'. *British Journal of Social Work*, 37: 491–514.

Whittaker, T. (1997). 'Rethinking elder abuse: toward an age and gender integrated theory of elder abuse'. In P. Decalmer and F. Glendenning (eds), *The Mistreatment of Elderly People*, 2nd edn (pp. 116–28). London: Sage.

World Health Organization (WHO) (2002). *The Toronto Declaration on the Global Prevention of Elder Abuse*, www.who.int/ageing/projects/elder_abuse/alc_toronto_declaration_en.pdf (accessed 16 December 2008).

— (2004). *The Economic Dimensions of Interpersonal Violence*. Department of Injuries and Violence Prevention, World Health Organization, http://whqlibdoc.who.int/publications/2004/9241591609.pdf (accessed 25 February 2009).

Yaffe, M.J., Weiss, D., Wolfson, C. and Lithwick, M. (2007). 'Detection and prevalence of abuse of older males: perspectives from family practice'. *Journal of Elder Abuse and Neglect*, 19: 47–60.
Yaffe, M.J., Wolfson, C., Weiss, D. and Lithwick, M. (2008). 'Development and validation of a tool to assist physicians' identification of elder abuse: the Elder Abuse Suspicion Index (EASI)'. *Journal of Elder Abuse and Neglect*, 20: 276–300.

10   Cyberbullying

Ian Rivers, Thomas Chesney and Iain Coyne

Since the mid 1990s developments in affordable personal computing and communication technology have resulted in the almost complete saturation of the household market in terms of internet connectivity and mobile telephone ownership. Most recent figures provided by the Office of Communications (Ofcom) indicate that, in the UK, while internet connectivity continues to rise, mobile telephony has almost reached saturation, with 73.5 million active subscriptions (1.25 subscriptions per head of the UK population; Ofcom, 2008). Within schools since 2002, it is estimated that 98 per cent of children and young people have had regular access to a computer (National Grid for Learning, 2002). As communication technologies have advanced and become a part of everyday life, the nature of social interaction has also changed. Where once a letter, memo or note, or a telephone call, would provide the means by which information was imparted with an expectation of a reply within a few days, today email, instant messaging and, of course, text messaging have become the norm, with the expectation of an immediate response. This is not only the way in which social interactions have changed among adults (both at home and in the workplace), it is also representative of the way children and young people now communicate with one another.

We have as yet to fully appreciate the fundamental changes to human communication and social interaction that technology has brought. For some, particularly older generations (i.e. those who were brought up prior to the mid 1990s), the virtual and material worlds represent separate and distinct entities (Turkle, 1995; Young, 1996a, 1996b); for those young people raised in societies where technology and gadgetry are the norm, the boundaries of these two worlds are less well defined, and in many cases have merged or become non-existent. Thus for many today 'reality' is not linked solely to the material world; it unquestionably co-exists in the virtual, and interactions between friends, adversaries or even strangers can continue from one world to another without boundary or hiatus. How we manage this 24/7 communication revolution is something we, as a society, have yet to address, particularly in cases where it is misused or abused.

A brief history of cyberbullying

Cyberbullying is not a new phenomenon. It has evolved with developments in internet connectivity and personal computer ownership. Before the term 'cyberbullying' was coined, aggressive online interactions were variously known as 'flaming', 'flooding', 'kicking' and 'spamming' (Garbasz, 1997; Turkle, 1995; Young, 1996a, 1996b). More recently within the online gaming world, cyberbullying has been better described as 'griefing' and 'trolling' (Warner and Raiter, 2005). 'Flaming' represents sudden explosions of anger and has primarily been a feature in computer-mediated communication (CMC). It is often emotionally charged and includes the expression of overtly hostile or insulting remarks in text form (Thompsen, 1994). In her meta-analysis of CMC, Li (2006d) reported that while female-only groups are the least likely to engage in this type of behaviour, male-only groups tend to use coarse or abusive language most often in chat exchanges. Unlike 'flaming', 'flooding' is not so much an exchange between two or more people as an attempt by one person to dominate the online environment by sending the same line of text several times (often in capital letters to emphasise a point or shout it out). 'Kicking' or banning was used a great deal in internet relay chat (IRC) as a means of temporarily or permanently restricting access to the chat environment following a complaint by a member of the online group or room. In principle, 'kicking' was introduced to offer service providers the means of ensuring that netiquette was observed; however, it quickly became a means for some 'chatters' to exclude those whom they did not like, or those who challenged their worldview. Finally, 'spamming', in only a short space of time, became a worldwide phenomenon and is still the bane of internet service providers. 'Spamming' includes the posting or emailing of non-existent business offers, scams to extort money, hoaxes, threats (particularly chain messages), virus alerts and confidence tricks (especially where false online identities are created to bait or ensnare a particular person or target groups of users such as children).

'Griefing' and 'trolling' (discussed in detail later in this chapter) are deliberate attempts by one online 'gamer' to harass one or more other 'gamers'. Sometimes this is done to procure an advantage or resource within the game context, but at other times it is the result of a 'gamer's' need for attention or a desire to establish her or his authority. In some respects 'griefing' and 'trolling' represent strategies that are perceived to guarantee success at the cost of others and in many ways are more closely aligned with our understanding of what constitutes 'bullying' than those behaviours that were common in IRC chat or other CMC environments.

Cyberbullying, as it is currently understood, first came to our attention in 2000 when researchers at the University of New Hampshire reported on a representative national sample of 1,501 American youths (Finkelhor et al., 2000). This study was perhaps the first to identify instant messaging, internet chat rooms and email as media through which bullying could be perpetrated. In the UK, the NCH (now Action for Children) charity was the first to report on mobile telephone text messaging as a form of bullying (NCH, 2002). Since then there have been several studies conducted in the USA and UK (Hinduja and Patchin, 2008; Kowalski et al., 2008; Patchin and Hinduja, 2006; Williams and Guerra, 2007; Ybarra and Mitchell, 2004). However, while these studies have used the term 'cyberbullying' to describe the behaviours investigated, researchers have varied in terms of the definitions of cyberbullying they used, the measure of prevalence they applied and, because technology has advanced in a relatively short period of time, the media and communication devices they investigated (Rivers and Noret, 2009).

Much of the early research on online aggression was conducted with adults, and indeed it was not until the later part of the 1990s and early part of 2000 that personal computers and mobile telephones were made more affordable and were bought by parents for children and young people to use. Initially, mobile telephones were bought by parents so they could be assured of the whereabouts and safety of their children (Ling, 2004). However, as these children and young people began to share their mobile telephone numbers and email addresses, and began to communicate via text and instant messaging, the behaviours that were witnessed in adult CMC became a feature of the online and messaging environments young people inhabited. Additionally, as the mobile telephone market grew, so too did the demand for the latest and most advanced handsets, which were transformed into fashion accessories and became essential to young people's status within peer-groups (Campbell, 2005). Ultimately, cyberbullying became an issue associated with children and young people rather than with adults and, as a result, greater attention has been paid to it.

Since 2002 there have been a number of studies of cyberbullying which have purported to show age and gender differences in online and mobile phone aggression (Hinduja and Patchin, 2008; Kowalski et al., 2008; Li, 2005; Patchin and Hinduja, 2006). However, as previously noted, these studies have differed in terms of the definitions of cyber-bullying they have used and the way in which prevalence has been established. In its widest sense cyberbullying can be defined as bully-ing behaviour that occurs through media and communication devices. It can include hurtful or abusive mobile telephone calls, text messages, email, abusive or threatening statements made in chat rooms, on bul-letin boards or via newsgroups. It can also include the posting of inap-propriate photographs, videos or comments on social networking sites, web pages and blogs. In online gaming, as we have already discussed, it can include inappropriate strategies that provide one person with an unfair advantage over one or more others, or establish her or his domi-nance in the game.

Given the varied ways in which cyberbullying can be perpetrated, and the fact that some of the technology and communication devices available today were not available in the late 1990s and early 2000s, it has been difficult to establish baseline prevalence rates. For exam-ple, in the USA Patchin and Hinduja's (2006) study of cyberbullying focused on 'wilful and repeated harm inflicted through the medium of electronic text' (p. 152). By way of contrast, in Canada, www.cyberbul-lying.ca has described this form of aggression as follows:

the use of information and communication technologies such as email, cell phone and pager text messages, instant messaging, defamatory personal web-sites, and defamatory online personal polling websites, to support deliberate, repeated, and hostile behavior by an individual or group, that is intended to harm others. (Li, 2007: 1779)

In the UK, Smith *et al.* (2008) described cyberbullying as 'an aggres-sive, intentional act carried out by a group or individual, using elec-tronic forms of contact, repeatedly and over time against a victim who cannot easily defend him or herself' (p. 376). While all of the behav-iours identified above are part of what we call 'cyberbullying', the fact that there has been a historical as well as methodological inconsistency across studies has meant that reported prevalence rates have varied dra-matically, from 4 to 36 per cent. Furthermore, those prevalence rates have been affected by the fact that researchers have not been consistent in terms of their measurement criteria. For example, while the majority of studies acknowledge that cyberbullying constitutes a repeated action on the part of one or more known or unknown perpetrators, rates of cyberbullying as featured in the literature have often included single or occasional reports, as well as those that have suggested a concerted campaign against an individual (Hinduja and Patchin, 2008; Kowalski *et al.*, 2008; Li, 2005, 2006b). In addition, while some studies have

asked children and young people to report on incidents of cyberbullying that have taken place in the last two months or term (Rivers and
Noret, 2009; Smith *et al.*, 2008), others have been less specific and have
simply asked about cyberbullying occurring *during school*, or having *ever*
happened (Kowalski and Witte, 2006; Li, 2005, 2006b).

Research on cyberbullying, young people and schools

Recognising that there are conceptual, methodological and historical
issues in interpreting the findings from various studies of what has been
called 'cyberbullying', it has become increasingly clear that it is an issue
for children and young people in schools today.

Using data collected from the Youth Internet Safety Survey (YISS),
Ybarra and Mitchell (2004) reported that 19 per cent of the 1,501
American youth who participated in the survey had been involved (as
either a perpetrator or victim) in some form of online harassment in the
previous year. By way of contrast, in the largest survey to be conducted
in the USA, Kowalski *et al.* (2008) found that 25 per cent of girls and 11
per cent of boys had been electronically bullied *at least once* in the past
two months (n = 3,767; Grades 6–8). Ybarra and Martin (2008, personal communication) reported that 28 per cent of their sample (aged
from 8 to 18 years) who used text messages had received harassing messages *more than once*. Li (2005), in her study of 177 Grade 7 students in
Canada, found that 24.9 per cent had been a victim of cyberbullying
(38.6 per cent were boys and 59.1 per cent were girls). In a follow-up
study of 264 students in Grades 7 to 9, she found that reports of victimisation did not differ significantly between the sexes (25 per cent for
boys and 25.6 per cent for girls), but that perpetration differed substan-
tively (22.3 per cent for boys and 11.6 per cent for girls; Li, 2006b).

In their online survey, Patchin and Hinduja (2006) studied the prevalence of different types of cyberbullying among 384 American youth.
Using 'wilful and repeated harm inflicted through the medium of elec-
tronic text' (p. 152) as their definition of cyberbullying, they found
that 29.4 per cent were victims. When these data were broken down
further, they reported that 21.9 per cent were bullied in a chat room,
13.5 per cent via computer text message, 12.8 per cent via email, 2.9
per cent via bulletin boards, 2.1 per cent via mobile telephone text messaging and 1.6 per cent in a newsgroup. Subsequently, in their study
of 1,378 internet users under the age of 18 years, Hinduja and Patchin
(2008) found that 32 per cent of males and 36 per cent of females were
victims of cyberbullying. Females were more likely than males to be
victimised by computer text message (19.8 versus 17 per cent), email

(13.0 versus 9.7 per cent) and mobile telephone text message (4.7 versus 4.0 per cent). Of those who reported perpetrating cyberbullying, boys were more likely than girls to victimise others in chat rooms (9.6 versus 7.3 per cent) and on bulletin boards (3.4 versus 2.4 per cent). In terms of the offline correlates of cyberbullying, Hinduja and Patchin suggested that it is linked to various school problems, including offline bullying, fighting, truancy, cheating in examinations and, interestingly, substance abuse (the consumption of alcohol or the smoking of marijuana). However, the exact nature of the relationship between these variables was not clear.

In the only longitudinal study conducted in the USA to date, Williams and Guerra (2007) reported on 3,339 young people in school Grades 5, 8 and 11 (2,293 of whom were followed up a year later) who were victims of internet bullying. Their findings suggested that it is rare in Grade 5 (4.5 per cent; 10–11 years of age) peaks at Grade 8 (12.9 per cent; 13–14 years of age) and then declines marginally in Grade 11 (9.9 per cent; 16–17 years of age). While the researchers did not find any single predictor of internet bullying, their results did suggest that all three of types of bullying they surveyed (physical, verbal and internet) were related to participants' normative beliefs about bullying and their approval of it, a negative school climate and negative peer support.

As we have noted previously, in the UK there have been several cross-sectional studies of cyberbullying. Research conducted by the children's charity NCH, entitled *Putting U in the Picture*, found that 20 per cent of the 770 young people they surveyed had been bullied through technology: 14 per cent through text messaging, 5 per cent in internet chat rooms and 4 per cent by email (NCH, 2005). A survey conducted by MSN with 518 young people found that 11 per cent were victims of cyberbullying (MSN, 2006).

Smith *et al.* (2008) reported on two cross-sectional studies conducted in the UK among secondary school-aged students (11–16 years). In the first of their studies with 92 students, they reported that 6.6 per cent were regularly victims and that there were no significant differences between the sexes. In their second follow-up study of 533 students, they reported that cyberbullying increased with age (4 per cent in Year 7 to 23 per cent in Year 11), with the most frequently reported forms of cyberbullying being instant messages (9.9 per cent), telephone calls (9.5 per cent) and text messages (6.6. per cent). They also determined that victims of cyberbullying were also victims of offline bullying, and that perpetrators of cyberbullying were also perpetrators of offline bullying.

In the only longitudinal study conducted so far in the UK, Rivers and Noret (2009) found that, while prevalence rates of receiving nasty

Table 10.1. *Receipt of nasty or threatening text messages and email, household uptake in mobile telephone ownership and internet connectivity*

Percentages	Year of study				
	2002	2003	2004	2005	2006
Household internet connection[a]	45.0	42.0	50.0	57.0	60.0
Mobile/ cell phone ownership[a]	82.0	80.0	85.0	89.0	90.0
Text/email bullying – Boys[b]	12.0	10.6	13.8	11.3	10.3
Text/email bullying – Girls[b]	14.1	14.3	18.8	21.3	20.8

Notes: [a] Data provided by Ofcom (2006).
[b] Data from Rivers and Noret (2009).

or threatening text messages and email *at least once* rose for girls across the five years of their study (from 14.1 per cent in 2002 to 20.8 per cent in 2006), overall rates of frequent receipt of nasty or threatening text messages and email (*once a week or more*) remained relatively stable for both boys and girls (ranging from 1 per cent to 1.8 per cent of the 2,500 11–13-year-olds that were surveyed per annum). Overall, for boys, rates of receiving nasty or threatening text messages and email *at least once* declined (from 12.0 per cent in 2002 to 10.3 per cent in 2006). Although only addressing text messages and email, Rivers and Noret also considered the UK's historical market uptake in internet connectivity and mobile telephone ownership as correlates of cyberbullying (Ofcom, 2006; see Table 10.1). Overall, they found that rises in the rates of text message and email aggression reported by girls mirrored rises in the number of households connecting to the internet ($r = 0.88$) and purchases of mobile telephones ($r = 0.96$), which suggested that it is only at the point of market saturation that robust estimates of prevalence can be made.

Comparable with Hinduja and Patchin (2008), Rivers and Noret (2009) also looked at the offline correlates of text and email bullying for victims and found that, among boys, reports of direct physical bullying predicted receiving nasty or threatening text messages and email *more than once*. Among girls, unpopularity at school was found to be the sole predictor.

Previous research on bullying in schools has suggested that there are both age and gender differences in the types of aggression perpetrated

218   *Ian Rivers, Thomas Chesney and Iain Coyne*

by young people (Besag, 2006; Nansel *et al.*, 2001; Rivers *et al.*, 2007). However it is unclear whether or not the same pattern of age and gender differences is a feature of cyberbullying.

Early research by Valentine and Holloway (2002) in the UK addressing children's use of information and communication technology (ICT) at school and at home illustrated that, among girls, expressed fears for personal safety online mirrored those offline fears they experience, particularly in the company of male strangers. Consequently, issues of personal safety were not absent from the minds of young people (especially young women) when they went online. However, comparable to offline social relationships, they were minimised or subverted through the establishment of friendship and intimacy where reciprocal sharing and mutual disclosure featured. Wolak *et al.* (2002) found, in their study of 1,501 youth internet-users in the USA, that many of the close online relationships that developed among their sample not only crossed gender lines (71 per cent) but also intersected with face-to-face social networks. Seventy per cent of the relationships formed were among similar-aged peers, although 8 per cent involved contacts who were older by five years or more. Nevertheless, of those who initiated face-to-face meetings *for the first time* with their online friends, the majority (77 per cent) were accompanied, though only 13 per cent by a parent.

More recent research has shown that female 'gamers' with more masculine identities are more accepting of aggressive, and, indeed, sexually aggressive, online behaviours than those who go online for social networking (Norris, 2004). By way of contrast, Companion and Sambrook (2008) have noted that, in online games, while males prefer more combat-orientated roles, females prefer less violent ones (e.g. those of a healer). However, in making these choices, Companion and Sambrook found that girls, rather than demonstrating a prosocial aspect to game play, were more likely to engage in solitary game play, and removed themselves from group-orientated interactions. The authors also hypothesised that female gamers were more likely to opt for non-violent roles because they eschew violent behaviour. However, as Taylor (2003) pointed out, women represent over 50 per cent of online gamers and find the fact that they can choose the gender of their online identity attractive, allowing for a wider 'frame' of behaviours and experiences.

The methodologies employed by researchers in their studies of cyberbullying to date have often failed to interrogate the similarities and differences between young people's offline identities and their online alter egos. Thus we do not know how many children and young people fundamentally change their identities online, either in chat rooms or in game scenarios. This ability, together with the ability of users to hide or change online identities with relative ease, has meant that it has been difficult to establish the gendered nature of cyberbullying and its relationship with more traditional forms of bullying (Rivers and Noret, 2009). Indeed, research suggests that in less than 50 per cent of cases do young people know the offline identity or gender of their online or mobile phone aggressor (Hinduja and Patchin, 2008).

Online games and virtual worlds

A relatively new form of cyberbullying has appeared in the form of virtual world *griefing*. While virtual worlds have been around since the 1970s, it is only recently that they have been accessible to general users, primarily as a result of widespread internet adoption and improved computer graphics which serve to give such worlds added realism. A virtual world is a persistent, computer-simulated, three-dimensional environment where many thousands of users meet together. Originally text-based and intended as a platform for game-playing, some have emerged into a general mode of social and commercial interaction. The most popular virtual world, with many millions of users, is Blizzard's *World of Warcraft*, a fantasy role-play game. Within Azeroth (the name given to the world within *World of Warcraft*), each user is represented by an avatar (users' animated or model representations of themselves) – a human warrior, or an Orc or some other fantasy creature – which can explore the world by walking, running, swimming or flying through it. Other worlds are based on science fiction fantasies. For example, Sony's *Star Wars Galaxies* gives users the opportunity to train to become a Jedi Knight.

Linden Lab's *Second Life* takes a different approach. It is one of several virtual worlds that do not sell themselves as games. The *Second Life* interface allows users to create 3D objects and program them with behaviour. For example, a user can create an object to look like a Porsche car, and then program it so it can be driven like a car. As such, *Second Life* is perhaps best described as an arena of creativity (Chesney *et al.*, 2009) that allows users to create any 'online life' they care to imagine. Unusually among virtual worlds, the intellectual property of user-generated content in *Second Life* is owned by the user who created it. In addition, *Second Life* has its own currency, the Linden dollar, which has a floating exchange rate with the US dollar. This has allowed many users to create objects and sell them to other users for real (i.e. offline) currency. Some users are able to make a living in this virtual world. However, the surge in virtual world user numbers has, predictably, brought with it new forms of cyberbullying or 'griefing'.

In an ethnographic study of the *Palace* (one of the first avatar communities), Suler (1997) identified the concept of cyber-deviance and suggested that severe deviance can result from the creation of avatars with the intention of victimising others or indecent language with the aim of antagonising others. Suler (1997) also suggests that those who are deviant will find ways to abuse the unique technical features within an online community and the standards set by the community for what is acceptable or unacceptable will define the level of deviance. Furthermore, a toxic disinhibition effect can emerge where, as a result of perceived anonymity, individuals express themselves more openly in an aggressive and abusive manner (Suler, 2004). This disinhibition effect can emerge from a number of factors, including a perception of invisibility; the asynchronous nature of communication; and dissociating the online persona from real-life persona.

Much of the work on griefing has examined virtual-world games, rather than the more general worlds such as *Second Life*. As noted earlier, Warner and Raiter (2005, p. 47) defined griefing in terms of, 'Intentional harassment of other players ... which utilizes aspects of the game structure or physics in unintended ways to cause distress for other players.' Within virtual worlds, Smith (2004) distinguishes between intra-mechanic conflict (direct consequence of the game rules) and extra-mechanic conflict (consequence of the games being social spaces, which does not emanate directly from the game). He argues that, whilst intra-mechanic conflict rarely results in wider griefing, extra-mechanic conflict is unwarranted and can cause distress. Smith suggests that grief play (intentional and severe harassment aimed at causing another person distress) is a form of extra-mechanic conflict found in virtual worlds.

One possible reason for grief play within virtual worlds emerges from the motivations of those playing the game. Foo and Koivisto (2004) identified four overall motivations for grief play:

- *Game-influenced* – this includes the protection afforded by anonymity; dissatisfaction with the game management; benefiting at the expense of others regardless of the outcome (greed); and a belief that the behaviour is tolerated or expected.
- *Player-influenced* – this includes a desire to put other players down (spite); victim vulnerability, especially if a player is new to the game; and revenge against those who have 'griefed' them.
- *'Griefer'-influenced* – this consists of a desire to establish and maintain group identity (codes, rites) and/or the enhancement and maintenance of reputation.

- *Self-influenced* – these are motivations based on the disposition of the 'griefer' and include current emotions; the need to exert power; the need for attention; and to experience enjoyment in disrupting others.

Unlike these gaming worlds, *Second Life* does not have many formal rules, but users are expected to avoid the following list of behaviours, known as the 'Big Six':

- *Intolerance* – using derogatory or demeaning language or images in reference to another resident's race, ethnicity, gender, religion or sexual orientation.
- *Harassment* – communicating or behaving in a manner which is offensively coarse, intimidating or threatening.
- *Assault* – pushing a resident or using a weapon such as a sword or gun to assault an avatar.
- *Disclosure* – disclosing information about a user (such as their real or First Life name).
- *Indecency* – swearing, nudity or the depiction of sex or violence in a so-called 'PG zone'.
- *Disturbing the peace* – disrupting scheduled events, repeated transmission of undesired advertising content, the use of repetitive sounds, etc.

In one study of *Second Life*, a series of in-world observations was made for three hours a day for five consecutive days, and instances of each of the 'Big Six' were readily witnessed (Chesney *et al.*, 2009). Thus, if we define griefing in terms of the 'Big Six' behaviours, then it is common. This same study also used a series of focus groups to examine the perceptions of victims on the impact of griefing. All the users who participated in the focus groups had direct experience of griefing. Overall, attitudes toward griefing fell into one of two camps: (1) griefing within this context is harmless fun, and (2) griefing is unacceptable. Those who felt it was harmless fun (who were in the minority) pointed to the anonymity of the interface as a reason not to 'take it personally'. Therefore, unlike the case of cyberbullying conducted by mobile telephone for example, users within *Second Life* do not normally know each others' identities. By way of contrast, those who saw griefing as unacceptable said that it disrupted their virtual world experience, which, in some cases, meant they were unable to chat with their friends, and in other cases meant loss of earnings because their business was affected. Examples of griefing provided by participants included verbal abuse, pushing the victim's avatar around and creating objects that repeatedly made annoying noises (very similar to flooding).

Chesney *et al.* (2009) identified three motivations for griefing. The first was that so-called 'griefers' want to show off their superior knowledge of the *Second Life* environment. This is very similar to offline bullying, where an imbalance of power is often cited as a defining characteristic of the relationship between perpetrator and victim. In griefing, however, this imbalance emerges from the knowledge gap between seasoned and new users. The second motivation for griefing was that people did it because of the online gaming culture: those who see *Second Life* as a game do what they would do in many other games (i.e. attack the people they meet), which conflicts with the intentions of those who want to do business or socialise with other residents. While combat is appropriate in other virtual worlds, such as *World of Warcraft*, it is less appropriate in *Second Life*. The last motivation derives from *Second Life* being a 'safe' and easy place to grief, and residents may grief simply because they can. The flip side of this third motivation is that the *Second Life* environment is a safer place to be griefed by other residents, with less severe potential consequences than other forms of bullying – online and offline.

Chesney *et al.* (2009) also found that, in terms of dealing with griefing, participants saw managing griefing as the responsibility of developers (Linden Lab), individual avatars and the resident community. In the main, *Second Life* users were happy to 'police' themselves and deal with griefing when it arose, not only through retaliation but also through ban lists. This does have implications in terms of the wider context of cyberbullying and particularly within communities such as Facebook or Myspace. For example, a group of users may start a ban or 'kick' list whereby a user or resident who griefs in one area can be banned from multiple areas. All that is required to be able to ban or 'kick' others is that the community owners (in this case, Linden Lab) cede the technical controls to the users. Other online communities such as Myspace or Bebo could in theory provide similar controls to allow community users to self-regulate. Alternatively, one of the possible control mechanisms that community owners could create for users is one that is founded upon reverse trust. Most people today are familiar with the eBay feedback system. It provides an opportunity for buyers and sellers to give feedback on the transactions. Good feedback means high trustworthiness, poor feedback indicates that there have been problems with distribution or payment. Self-regulated ratings would provide users with an opportunity to assess the content within their community and, if a threshold was reached (i.e. enough people felt the content was indicative of cyberbullying, for example), the offending page could fall down search engine lists, or be banned altogether.

This emerging research into virtual worlds provides insights for those investigating other forms of cyberbullying and it is becoming increasingly important, as already some commentators (e.g. Castronova, 2001) have suggested that 3D virtual worlds such as *Second Life* will become the dominant way in which we will access information over the internet. If indeed this is to be the case, further consideration of the darker side of online communication is required.

Theorising cyberbullying

Much of the research that has been done on 'cyberbullying', as in any form of bullying, has been applied with little consideration of the theoretical ideas that may explain this phenomenon. In their study of text-based aggression, Hinduja and Patchin (2008) indicated that the theories that underpinned their study were drawn primarily from criminology. They suggested that 'cyberbullying' was a learned behaviour and among perpetrators it could be explained as the manifestation of a latent trait such as low self-control. While researchers have debated whether or not perpetrators of bullying have low self-esteem, a few studies have indicated that some display a high degree of control over the environments they inhabit, and have well-developed social skills (see, for example, Sutton *et al.*, 1999). For victims of 'cyberbullying', researchers agree that a sense of worthlessness together with a sense of disempowerment permeates (Ybarra *et al.*, 2008). Interestingly, and illustrative of the argument presented earlier in this chapter, Patchin and Hinduja also argued that issues such as race and, more pertinently, gender are less relevant online, as the environment is to all intents and purposes cultureless and genderless and provides an opportunity for the individual to interact with others anonymously, or as someone older or younger than him or herself, or indeed as a member of the opposite sex.

Early researchers of online communication suggested that those behaviours that intimated aggressive or sexual content in text format may not have been meaningful because they were not 'real', i.e. they did not occur in the material world (Turkle, 1995). Thus, comparable with Chesney *et al.*'s (2009) observations on activity in *Second Life*, text-based griefing may have been perceived by some as nothing more than harmless fun. Yet, even within the context of *Second Life*, intimate relationships between users can be forged online, which can have a significant impact upon established relationships offline. How this intersectionality between the online and the offline world occurs is something that has yet to be explored; however, it would seem that there is an association between the material world and those virtual environments that portray an approximation of reality or indeed mirror it when compared to those that do not. Thus, the greater the intersection between the material and the virtual, it may be possible to argue, the greater the danger of harm being caused.

Psychologically, Young (1996a) has suggested in his online papers that, while the material world provides us with reference points that contain or regulate behaviour, when those boundaries no longer exist or are not apparent, extremes of behaviour can follow, often without the need for justification, which, in turn, negates the sense of guilt. This can be seen most clearly in the case of the suicide of 13-year-old Megan Meier, a young woman with a history of clinical depression, who began an online relationship with a 16-year-old boy 'Josh Evans' on Myspace. 'Josh Evans' later turned out to be the mother of one of Megan's former friends, who had created him together with her daughter and an 18-year-old employee. The purported intention of creating this false account was to lull Megan into a false sense of security, to obtain private information from her and then use it to humiliate her. This they did. The final message Megan received from 'Josh Evans' read, 'Everybody in O'Fallon knows how [sic] you are. You are a bad person and everybody hates you. Have a shitty rest of your life. The world would be a better place without you.' Megan hanged herself on 17 October 2006. In the end, Lori Drew (the mother and chief creator of 'Josh Evans') was prosecuted and found guilty of accessing a computer without authorisation on three occasions, though she was not found guilty of criminal conspiracy. However, it is the reported lack of remorse shown by Lori Drew and the absence of an apology that shocked the local community in Dardenne Prairie, Missouri where the Meiers and Drews lived, and more widely America itself.

The fact that the creation of a false online identity by one person in collaboration with two others can have a profound effect upon the life of a fourth person was not lost on Young, even though he was writing a decade earlier. He argued that, 'one of the most striking features of email forums and letters is that people can experience almost no impediment to expressing themselves – for good or ill – because it all feels as if it is happening in the head' (Young, 1996a, p. 4). Thus, from the perspective of the perpetrator, the real harm caused by a confrontational or abusive exchange with another person sitting at another computer in another room, in another house, is questionable at best.

Issues in policy directions

Following the death of Megan Meier, in the USA there followed a raft of bills at town, county, state and national legislature levels to combat cyberbullying. On 22 May 2008, Democrat Congresswoman Linda Sanchez introduced HR (House of Representatives) 6123, the 'Megan Meier Cyberbullying Prevention Act', to amend Title 18 (Crimes and Criminal Procedure) of the United States Code to include cyberbullying as a crime. In an independent review sponsored by the UK government, Tanya Byron, a clinical psychologist and media personality, was asked by the prime minister to consider the risks of exposure to potentially harmful or inappropriate material on the internet and in video games. In her report, popularly known as the *Byron Review* (Byron, 2008), she argued that debates surrounding the harm caused to children and young people by new technologies is unhelpful; instead, she argued that there is a need to find ways of empowering those who use technology to manage risk effectively. Based upon a review of developmental neuropsychological studies, she argued that age-related restrictions or classifications of video games are necessary to limit exposure to violent media at likely stages in development. In addition, she recommended a more stringent regulation of the internet, and the introduction of a classification scheme that locks out searches that are inappropriate or unsafe. Unfortunately, only brief mention was made of cyberbullying and, rather than address issues relating to the teaching of ICT in schools, she recommended that those institutions responsible for the training of teachers should raise the level of knowledge around e-safety and assess that knowledge against professional standards of competence. Further, she argued, somewhat punitively, that schools and, by implication, departments of education where teachers are trained, should be inspected and assessed 'on performance in regard to e-safety' (p. 9).

In her summary, Byron (2008) strongly asserted that, rather than blame technology for the abuses that take place, the impetus rests with others to help children and young people manage most of the risk they encounter online and in video games. But how do we qualify risk? In the case of Megan Meier, a friendly online relationship turned sour, and deliberately so. Moreover, Megan's parents had taken precautions to protect their daughter. She was supervised by her mother when she went online, therefore the risk was minimised and the outcome was unforeseeable. Byron argues that, 'we need to take into account children's individual strengths and vulnerabilities, because the factors that can discriminate a "beneficial" from a "harmful" experience online and in video games will often be individual factors in the child' (p. 3). How we manage these 'individual strengths and vulnerabilities' has yet to be answered. However, as we move towards the closer regulation of some forms of material on the internet, Ybarra *et al.* (2008) have a salutary lesson for legislators, teachers and parents to learn. Some of that 'risk' young people encounter exists within mainstream media (news sites and web pages) that are used for homework, humanities, social studies and history projects. Stories, pictures and commentaries on topical issues such as religious discrimination, war, death and terrorism can be accessed by children and young people legitimately, and these can include graphic images and descriptions. In the end, the question arises, should we regulate these more stringently as well?

Although guidance materials for teachers and parents concerning e-safety are pivotal to the management of 'risk', and should include advice on strategies to block or challenge inappropriate messages, requests and web-posts, and offer generic guidance on appropriate usage and conduct (netiquette), cyberbullies should also be aware that anonymity is not a safeguard against exclusion from school or a criminal record. Increasingly, in the UK, parents and young people are reporting hateful messages they receive via mobile telephones or email to the police, who can then track individual internet protocol (IP) addresses or mobile telephone numbers through service providers, even where the sender's identity is unknown or has been blocked.

Current interventions

Since the very first studies that identified the potential for both online and mobile phone harassment, various mobile telephone companies and internet service providers (ISPs) have been keen to be seen to address this problem. The majority of interventions currently on offer provide 'what to do' suggestions if a child or young person is the victim of cyberbullying. For example, www.reachout.com.au, an advice and support facility for Australian youth, recommends the following actions:

- Keep a record (time and date). This may help you (or the police) to find out who is sending the messages.
- Tell someone. Talk to someone you trust, a parent, friend, school counsellor or teacher. Check out the Finding Help section for more info on how these people can help.
- Contact your phone or Internet service provider and report what is happening. They can help you block messages or calls from certain senders.

- If messages are threatening or serious get in touch with the police. Cyberbullying, if it's threatening, is illegal. You don't need to put up with that!
- Don't reply to bullying messages. It'll only get worse if you do. By replying the bully gets what he or she wants. Often if you don't reply the bully will leave you alone.
- Change your contact details. Get a new user name for the Internet, a new e-mail account, a new mobile phone number and only give them out to your closest friends.
- Keep your username and passwords secret. Keep your personal information private so it doesn't fall into the hands of someone who'll mis-use it.

In the UK in 2008, the charity Beatbullying launched 'CyberMentors', an online and, for students in participating schools, face-to-face service providing victims of all forms of bullying with a peer mentor to whom they can talk about their experiences. By way of contrast, Childnet International has provided students, parents and teachers with information on how to contact mobile telephone companies, social networking sites, video-hosting sites, MSN and chat room service providers in situations where aggressive or hurtful comments are sent or posted, or where images or videos are uploaded (Childnet International, 2007). Guidance provided by the UK government has included discussion of the need for acceptable use policies (AUPs), as well as an overview of current legislation linked to the misuse of technology (Department for Children, Schools and Families, 2007). However, it remains to be seen whether the guidance materials and interventions currently on offer will have the desired effect of reducing cyberbullying.

Summary and conclusions

Cyberbullying has a long history. Since the 1970s when the first interactive games were created, the potential for one person to harass or dominate a virtual environment has existed. Rapid developments in technology, increased affordability and the move from fixed to mobile interfaces has resulted in a rise in reports of abusive or threatening interactions and messages by children and young people. However, what research we have suggests that frequent exposure to abusive or threatening online or text-message content may not be as widespread as first thought. As technology becomes more a part of everyday lives, it will be necessary for us to manage our virtual interactions with others more effectively, and future efforts should focus on how best to advise users in their management of those interactions. As we have noted, exposure to risk will not vanish with the imposition of online safeguards. Aggression may be used as part of a resource collection strategy in an online game or virtual world. It may feature in 'spur of the moment' or ill-advised email and text messages. It may be inadvertently suggested by the use of CAPITALS or exclamation marks (!) in conversations and posts. Aggression is a human trait and it is necessary for us to understand its changing nature as our worlds move from the material to the virtual.

REFERENCES

Besag, V.E. (2006). *Understanding Girls' Friendships, Fights and Feuds: A Practical Approach to Girls' Bullying*. Maidenhead: Open University Press.

Byron, T. (2008). *Safer Children in a Digital World: The Report of the Byron Review*, www.dcsf.gov.uk/byronreview (accessed 5 October 2008).

Campbell, M.A. (2005) 'Cyber bullying: an old problem in a new guise?' *Australian Journal of Guidance and Counselling*, 15: 68–76.

Castronova, E. (2001). *Virtual Worlds: A First-hand Account of Market and Society on the Cyberian*. CESifo Working Paper Series No. 618, http://papers.ssrn.com/sol3/papers.cfm?abstract_id=294828.

Chesney, T., Coyne, I., Logan, B. and Madden, N. (2009). 'Griefing in virtual worlds: causes, casualties and coping strategies'. *Information Systems Journal*, 19: 525–48.

Childnet International (2007). *Cyberbullying: A Whole-school Community Issue. When and How to Contact the Service Provider*, www.digizen.org/cyberbullying/overview/contact.aspx (accessed 18 May 2009).

Companion, M. and Sambrook, R. (2008). 'The influence of sex on character attribute preferences'. *CyberPsychology and Behavior*, 11: 673–74.

Department for Children, Schools and Families (2007). *Cyberbullying. Safe to Learn: Embedding Antibullying Work in Schools*, www.teachernet.gov.uk/_doc/11909/CYBERBULLYING.pdf (accessed 18 May 2009).

Finkelhor, S. Mitchell, K. and Wolak J. (2000). *Online Victimization: A Report on the Nation's Youth*, www.unh.edu/ccrc/Youth_Internet_info_page.html (accessed 12 April 2009).

Foo, C.Y. and Koivisto, E.M.I. (2004). 'Grief player motivations'. Paper presented at the Other Players Conference, Denmark, December.

Garbasz, Y. (1997). *Flame Wars, Flooding, Kicking and Spamming: Expressions of Aggression in the Virtual Community*, www.personal.u-net.com/~yandy/papers/PSA.html (accessed 12 April 2009).

Hinduja, S. and Patchin, J.W. (2008). 'Cyberbullying: an exploratory analysis of factors related to offending and victimization'. *Deviant Behavior*, 29: 129–56.

Kowalski, R.M. and Witte, J. (2006). 'Youth internet survey'. Unpublished manuscript, Clemson University.

Kowalski, R.M., Limber, S. P. and Agatston, P.W. (2008). *Cyberbullying: Bullying in the Digital Age*. Malden: Wiley/Blackwell.

Li, Q. (2005). 'Cyberbullying in schools: nature and extent of adolescents' experience'. Paper presented at the Annual American Educational Research Association Conference, Montreal, April.

(2006a). 'Computer-mediated communication: a meta-analysis of male and female attitudes and behaviors'. *International Journal on E-Learning*, 5: 525–70.

(2006b). 'Cyberbullying in schools: a research of gender differences'. *School Psychology International*, 27: 157–70.

(2007). 'New bottle but old wine: a research of cyberbullying in schools'. *Computers in Human Behavior*, 23: 1777–91.

Ling, R. (2004). *The Mobile Connection: The Cell Phone's Impact on Society*. San Francisco, CA: Morgan Kaufmann.

MSN (2006). *MSN Cyberbullying Report: Blogging, Instant Messaging, and Email Bullying amongst Today's Teens*, www.msn.co.uk/cyberbullying (accessed 6 October 2008).

Nansel, T., Overpeck, M., Pilla, R.S., Ruan, W.J., Simons-Morton, B. and Scheidt, P. (2001). 'Bullying behaviors among US youth: prevalence and association with psychosocial adjustment'. *Journal of the American Medical Association*, 285: 2094–100.

National Grid for Learning (2002). *Young People and ICT: Findings from a Survey Conducted in Autumn 2001*. London: Department for Education and Skills.

NCH (2002). *NCH National Survey 2002: Bullying*, www.nch.org.uk/itok/showquestion.asp?faq=9andfldAuto=145 (accessed 1 September 2003).

(2005) *Putting U in the Picture: Mobile Bullying Survey*, www.stoptextbully.com/files/textbully_inserts.pdf (accessed 12 October 2008).

Norris, K.O. (2004). 'Gender stereotypes, aggression, and computer games: an online survey of women'. *CyberPsychology and Behavior*, 7: 714–27.

Ofcom (2006). *Communications Market Report*. London: Ofcom.

(2008). *Communications Market Report*. London: Ofcom.

Patchin, J. and Hinduja, S. (2006). 'Bullies move beyond the schoolyard: a preliminary look at cyberbullying'. *Youth Violence and Juvenile Justice*, 4: 148–69.

Rivers, I. and Noret, N. (2009). '"I h 8 u": findings from a five-year study of text and e-mail bullying'. *British Educational Research Journal*, iFirst Article, 1–29.

Rivers, I., Duncan, N. and Besag, V.E. (2007). *Bullying: A Handbook for Educators and Parents*. Westport, CT: Greenwood/Praeger.

Smith, J.H. (2004). 'Playing dirty – understanding conflicts in multiplayer games'. Paper presented at the 5th Annual Conference of the Association of Internet Researchers, Sussex, September.

Smith, P.K., Mahdavi, J., Carvalho, M., Fisher, S., Russell, S. and Tippett, N. (2008). 'Cyberbullying: its nature and impact in secondary school pupils'. *Journal of Child Psychology and Psychiatry*, 49: 378–85.

Suler, J. (1997). 'The bad boys of cyberspace'. In *The Psychology of Cyberspace*, http://users.rider.edu/~suler/psycyber/badboys.html (article originally published 1997).

(2004). 'The online disinhibition effect'. *CyberPsychology and Behavior*, 7: 321–26.

Sutton, J., Smith, P.K. and Swettenham, J. (1999). 'Social cognition and bullying: social inadequacy or skilled manipulation?' *British Journal of Developmental Psychology*, 17: 435–50.

Taylor, T.L. (2003). 'Multiple pleasures: women and online gaming'. *Convergence: The International Journal of Research into New Media Technologies*, 9: 23–45.

Thompsen, P.A. (1994). 'An episode of flaming: a creative narrative'. *ETC: A Review of General Semantics*, 51: 51–72.

Turkle, S. (1995). *Life on the Screen: Identity in the Age of the Internet*. London: Phoenix.

Valentine, G. and Holloway, S.L. (2002). 'Cyberkids? Exploring children's identities and social networks in on-line and off-line worlds'. *Annals of the Association of American Geographers*, 9: 302–19.

Warner, D.E. and Raiter, M. (2005). 'Social context in Massively-Multiplayer Online Games (MMOGs): ethical questions in shared space'. *International Review of Information Ethics*, 4: 46–52.

Williams, K.R. and Guerra, N.G. (2007). 'Prevalence and predictors of internet bullying'. *Journal of Adolescent Health*, 41: 14–21.

Wolak, J., Mitchell, K.J. and Finkelhor, D. (2002). 'Close online relationships in a national sample of adolescents'. *Adolescence*, 37: 441–55.

Ybarra, M.L. and Martin, S. (2008). 'Unwanted sexual and harassing TXTs: a national survey of children and adolescents'. Personal communication.

Ybarra, M.L. and Mitchell, J.K. (2004). 'Online aggressors/targets, aggressors and targets: a comparison of associated youth characteristics'. *Journal of Child Psychology and Psychiatry*, 45: 1308–16.

Ybarra, M.L., Diener-West, M., Markow, D., Leaf, P.J. and Hamburger, M. (2008). 'Linkages between internet violence and seriously violent behavior: findings from the Growing Up with the Media national survey'. *Pediatrics*, 122: 929–37.

Young, R.M. (1996a). *NETDYNAM: Some Parameters of Virtual Reality*, www.human-nature.com/rmyoung/papers/paper17.html (accessed 12 April 2009).

(1996b). *Psychoanalysis and/of the Internet*, www.human-nature.com/rmyoung/papers/paper36.html (accessed 12 April 2009).

11 An overview of bullying and abuse across settings

Iain Coyne and Claire P. Monks

In editing this book, we have illustrated that bullying and abuse emerge over the lifespan of human beings. It is identified within each of the settings detailed in the book and has serious mental and physical consequences for those involved, as well as associated costs for families, schools, organisations and society. Our vision was to obtain subject matter experts' perspectives on current research and practice within each of these different contexts, as well as debate possible avenues of research and practice that may cross settings. In creating this reference, our vision is that individuals interested in bullying and abuse in one specific context may learn from other contexts and consider adapting methodologies, models, interventions, and so forth to their own area of research or practice. Whilst we accept there will be contextual limitations and unique elements to different settings, we also argue that a greater appreciation of bullying and abuse more widely may enable us to develop common theoretical frameworks and interventions to better understand and reduce this phenomenon.

We are conscious that the book should not spread panic or present the idea that the human experience is plagued with abuse, bullying and neglect. Whilst this is theoretically possible, we cannot envisage the likelihood that the same individual will become a continual victim who is bullied or cyberbullied at school and at home by their siblings, is taken into care and bullied by other children, then, as they develop and start to form relationships, is abused by their partner. As a result of their background they become involved in crime, resulting in prison bullying and, after leaving prison and emerging into the world of work, they face further victimisation. Finally, as they become an older adult, exposure to abuse from family or from other caregivers starts to develop. The likelihood of this life history developing would be remote, and interventions outlined in the previous chapters would stop the potential for perpetual abuse at an earlier stage.

Further, we do not want parents, adolescents, employees or family members of older adults to become fearful of the social contexts they or their relatives will face throughout life. There is by no means an inevitability to the suffering of abuse in these contexts, because, as prevalence rates tend to illustrate, many individuals are not targets of severe levels of bullying and abuse.

However, this volume does indicate that some individuals encounter abusive behaviours and systematic and enduring bullying, at school, at home, at work or in other contexts. With this in mind, this final chapter synthesises and compares the research presented in Chapters 2 to 10. We draw conclusions regarding defining bullying, developmental changes, risk factors, measurement of bullying, individual and situational antecedents and interventions to reduce bullying across the different contexts. Further, we discuss the role of theory in furthering our understanding of the phenomenon.

The research life cycle

Systematic research into bullying and abuse in many of these different contexts is relatively new, with the majority of advances in research and practice emerging from the 1990s to the present day. It is evident, as Smith (Chapter 3) illustrates, that school bullying has led the way. Through the 'phases of research' identified by Smith, school bullying research has matured and developed into a large-scale international programme, with a vast amount of research evidence and what appears to be well-developed interventions showing some positive outcomes. However, as Smith recognises, there is still much work to be done in school bullying, especially with the advent of cyberbullying. Learning from successes and failures, as well as accounting for new types of bullying, means that there will always be a need to consider different approaches to measuring the behaviour; revise our conceptualisations of the behaviour; develop and test causal models of bullying; and evaluate and enhance intervention strategies to reduce the behaviour.

Using the analogy of a product life cycle, Smith's waves of school research can be mapped on to each life-cycle phase. The first wave characterised by building awareness of the behaviour maps to the introduction phase of a product life cycle; the second wave of increasing knowledge across different countries represents the growth phase of a product; and the third wave of an established research programme equates to the maturity phase of a product. Arguably through the 'development of new product features' (e.g. cyberbullying), research on school bullying has not yet reached the final product life-cycle phase of decline. Taking this approach one step further, we propose a tentative

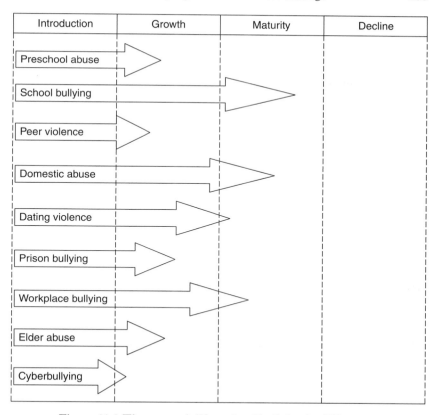

Figure 11.1 The research life cycle of bullying in different contexts
(c. 2010)

classification of phases of the research life cycle for bullying research in other contexts (see Figure 11.1).

This classification highlights the progression from descriptive survey research identifying prevalence rates and risk factors (introduction); through identification of antecedents and use of multi-method approaches to data collection (early growth); towards the development of theory and identification of interventions (later growth); to the development and evaluation of interventions (maturity). Some research areas are developing fast, others are just starting out and some have a long history of investigation. We are conscious that some readers and experts in these fields may not agree entirely on this classifications and we also acknowledge that there are limitations to a simple classification such as this (for example, as Walsh and colleagues identify in Chapter 9, there is a 30-year history of studying older adult maltreatment even though research on elder abuse *per se* is more recent). However, researchers and practitioners working within one environment may be able to learn from the methods adopted, tools used, theories tested and interventions developed in the other environments. Having a sense of where their area and related areas of interest stand currently provides a research agenda for these individuals going forward.

Defining bullying

Terminology

It is naive to imagine ever achieving an agreed cross-context definition of 'bullying' covering the range of behaviours experienced and unique contextual elements. Whilst bullying is the preferred term used in some of the contexts (e.g. school, workplace, prison and cyber), in other areas broader concepts are considered (e.g. peer violence, elder abuse, peer victimisation, dating violence). Within school, cyber and work contexts, bullying tends to be examined as a specific phenomenon (mostly as a result of the criteria used to define the behaviour), whereas in these other areas it is seen within the wider context of abusive or violent behaviour. In the latter cases, the authors argue for contextual reasons for taking such an approach: Monks (Chapter 2) suggests young children have an over-inclusive definition of bullying; Barter (Chapter 4) argues that the peer culture in care homes needs to be accounted for; and both Ireland (Chapter 7) and Walsh *et al.* (Chapter 9) indicate that frequency, duration and intent as criteria for defining bullying may not always apply in prison or elder abuse contexts.

This begs the question of whether bullying comprises a set of unique behaviours which are context-specific (and hence can only be examined within that setting) or whether our traditional approach to defining 'bullying' is too restrictive and limits our ability to include other behaviours. Perhaps, as Ireland suggests, we should consider bullying an 'umbrella term', which allows researchers, practitioners and other relevant stakeholders to account for other abusive and violent behaviours that at present do not fit the traditional conceptualisation of bullying. Bullying as currently defined is distinct from other types of abusive behaviour, yet need this be the case?

Defining criteria

Building on this debate, let's consider the defining features of 'power imbalance', 'intent' and 'repetition' attributed to traditional notions of bullying and how these are represented, if at all, across the different social contexts. First, across most of the environments discussed a power imbalance is represented. Whilst this imbalance tends to be more strongly characterised in definitions of school and workplace bullying, domestic violence and cyberbullying, it also emerges within elder abuse (specifically in relation to trust), peer violence (especially in the context of high-level behaviours), prison bullying and dating violence (in terms of dominance–submissiveness–control). However, Ireland questions the notion that inequalities in power should *always* be a defining feature of bullying, as 'baroning' in a prison context is not based on an overt imbalance of power. Further, Monks suggests there are fewer well-developed classroom hierarchies in preschool children and a more fluid nature to victim status. This implies that social hierarchy and the resulting dominance and power associated with this is not as strong a force in this environment as within other bullying contexts. Therefore, one could also question if bullying *always* requires a power imbalance. Indeed, as Coyne (Chapter 8) points out, power imbalance is nowadays not a main feature of practitioner or lay definitions of workplace bullying.

Second, intent is a controversial issue within bullying research and is not explicitly stated across all the settings discussed in this book. The premise is that, in order for bullying to occur, the perpetrator chooses to engage in abusive behaviour towards another individual and understands the impact of their actions (intends to harm). Clearly, predatory workplace bullying and the concept of social cognition in school/preschool bullying point to a planned, intentional nature to bullying. On the other hand, conflict-related bullying suggests an initial unplanned intention to bully, and the lack of empathy and poor social cognition in perpetrators of school bullying implies no intention to cause harm to another. Additionally, within elder abuse and prison bullying, respectively, unintentional abuse can develop. In elder abuse this is seen as a result of lack of experience, ability or ignorance on the part of the caregiver, whilst in prison bullying it manifests itself in prisoners engaging in behaviour without considering the consequences of their actions.

Third, frequent and enduring negative acts are seen as bullying. Therefore, one-off incidents, because of their lack of systematic targeting and escalation of conflict, cannot be deemed to be bullying. Whilst abusive behaviours in residential care homes, in domestic situations, in dating relationships, by prisoners, towards older adults and in cyberspace may include an element of repetition, they also allow for one-off incidents to be considered as abuse. For example, prison bullying need not always be repeated, as 'the *fear* of being aggressed, rater than the actual incidence, [may be] considered of more importance in determining bullying' (Ireland, this volume, p. 138). Further, in preschool bullying targets are not repeatedly victimised and victim status is less stable. Initially, the repetition criterion implies that traditional bullying is a very different concept from elder abuse, prison bullying, domestic abuse, and so on. Yet, as with other defining criteria, restricting ourselves to such a feature may cause criterion deficiency in our conceptualisation of bullying. There is not universal agreement on repetition even within the school and workplace bullying fields. For example, Smith (Chapter 3) pinpoints difficulties in extending the notion of repetition (and power imbalance) to school cyberbullying contexts as this may involve a single act by an aggressor that is 'repeated' by others. Therefore, researchers may need to consider what they actually mean by repetition and focus on other possible angles, such as fear of repetition or repetition by others.

Overall, the defining criteria of repetition, power imbalance and intention seen in traditional definitions of bullying feature to some extent in abusive behaviour in other contexts discussed in this book. However, experts within these areas propose different terms and definitions and even detail why their research areas cannot be viewed as bullying. This differentiation partly stems from the inappropriateness of traditional bullying definitions (mostly based in school and working contexts) in these other settings – whether because there is sometimes no repetition, no power inequity or no intent. Perhaps, rather than trying to espouse differences, what is needed is recognition of the similarities between these concepts and a re-analysis of our traditional approach to defining bullying. After all, even in these 'traditional' contexts there is no universal agreement on what constitutes bullying, and it is evident that such a view would face problems when applied to newer forms of bullying (e.g. cyberbullying). The discussion of related abusive behaviours in this book may have opened up our eyes to the possibility that 'bullying' is a wider concept than we initially envisaged.

Typologies of behaviour

As well as considering the definitions and terminology used across the contexts, types of behaviours experienced may also help to provide

Table 11.1 *A typology of bullying and abuse across different social contexts*

	Physical	Verbal	Emotional[1]	Sexual	Neglect	Other
Preschool	✓	✓	*a*	✗	✗	
School	✓	✓	✓	✓	✗	
Peer violence	✓	✓	✓	✓	✗	
Domestic abuse	✓	✓	✓	✓	✓	
Dating violence	✓	✓	✓	✓	✗	
Prison	✓	✓	✓	✓	✗	Theft-related
Workplace	✓	✓	✓	✗	✗	Work-related; organisational
Elder abuse	✓	✓	✓	✓	✓	Financial; medical; systemic institutional
Cyberbullying	*b*	✓	✓	✓	✗	

Notes: [1] Emotional includes relational and indirect abuse (such as social exclusion and spreading rumours).
a = Only direct forms of emotional abuse appear in preschool victimisation.
b = Physical abuse tends not to be common through technology, but may occur as a consequence of cyberbullying. However, 'happy slapping' and physically attacking an avatar in online worlds (e.g. *Second Life*) could be perceived as physical bullying.

researchers and practitioners with a sense of the relatedness of bullying to other forms of violence and abuse. Table 11.1 provides an account of the different categories of bullying and abuse across the nine environments. Whilst specific incidences of behaviour differ in each context, there is concordance that physical, verbal and emotional behaviours underlie the concepts of bullying, abuse or violence proposed in each setting. Yes, there is disparity at actual specific behaviour level and, yes, there are different prevalence rates for categories across the contexts (e.g. physical bullying is more prevalent at preschool and school than at work). However, it is evident that whatever environment we are considering (school bullying, domestic violence, dating abuse or elder abuse), we are considering a behaviour that comprises the same elements of physical, verbal and emotional abuse and which suggests more of a convergence than divergence between settings.

Conversely, neglect is seen only within domestic abuse and elder abuse, whilst other types (e.g. theft-related, work-related and financial) appear to be unique to only one context. Sexual abuse is interesting, as this is clearly seen as a type of abuse within all environments with the exception of preschool and work. It is to be expected, given their age and developmental level, that preschool children are unlikely to engage in sexual forms of abuse and hence this would explain why this type is not considered within this context. However, within work contexts sexually abusive behaviours are conceptualised more within the notion of sexual harassment than bullying (partly because sexual harassment need only be a one-off incident and hence does not fit the criteria of persistency).

Perhaps akin to cross-cultural research, the conceptualisation of bullying and abuse can be visualised with etic (universal) and emic (culture- or context-specific) dimensions. Etic elements allow us to consider cross-context similarities and explanations. Emic dimensions highlight differences across settings. As suggested, bullying may or may not be the most appropriate term to use and current definitions may need to be revised. Developing a definition around a term which is culturally (and contextually) sensitive has resulted in a wide variety of related, yet different, concepts being proposed and researched. Perhaps it is time to consider a more etic-based higher-level conceptualisation of bullying which allows for cross-fertilisation of ideas, as well as to accept that such a conceptualisation will also have emic dimensions.

Overall, in terms of defining the concept of bullying/abuse across contexts, we are left with three options:

- acknowledge that we are essentially looking at the same concept and develop an all-encompassing term and defining criteria which cross the different contexts;
- recognise that the above is impossible and that the concepts are very different and unique to each context;
- identify core features which span all contexts and refine definitions to capture these. Additionally, highlight context specific elements which researchers and practitioners in these settings also need to consider.

Prevalence

Whilst in some cases victim prevalence rates across contexts are relatively small (e.g. 1–5 per cent), in other studies rates of 20, 53 and even 90 per cent have been reported. This is partly a result of the methodology used, as well as situational characteristics. Notably, rates of bullying may be especially high in the more constrained situations of the home, residential care settings and prisons. Given these issues, it is not practicable to provide a comparative account across the different contexts of the level of victim status, other than to acknowledge that in some cases a large proportion of the population being studied face some level of bullying and abuse. In a similar vein, perpetrator rates (although not reported routinely) show variability from a lower estimate of 2 per cent to a higher rate of 50 per cent. Even less considered, bully-victim rates are estimated at 14 per cent in preschool, 45 per cent in prisons and 66 per cent in domestic violence settings.

Prevalence rates suggest a developmental change in rates of physical bullying. Physical bullying appears to decline as individuals become older. This can in part be understood in terms of the developmental model of Björkqvist *et al.* (1992), and, in relation to adult bullying, it may be a function of the 'effect–danger principle', in that the risk of being caught physically bullying is higher and the penalty more severe than indirect forms of bullying (Ireland, Chapter 7). However, physical bullying rates are not a simple linear function of age. As Naylor *et al.* and Ireland and Walsh (this volume) all show, rates of physical bullying can be substantial in adult relationships. Further, physical bullying generally does not occur within cyber contexts, even though most cyberbullying research focuses on children and young people. Unfortunately, prevalence rates for the other forms of bullying are not provided across all environments, although within care home and domestic environments there are some differences in rates between types of abusive behaviour.

A fairly consistent finding is a lack of gender differences in overall victim rates. It appears that, in the main, both genders are equally likely to be targets of bullying and abuse. Within domestic and elder abuse contexts, some evidence points to a higher rate of victimisation for females – although in sibling abuse the opposite effect is seen. Another similarity is the result that, in most environments, perpetrators are more likely to be males than females, especially when it involves physical and sexual forms of bullying.

There are sex differences in the methods of bullying employed, particularly among children and adolescents. Within schools, residential homes and juvenile dating, female bullies tend to be more likely to use relational forms of attack (e.g. rumour-spreading and social exclusion), whereas male bullies are more likely to employ direct forms of bullying (e.g. physical and verbal bullying).

Data on age trends are more of a mixed bag. As already suggested, in general, adolescents and adults use more indirect forms of bullying, whereas young children are more likely to use direct and physical forms of bullying. In a school context, victim rates decline as children grow older, whereas perpetrator rates are unchanged. Smith suggests that pro-bullying attitudes increase up to about age 14 to 15, after which they decline. To some extent this is mirrored in cyberbullying, with a peak at around age 13 to 14 and a decline at 16 to 17 (Rivers *et al.*, Chapter 10) and within dating violence, which decreases between ages 16 and 18 (Ortega and Sánchez, Chapter 6). In workplace bullying and elder abuse, the evidence so far points to older adults being more at risk, whereas in domestic abuse younger siblings and children aged 8 to 15 are more likely to be victims.

Methodological issues

Methodological problems in relation to identifying rates of bullying and abuse are prominent throughout the chapters in this book. Before discussing this further, it is worth praising the wide variety of methods used across the different settings. Methodological variability illustrates how researchers have attempted to understand the complex phenomenon of bullying and provides insight into the maturity of the research programme within each context. Different approaches to collecting data, which allow researchers to delve deeper into one perspective or collect information from different perspectives, have undoubtedly advanced our knowledge of bullying and abuse.

As is to be expected, initial investigations used a cross-sectional self-reported survey method as a means of describing the phenomenon of bullying and abuse. These have been the foundations of bullying research in the different settings, and, even though there are limitations on their usefulness (e.g. their reliance on one perspective, usually the victim), they are likely to continue to be used for investigating and describing bullying and abuse. As Smith argues, their use in identifying incidence rates helps to raise awareness of bullying and offers a form of publicity, which leads to interventions and action and helps to provide a baseline for monitoring the effectiveness of interventions. Across many settings, advances have been made from simple one-item methods (e.g. 'have you been bullied?') to the use of definitions followed by self-report items, and the development of more psychometrically sound scales of bullying behaviours. Additionally, some contexts have also adopted more longitudinal or two-wave designs to better test predictive models and the stability of bullying over time. However, such designs tend to be the exception rather than the norm.

Aside from the ubiquitous survey method, other approaches used include parent-reports, teacher-reports, peer-reports, observation methods, sociometry (peer nomination), contrived play settings, focus groups and interviews. Whilst a number of these have been developed to obtain data from particular groups (e.g. young children), it is evident that some cross settings. Knowledge of the different methodologies used within other contexts and consideration of the positives and negatives of such methods could help researchers in other domains evaluate how they collect data on bullying. For example, very little use of participant roles and peer nominations have been used in a working context, with some authors arguing that organisational politics and idiosyncratic biases undermine the nomination of individuals – especially if those potentially nominated are managers. Additionally, there is hardly any consideration of bully-victims as a group (and, as Ireland shows, these comprise the largest group in prison samples), let alone notions of 'reinforcer', 'defender' or 'bystander'.

However, variations in approaches used or criteria adopted to identify victims and perpetrators have meant that, within a particular context, comparison across countries, regions, school types, organisational sectors, and so forth has become impossible. Specifically, common problems reported are variations in the duration level used, differences in the frequency level used and the variety of definitions adopted to capture the same concept. Other issues include the use of different measurement scales; a focus on restricted samples (e.g. clinical samples); non-random designs; and, in cyberbullying, the inclusion/exclusion of different media.

As a result, prevalence rates differ widely across studies and hence identification of victims, perpetrators, bully-victims, and so on is tinged with an element of unreliability. Clearly, this has knock-on effects when identifying risk factors, antecedents, theoretical models and interventions. To some extent this is a fundamental problem of research in the area of bullying and abuse, especially as many of the differences seen revolve around the definition of bullying and abuse. If frequency and duration are key components of a definition of bullying, why do researchers use such varied levels to capture these key aspects? Can we ever have an agreed duration and frequency rate which dictates the research agenda (for example, in workplace bullying, weekly for at least six months has often been used)? If not, why is this a fundamental part of a definition? We likely could never develop a repetition 'rule' or 'law' which should be used in all research designs, but we may be able to have more agreement on boundaries of acceptable criteria. This may detract from the notion of bullying being a separate concept from other related areas, and there is likely to be resistance to this. However, as it currently stands, the research area of bullying and abuse is always going to be open to methodological criticism.

To some extent, agreement on criteria is currently emerging within several contexts as research programmes mature. Part of the methodological criticism has related to historical research studies and this has promoted recent developments in methods to counteract some of the issues identified. For example in cyberbullying, as the technology has advanced, there has been a need to broaden definitions to include new technology. As a starting point, it would be a positive move for each area to have some consistency in criteria used in prevalence studies going forward which will enable more accurate assessment of differences across countries and groups and over time. Perhaps knowledge of approaches used in others areas could provide the impetus for a rethinking of the criteria used in prevalence studies.

Risk factors/antecedents

Gender and age as risk factors have already been detailed, as they are the most commonly considered factors across the different settings. Other risk factors outlined include job level, type of organisation, substance abuse, a history of bullying/abuse, socioeconomic status, educational level (of abuser), disability (victim) and mental illness. Nevertheless, such factors are not consistently seen in all studies, and demographic risk factors *per se* may not be directly related to bullying and abuse. Rather, they may interact with other antecedents in explaining how bullying and abuse emerge.

Situational/environmental factors

Within some settings (e.g. workplace, prison and care homes) there has been more of a focus on explaining bullying and abuse from a situational perspective. Although not necessarily represented across all settings, situational antecedents seen in the previous chapters can be classified into five categories: family/home environment; peer-relations; dominance and leadership; culture and climate; and societal context.

As may be expected, family/home factors have been identified more within the child and young adult bullying contexts than the adult contexts. Specifically, evidence suggests that exposure to family conflict and aggression, insecure attachment to primary caregiver and an autocratic/punitive parenting style relate to aggressive behaviour in preschool, school, dating, domestic, care-home and elder abuse contexts. Parental neglect, over-protective families, exposure to violence in the home and insecure attachment have also been found to relate to victim status (however, in the latter case, this is not a universal finding). The home context the child grew up in or is currently still facing may cause stress and strain, which may then manifest itself in aggression and anger towards others. By contrast, the context may provide a model for what is perceived as acceptable or normal behaviour, which then guides the child's behaviour in other social settings.

In terms of the peer context as an antecedent of bullying, Ortega and Sánchez (Chapter 6) suggest that violence against peers and witnessing violence in peer-groups predicts dating violence. More focus, though, has been on peer-rejection and its relationship to perpetrator and victim status. Rejection by peers may result in bully or victim status in preschool, school and working contexts. Social isolation as a result of peer-rejection has been mooted as an explanation of why an individual becomes a scapegoat for others' aggression. Such an individual becomes the outsider, an easy target, an acceptable target, has few friends (hence a lack of social support), which creates a power imbalance between the perpetrator(s) and the individual. Nevertheless, this is not a consistent finding because, in preschool contexts, the unstable nature of victim status may mean that differences in sociometric status will not emerge and, in a working context, Coyne et al. (2003) found victims were generally rated as preferred people to work with and not outsiders.

Peer rejection also correlates with aggressive behaviour, but this seems to impact more in infant and junior school than secondary school. What is not so clear, partly thanks to the cross-sectional approach used in many studies, is whether peer-rejection causes an individual to behave aggressively or whether aggressive behaviour causes the individual to be rejected by peers. In preschool children, evidence points more towards the latter direction. However, laboratory studies on aggression show that manipulation of social exclusion caused participants to behave more aggressively towards another person (Twenge et al., 2001). Perhaps, as Dodge et al. (2003) propose, a more cyclical relationship exists whereby aggression predicts peer-rejection, which in turn increases aggressive behaviour. Possibly in an attempt to be more popular, or because their perception of what is acceptable behaviour is modelled on their home experiences, the aggressor behaves in an inappropriate manner, which is perceived negatively by peers, who then isolate this individual. As a result, the aggressor reacts in an even more aggressive manner and the cycle of rejection and aggression continues.

In a schooling context, bullies can sometimes have high status in peer-groups, whilst at work the perpetrator may be perceived as an effective and valued member of staff (with the victim seen as the troublemaker). Indeed, Monks (Chapter 2) suggests that some bullies who use aggression selectively and in a socially skilled manner are socially dominant and perceived as popular. Therefore, position in the social hierarchy

may 'moderate' the relationship between aggression and peer perceptions, especially when the perpetrator uses a combination of aggressive
and affiliative strategies.

Extending the idea of status and hierarchy, another category of
antecedents revolves around power, dominance and leadership. Barter
(Chapter 4) discusses peer-group hierarchies in relation to the inherent and accepted top-dog mentality within care homes. She explains
that peer hierarchies enable young people to boost their reputations,
boost, enhance or diminish those of others and have influence with
staff. Perhaps of real concern was the acceptance of the inevitability of
a hierarchy by victims of bullying and by staff. Barter's work suggested
staff used the hierarchy as a way of controlling young people in care
homes.

Additionally, an individual becomes a target as a result of their vulnerability in relation to a perpetrator's ability to wield a higher level
of power. Across the different contexts, power imbalances may be due
to organisational level (work); inequality in social and economic status
(elder abuse); physical aspects, such as height (school); knowledge of
technology (cyberbullying); age (domestic abuse and care-home contexts); and patriarchal perspectives (dating abuse). Overall, the need for
power coupled with the acceptance or inherent nature of power hierarchies in the environment seems to promote bullying and aggression.

To some extent, leadership builds on the theme of power. In a working context, this often emerges in relation to an autocratic leadership
style. A style focused on power, dominance and control creates an environment which accepts bullying and where victims are fearful of com-
plaining or criticising (Hoel and Salin, 2003). Further, in care homes,
the use of intimidation and control by staff promote more violence
within the home, and in prisons, overt security measures (arguably a
measure of dominance) increase hostile behaviour. However, poor leadership is not all about the use of too much power and control, as it can
also relate to a lack of leadership or ineffective leadership. In particular,
a *laissez-faire* leadership style (work), the encouragement of peer hierarchies (care home) and the predictability of staff supervision (prison)
mean 'leaders' subconsciously give permission for bullying to persist
through a perception that it is acceptable or that little punishment will
follow for those engaging in it.

We have already touched on culture and climate as antecedents of
bullying in respect of peer hierarchies and leadership style. However,
here we focus more on the social environment in terms of competition,
stress and strain, conflict and change as possible antecedents to bullying

and abuse. While specific cultural factors may differ across contexts, it is evident that culture provides the enabling, motivating and precipitating processes for bullying to occur (Salin, 2003). Competitive, non-supportive, stressful and strained environments promote bullying and abusive behaviours. These environments provide a sense of justification for the behaviour; create frustration and inappropriate aggressive responses to the frustration; or become perceived as risk-reduced places to engage in such behaviours. Even though in this volume the contexts discussed vary widely, the role that culture plays in promoting bullying is a strong feature throughout.

The final antecedent of social/community context goes one step beyond the more proximal measure of environmental culture. A culture of violence and/or acceptance of violence in the local community or wider society will promote engagement in bullying as this is the behavioural model children, adolescents and adults will have assimilated into their own approach to life. Akin to environmental culture, social norms endorse the perception that bullying and abuse is an acceptable behaviour in society. Portrayals of violence in the media, in films, in computer games and by famous individuals in society may create the impression that it is acceptable to bully someone. Although authors in each setting did not explicitly cite social context as an antecedent, societal norms will impact on each and every setting outlined in this volume. Cyberbullying is interesting as this can cross society and cultural contexts. However, even here online communication and gaming has its own 'society norms' (Kayany, 1998).

An excellent example of the role of societal norms in promoting bullying and abuse comes from the elder abuse context (Walsh *et al.*, Chapter 9). Here, ageism and political economy theory indicate how society can create negative attitudes towards and stereotypes of the older adult (which in turn justifies aggression), or how they create a forced dependency and marginalisation on the part of the older adult towards others (which in turn reduces their power and increases their vulnerability). Perhaps we all need to consider the society context more fully in relation to bullying and abuse. One wonders if institution-level interventions will ever be truly successful if, at the society level, there is an implicit or explicit acceptance of bullying and abuse.

Situational factors are a key element of bullying and abuse across the different contexts, and they range from the more proximal, dyadic/family contexts to the more distal society contexts. However, situational factors are only one element in explaining bullying and abuse. We now turn to discussing individual components of the victim and perpetrator as antecedents to bullying.

Victim characteristics

Before synthesising the research on victim characteristics, we have to touch on the issue of victim-blaming. Some authors reject the notion that individual differences may explain why someone is a victim and claim that those who subscribe to this view are blaming the victim for their situation. However, not everyone reacts in the same way given the same situational/environmental context and not everyone becomes a victim or a perpetrator. Further, research has shown that if we can identify possible individual factors which may make someone more vulnerable to bullying, we are able to provide targeted interventions towards these 'at-risk' groups. Whilst bullying may be 'caused' by environmental factors, there still needs to be someone or some group who are the focus of the behaviour and we as researchers and practitioners should understand why these individuals or groups are targeted.

Evidence illustrates that dispositional elements to victimisation include depression, anxiety, low self-esteem, poor social skills, conflict avoidance and low ability levels. Further, within school, child abuse and elder abuse contexts, disability or cognitive/physical impairment has been shown to relate to victim status. Two theoretical arguments are often proposed to account for these findings. The first suggests that some individuals are targeted because they are vulnerable, unable to defend themselves and hence are easy targets (submissive victim). The perpetrator preys on this vulnerability or the vulnerability allows the perpetrator the freedom to engage in bullying without fear of retribution or punishment. The second argument suggests that victim disposition or behaviour may provoke anger and aggression in others as a result of envy, annoyance or from clashing with social norms guiding appropriate behaviour (provocative victim). This may result in the victim being viewed as a justified target.

Although there is increasing evidence suggesting a victim component to bullying and abuse, one of the main criticisms is the lack of longitudinal or two-wave designs which actually examine the directional hypothesis. Given the difficulties in running such studies and possible ethical issues of allowing bullying to continue, cross-sectional studies have been the norm. This approach does not fully answer the question of whether disposition explains why someone is a victim or whether being a victim results in changes to disposition.

Perpetrator characteristics

In a similar vein, a dispositional component to perpetrator status suggests that individuals high in anger, aggression, stress, defensive egotism and lacking control of anger and other emotions are more likely to engage in bullying than individuals with the opposite disposition. Such individuals are unable to vent their anger appropriately and resort to bullying and abuse as a way of regulating their emotions – likely directed at the individual they perceive as the cause of their anger. However, in preschool, school and work contexts, some perpetrators may actually score highly in social intelligence or political behaviour and, rather than bullying being a consequence of an inability to regulate emotion, it is a planned and purposeful act to achieve a particular end result. In child and elder abuse contexts, there is evidence to suggest that perpetrators have themselves been exposed to a history of abuse. Perhaps this exposure creates a model within the perpetrator of what is normal or acceptable behaviour, which they then enact on others.

Defender characteristics

An interesting aside is the notion of defender characteristics (Smith, Chapter 3). Smith suggests defenders have high levels of empathy coupled with high sociometric status and a feeling of being empowered to defend the victim. Given that defenders are neither victims nor perpetrators, perhaps we could focus on examining more closely the individual elements of this role in relation to other contexts. Intervention-wise, it may be possible to 'train' individuals to become defenders of the victim rather than victims or perpetrators, and knowledge of individual characteristics which underlie this role would be an advantage.

The notion of an individual component to victim/perpetrator status is controversial and, as discussed, there are methodological problems with the research. However, across most of the contexts there is a consideration of the role the individual plays in bullying and abuse and, whilst situational components may explain the emergence of bullying and abuse, individual differences could explain who the likely 'players' will be in the situation. Further, as the dyadic model of Aquino and Lamertz (2004) proposes, the interaction between victims and perpetrators in relation to individual differences may predict the types of bullying enacted, which could result in different methods of coping, different outcomes for both parties and different interventions. It would be interesting to see if this model can transfer to other contexts.

Theoretical explanations

Whilst so far situational and individual antecedents have been discovered separately, many acknowledge that these explanations alone are too simplistic to capture the phenomenon of bullying and abuse. To that end, a number of theoretical models have been proposed to explain bullying and abuse which try to capture all or separate elements of the bullying process. It must be said that, although models have been suggested, this is perhaps one aspect where systematic research is lacking and often theories are proposed without any empirical evidence to support them. Across the contexts we see two approaches: the application of general psychological models to bullying and abuse and the development of specific contextual models explaining bullying. The following discussion focuses on assimilating the various models proposed into broader theoretical approaches and concentrates on those that emerge across a number of settings.

Attachment theory/parental style

Attachment theory hypothesises that attachment to parents/caregivers provides a child with an internal working model (IWM) which guides their relationships with others throughout their life (Main *et al.*, 1985). Insecure attachment may result in an individual responding to others with hostility and aggression. Whilst this model tends to be related to child and adolescent bullying, as the theory promotes the relative continuity of the IWM over time (Goldberg, 2000), it could also explain adult forms of bullying and abuse. For example, perhaps the way a manager relates to their employees at work may be influenced by their insecure attachment to their parents when young? Linked to attachment, parental styles (especially harsh/autocratic styles) may cause an individual to behave in an aggressive manner. Similar to attachment theory, this provides the child with a working model of what is acceptable behaviour when dealing with others. Taking a work context again, although parental style is not considered, researchers do look at leadership and especially autocratic leadership style. If one can envision the organisation as 'the parent' when an individual is at work, then we would expect autocratic and harsh management styles to predict bullying behaviour at work. Whilst attachment theory may explain who will likely become a victim and who a perpetrator (although evidence is limited on its ability to distinguish between them), there is not enough evidence as yet to assess its effectiveness across different contexts.

Evolutionary theory

An evolutionary approach to bullying and abuse has been suggested across a number of contexts. Bullying and abuse can be seen as having costs and benefits and being adaptive for an individual doing the bullying. For example, Ireland (Chapter 7) shows how bullying behaviour may operate as a survival mechanism in a prison setting, and Einarsen and Mikkelsen (2003) discuss from an evolutionary perspective how fear of ostracism and its associated anxiety causes negative outcomes for the victim of workplace bullying. Further, Naylor *et al.*, Ortega and Sánchez and Walsh *et al.* (this volume) propose a feminist/patriarchal approach to understanding sex differences in aggression. The gendered imbalance of power and rigid/sexist attitudes about male and female roles could explain domestic violence, dating violence or elder abuse towards women. However, this latter notion does not explain violence towards males in these contexts. Bullying as a survival mechanism is an interesting and worrying notion, as it suggests that it is inherent within human social situations. However, in contrast, prevalence rates suggest bullying is not always a common occurrence and that for many people a 'need to survive' does not always manifest itself in aggression and violence. Additionally, the sexual selection notion of evolutionary theory does not always apply, as gender differences in victim rates especially are not universally seen.

Social learning theory

We have already touched on social learning theory (SLT) when discussing antecedents of bullying and abuse. SLT may explain why parental style relates to aggressive or non-aggressive behaviour. Through observation, role modelling and reinforcement, a child learns how to act in social situations. As a result of rewarding or ignoring a child for engaging in aggressive acts or by engaging in harsh/assertive parenting, a child starts to view aggression as the model behaviour and then uses this in their relationships with others. The impact of family background characteristics (from an SLT perspective) especially relate to involvement in bullying at preschool and school, sibling abuse, bullying within care homes and dating violence, but it may also be applied to adult bullying. Modelling of behaviour is not just restricted to family background, as it can also include peer-relationships, the work environment (e.g. a culture of acceptance of bullying) and the wider community/society (the acceptance of aggression in the local community or wider society). Even within a cyber context the notion of a 'hacker norm' (Kayany,

1998) exists, which provides a model for behaviour online. Given this, SLT is perhaps one theoretical model which has the capacity to cross all the different contexts, and more consideration of this approach in these different settings is needed.

Socio-cultural theories

Moving away from the more individual factors, socio-cultural theory focuses on understanding the importance of situational factors in behaviour. Here, bullying is embedded within the culture of the organisation where it is taking place and is a function of the system rather than individuals within it. This approach is particularly promoted within care homes, prisons and workplaces, with bullying seen to be prevalent when the culture within the organisation is non-democratic, hierarchical, supportive of bullying, competitive, strained and stressful. Within a working environment, these characteristics are hypothesised to cause bullying either through a stressor perspective (in particular, the frustration–aggression model) or through a conflict escalation perspective. Interestingly, these two approaches have also been seen in other contexts. Walsh *et al.* (Chapter 9) suggest the stress experienced by a caregiver may cause them to react aggressively, and Ortega and Sánchez (Chapter 6) suggest conflict theory as an explanation for dating violence.

Ecological/interactional models

Across many contexts a more unified approach to understanding bullying behaviour emerges, which takes account of the interaction between individual, organisational, interpersonal and societal factors. This model offers a more complex approach to understanding bullying and abuse, and suggests a dynamic and process component to such behaviour. Individual factors explain why a person reacts in the way they do or why they become a target/perpetrator; organisational factors provide the setting for bullying-type behaviours to emerge (e.g. hierarchical structure, change, stress, etc.); interpersonal factors explain the dynamic interplay between dyads or groups which causes conflict to escalate; and societal factors provide a 'model' of what is deemed acceptable or unacceptable behaviour in society. Whilst specific models vary, most tend to include these components in their design and propose that the interplay between these factors causes bullying and abuse (although society factors are not universally included). This theoretical stance is promising as it suggests a multi-dimensional approach directed at various levels: the individual (bully, bullied and onlookers); the immediate peer-group, family or workforce; the culture or climate of the setting; and, beyond, the general societal context. Variations are seen across the different settings outlined in this book, and perhaps a more unified interaction theory could be developed synthesising these contextual-dependent interactional models. This will be difficult because, in many of the settings discussed, such models have not yet been fully tested. To try to then test across contexts may be one step too far at the current stage. However, further research focused on developing this approach and clarifying the interactions between each factor across different settings may help to develop a more integrated theory of bullying and abuse across contexts.

In the current debate, we have not discussed each theory proposed in detail (such as social cognition, social identity theory, political economy theory, etc.), but have, rather, synthesised them into a number of broader approaches. Some are more general psychological approaches focused on the individual (e.g. attachment theory), and others focus on the situational component which includes more general psychological theories (such as stressor or conflict models). We propose that the final interactional model is a more fruitful avenue of research to follow and one which researchers in the different settings should start to explore further. Theoretical developments in most settings discussed in this book are in their infancy, so now is perhaps the best time to start thinking about this from a wider perspective.

Interventions

Early intervention is paramount in helping to reduce bullying and abuse in all settings, but it is unlikely that such behaviour will ever be eliminated. Given its complex nature and interplay of various antecedents, a full-scale intervention approach that captures all these aspects and is adopted and recognised by all parties is a nirvana. Indeed, as Smith (Chapter 3) illustrates, school-based interventions, whilst showing positive results, are modest at best. The commitment towards, the length of and the ownership of the intervention, as well as the community context, are all factors which moderate the effectiveness of the intervention. Acknowledging the fact that we may never eradicate bullying is an important step for researchers, practitioners and other relevant stakeholders to take. Attention should be focused on ways to reduce bullying and the impact of such behaviour on individuals, organisations and wider society. People will still be bullied and bully, but we need to find solutions which reduce their chances of being victims or perpetrators and which provide better help, support and rehabilitation for all those involved.

Similar to the theoretical discussion, the development and especially evaluation of interventions within each setting is limited. Partly, this is a result of the lack of theory to guide interventions and partly a result of where the research is currently within each context. However, all authors touch on the notion of intervention and provide options for those working within the bullying and abuse field. Synthesising the variety of methods presented, five major strategies emerge: cultural change; appropriate training; mentoring and peer-support systems; mediation/conflict resolution; and counselling/rehabilitation. Note that these are not mutually exclusive methods and often operate in tandem; for the purpose of this section, however, we discuss each in turn as their focus differs slightly.

Cultural change

Based on the notion of a situational component to bullying and abuse, cultural change interventions attempt to change the underlying situation within an environment, from one accepting or promoting bullying and abuse to one which reduces the potential for abusive behaviours and which details clearly that bullying is not acceptable. These include whole-school interventions, dignity at work policies, cultural change policies in care homes and prisons and acceptable use policies in cyber-bullying settings. Further, within elder abuse and dating violence we can see this method in terms of changing family attitudes towards older relatives or adolescents' attitudes to partner violence. In developing a policy, not only does an organisation/institution raise awareness of bullying and abuse, it also sets clear boundaries for what it sees as acceptable behaviour and a clear process for dealing with bullying and abuse. However, culture is notoriously difficult to change given the way it is embedded into the operations of the institution and the people within it. Cultural change approaches will only work if there is support, commitment and participation on the part of all relevant stakeholders (e.g. employees and managers; teachers and children; care-home staff and residents; prisoners and prison staff; older adults and carers).

Training

Training is a key feature of any bullying intervention as it promotes understanding of what constitutes bullying and abuse and provides information on the policy adopted within the particular institution.

This functions as part of the raising-awareness element of cultural change, but can also help to foster buy-in by everyone involved. It alerts individuals to the phenomenon of bullying – its antecedents and consequences – promotes positive behaviour, up-skills those involved in dealing with bullying in the correct ways to work and informs everyone about what to do when facing bullying.

However, training can also be targeted at individual differences which promote victim vulnerability or perpetrator dominance. These can include training to enhance social skills, assertiveness, communication, emotional regulation and conflict management. These methods attempt to reduce bullying by promoting behavioural change, which results in an individual being less vulnerable to aggressive acts or less likely to respond to stressful situations in an inappropriate/aggressive manner.

Mentoring and peer support

So far, we have really only discussed preventative interventions aimed at trying to create a culture where bullying is reduced or where individuals are not likely to engage in it. Mentoring often assumes that bullying has already taken place and hence could be seen more of a supportive intervention. Especially evident here is the use of peer mentoring or buddy systems. Such methods normally pair up a younger or less experienced individual with an older/more experienced individual, who then provides informal, confidential support and advice. The mentor is able to provide an element of social support for a victim of bullying, but can also be seen as a model to guide appropriate behaviour. Mentoring does not even need to be face-to-face, as Rivers *et al.* (Chapter 10) identify in relation to Beatbullying's 'CyberMentors' project in the UK.

Peer support extends beyond just mentoring and can include challenging bully behaviour, peer counselling, listener schemes and group interventions. Peer-group pressure can prove to be a strong influence on individual behaviour. Taking the notion of social identity theory, an individual breaking peer in-group norms of acceptable behaviour would be seen as part of an out-group and may be ostracised. Given this, peer-group methods may even have more of an effect on individual behaviour than organisational policies.

Mediation and conflict resolution

Approaches adopted here revolve around providing an environment which allows all parties to come together to try to understand each other's position and to resolve conflict. In a workplace context, a number of organisations have created dignity at work advisers who provide this informal contact mechanism and who can work with victims and perpetrators to try to find solutions to problems. Within a residential home environment, a restorative justice approach has been used. As Barter (Chapter 4) summarises, this approach allows all parties to have their say and to be involved in resolving the conflict. However, although evidence supporting its use for resolving conflict is favourable, this approach does incur some problems in trying to resolve actual bullying. Further, Ortega and Sánchez (Chapter 6) show how conflict resolution strategies are fundamental components of juvenile dating intervention programmes.

Mediation is a useful technique for resolving conflict, although its impact is limited when conflict has escalated too far. Fisher and Keashley (1990) argue that if conflict has reached a destructive or segregation phase, mediation is unlikely to work. Here, a more direct and strong approach is required to stop further escalation and to motivate the parties to want to work together.

Counselling and rehabilitation

Such interventions are aimed at trying to help victims and perpetrators to recover from the impact of bullying and rehabilitate back into their particular setting. In effect, this can be seen as the end stage of intervention as it assumes that preventative and supportive mechanisms have failed or were not in place. A variety of therapeutic techniques could be used (e.g. cognitive behaviourial therapy) to try to reduce the ongoing impact of bullying on a victim or to try to resolve underlying problems within a perpetrator. Whilst such approaches do not stop initial bullying and abuse, they may be able to reduce further cases of abuse and reduce the trauma suffered by individuals as a result of exposure to bullying and abuse.

As well as interventions proposed here, in many cases there is a legal aspect to bullying and abuse. A fuller discussion of the legal side of bullying and abuse is beyond the scope of this book as many different laws operate given the different settings and different countries. Further, in elder and domestic abuse contexts we see the notions of surveillance, adult and child protection and the inclusion of other services (e.g. police, social support, etc.). These are clearly important interventions, but our focus was more on those aspects which operate at the micro-level and which have the capacity to cross the different contexts. Given this, we have also neglected to discuss interventions at society or community level, even though changing perspectives of society may actually reduce bullying and abuse. To make an impact at this level is challenging and requires the support of a wide range of people, including politicians, professional bodies, the media, religious groups, charities, and others.

Regardless of the intervention strategy adopted, it is evident that support and commitment is needed from all relevant stakeholders and there is also a need to ensure the continued and long-term implementation of such a programme. This clearly requires investment in terms of time and money but, as a number of authors identify, the potential cost of bullying and abuse on individuals, institutions and society provides the 'business case' for such an investment.

Conclusion

Bullying and abusive behaviours occur in a variety of contexts during childhood, adolescence and adulthood. Whilst each area is at a different stage in its research programme, we currently have a good base of research into bullying and abuse in a variety of settings. Hopefully, we have achieved our aim for this book of bringing together knowledge from diverse research programmes and identifying avenues for future research and practice. Earlier, we proposed three routes for researching bullying across contexts, ranging from diversification to unification. Our thesis is that the third option may be a particularly fruitful way forward for research and practice. Greater sharing of ideas, knowledge and practice by researchers and practitioners across these different settings, and further comparison of similarities and differences in methods and approaches may help advance the field to mutual benefit. All areas need to further develop the role of theory, as this will likely make interesting contributions to improving our understanding and provide a stronger knowledge base from which to develop interventions and preventative measures.

REFERENCES

Aquino, K. and Lamertz, K. (2004). 'A relational model of workplace victimization: social roles and patterns of victimization in dyadic relationships'. *Journal of Applied Psychology*, 89: 1023–34.

Björkqvist, K., Lagerspetz, K.M. and Kaukiainen, A. (1992). 'Do girls manipulate and boys fight? Developmental trends in regard to direct and indirect aggression'. *Aggressive Behavior*, 18: 117–27.

Coyne, I., Smith-Lee Chong, P., Seigne, E. and Randall, P. (2003). 'Self and peer nominations of bullying: an analysis of incident rates, individual differences and perceptions of the working environment'. *European Journal of Work and Organizational Psychology*, 12: 209–28.

Dodge, K.A., Lansford, J.E., Salzer Burks, V., Bates, J.E., Pettit, G.S., Fontaine, R. and Price, J.M. (2003). 'Peer rejection and social information-processing factors in the devleopment of aggressive behavior problems in children'. *Child Development*, 74: 374–93.

Einarsen, S. and Mikkelsen, E.G. (2003). 'Individual effects of exposure to bullying at work'. In S. Einarsen, H. Hoel, D. Zapf and C.L. Cooper (eds.), *Bullying and Emotional Abuse in the Workplace. International Perspectives in Research and Practice* (pp. 127–44). London: Taylor and Francis.

Fisher, R.J. and Keashly, L. (1990). 'Third party consultation as a method of intergroup and international conflict resolution'. In R.J. Fisher (ed.), *The Social Psychology of Intergroup and International Conflict Resolution* (pp. 211–38). New York: Springer-Verlag.

Goldberg, S. (2000). *Attachment and Development*. London: Edward Arnold.

Hoel, H. and Salin, D (2003). 'Organisational antecedents of workplace bullying'. In S. Einarsen, H. Hoel, D. Zapf and C.L. Cooper (eds.), *Bullying and Emotional Abuse in the Workplace. International Perspectives in Research and Practice* (pp. 203–18). London: Taylor and Francis.

Kayany, J.M. (1998). 'Contexts of uninhibited online behaviour: flaming in social newsgroups on Usenet'. *Journal of the American Society for Information Science*, 49: 1135–41.

Main, M., Kaplan, N. and Cassidy, J. (1985). 'Security in infancy, childhood, and adulthood: a move to the level of representation'. In I. Bretherton and E. Waters (eds.), *Growing Points of Attachment Theory and Research*. Monographs of the Society for Research in Child Development, vol. 50 (pp. 1–2).

Salin, D. (2003). 'Ways of explaining workplace bullying: a review of enabling, motivating and precipitating structures and processes in the work environment'. *Human Relations*, 56: 1213–32.

Twenge, J.M., Baumeister, R.F., Tice, D.M. and Stucke, T.S. (2001). 'If you can't join them, beat them: effects of social exclusion on aggressive behaviour'. *Journal of Personality and Social Psychology*, 81: 1058–69.

Index

258   Index